ESCROW

PRINCIPLES and PRACTICES

Sherry Shindler Price

This publication is designed to provide accurate and current information regarding the subject matter covered. The principles and conclusions presented are subject to local, state and federal laws and regulations, course cases and revisions of same. If legal advice or other expert assistance is required, the reader is urged to consult a competent professional in that field.

Publisher*: Pollyanna Fields*
Technical Writer and Editor: *Nora Boyle*
Creative Editor and Production Coordinator: *Judy Hobbs*
Sr. Graphic Design: *Dria Kasunich*
Graphic Design: *Susan Mackessy*

Ashley Crown Systems, Inc.
22952 Alcalde Drive
Laguna Hills, California 92653

Printed in the United States of America
ISBN: 0-934772-48-7

TABLE OF CONTENTS

Chapter 5 Contracts   151

Chapter 6 Local Variations   173

Chapter 7 Escrow Instructions   197

Chapter 15 The Escrow Folder

425

Preface

Whether you are reading this book to increase your knowledge about escrow for the purpose of beginning anew career, using it to satisfy a requirement for your real estate broker's license or simply wanting to learn more, as a consumer, about the fascinating subject of escrow, you will find the information presented in this book to be useful. While the book is written with the beginning student of escrow in mind, inquiring consumers also will find answers to their questions about the subject.

While featuring Northern and Southern California escrow practices and other particular California laws affecting the practice of escrow, practitioners in any state will benefit from the basic information presented here regarding the processing of the transfer of real property by a neutral third party, whether that party is an escrow officer, real estate broker, title insurer or an attorney.

About the Author

Sherry Shindler Price brings a rich background in real estate and education to the creation and production of this book. Her 23 years in the real estate profession include eight years of specialization investment properties and residential sales.

A California Community College Real Estate Instructor since 1986, Sherry also has used her experience in the real estate industry as a framework for writing test items for state licensing examinations, authoring *California Real Estate Principles*, reviewing numerous real estate textbooks for major publishers and preparing a series of continuing education courses for private schools. A well-known real estate lecturer and educator, Sherry contributes extensive knowledge to this project.

She holds a bachelor of science degree in education from Long Beach State College, a California Real Estate Broker's License and a California Community College Lifetime Instructor's Credential.

Acknowledgments

The author would like to thank the real estate professionals and editors who contributed to the earlier edition of this textbook. Contributors to the earlier edition include Peter Meade, Joan Thompson, and Norma Hurlick.

Escrow Principles and Practices, 4th edition was the result of teamwork from the publisher, educators, and other professionals to make this textbook the best in real estate escrow. Special thanks to Leigh Conway, Nora Boles, Judy Hobbs, C Dria Kasunich, Susan Mackessy, and Cynthia Simone Communications for their experience and skill in bringing together the material content, illustrations, and layout.

Finally, the author would like to acknowledge the California Department of Real Estate and others for the forms and contracts printed throughout the textbook.

chapter **1**

WHAT IS ESCROW?

Focus

Pre-Test

The following is a self test to determine how much you know about escrow and title professionals before reading this chapter. Take it without studying, then read the material presented in the text. At the end of the chapter you will find a repeat of this exam. Test your knowledge by answering the questions again, then check your improvement. (The answers are found at the end of the book.) Good luck.

True/False

1. An escrow is a short-lived trust arrangement.

2. When there is a conflict between signed instructions and the original agreement, the original contract will prevail.

3. Escrow holds documents, conditionally, until all terms of the escrow are met.

4. A buyer or a seller can change escrow instructions unilaterally.

5. A real estate broker has authority to amend escrow instructions.

6. An escrow agent operates as a dual agent.

7. A beneficiary statement is requested if an existing loan is going to be assumed.

8. Prorations usually include principal and interest.

9. The escrow holder gives closing statements to the buyer and seller at the end of the escrow.

10. The escrow holder must return any funds to buyer or seller if requested to do so by either.

Introduction

The term "Escrow" describes a temporary trust arrangement between parties wishing to transact business and exchange money or property. Escrow, from the French word for scroll, is the process where a neutral third party collects all the documents to affect that transfer of property and money, and to make sure the buyer and seller agree to terms.

To "open escrow" means to name an escrow holder, otherwise known as an escrow company, or some other eligible person, such as an attorney, to act as the impartial agent between both buyer and seller. Escrow reduces the potential risk of fraud by acting as a trusted third party that collects, holds, and disburses funds according to buyer and seller instructions. Funds and documents are placed in the custody of the escrow officer for delivery to a grantee only after certain conditions are met.

As a trust arrangement between parties, escrow is the final stage in a transaction between buyer and seller, usually exchanging real estate. The seller "grants" the property to the person, the buyer, who must prove he has sufficient funds to pay for it.

When all relevant documents and monies are collected, they are reviewed, and joint escrow instructions are exchanged between the parties to sign. The conditions of the sale are set in writing as directed by the principals within the law. When these conditions are not met, they are said to 'fall out of escrow,' or, where one of the parties is unable to satisfy the conditions of the purchase and sale contract.

The escrow instructions reflect the understanding and agreement of the principals, who may not always be the buyer and seller, because transactions involving the sale of real estate are not the only kind that requires the use of an escrow. Any time a neutral third party is needed to handle documents or money, such as in the transfer of real property, loans, sale of trust deeds, or bulk sales and sales of a business or business opportunities, an escrow might be required.

In this chapter, escrow as it relates to the sale of real estate is covered. No one is required by law to use an escrow for any of the above transactions, including the sale of real property. However, when a buyer and seller reach an agreement about the sale of property, including terms and price, it is advisable for a neutral third party to handle the details of completing the sale.

Misunderstandings, criminal intent, and negligence, on the part of the principals may incur loss to one or both parties if the contract is not handled by an outside escrow professional.

After instructions are signed, the escrow holder reviews and insures they are upheld, by requesting all parties involved to observe the terms and conditions of the contract. The escrow holder coordinates communication between the principals, the agents, and any other professionals -such as the lender or title company whose services are called for in the instructions.

Briefly, the entire process entails the following: The offer to buy a property is usually the purchase agreement that is accepted and signed by all parties. Then escrow is opened. The buyer deposits money into the escrow account, which is held in trust by the escrow company. Then, there is a contingency period, when all conditions in the purchase agreement are executed. These typically include approvals, title reports, loan approvals, appraisals, physical inspections, pest and termite reports, and certifications.

Homeowner's insurance, fire insurance, and other local requirements are updated, paid, and renewed. After all conditions are met, the loan documents are signed and the closing costs are paid. The deed is then recorded. *Escrow closes* when the escrow holder receives confirmation that title was recorded at the county recorder's office and the new owner takes possession of the property.

Requirements for a Real Estate Transaction

A real estate transaction usually starts at the time a broker obtains a listing from a property owner. The most common type of listing is an Exclusive Authorization and Right to Sell. With this type of listing, the seller must pay a commission no matter who sells the property—even if the owner makes the sale. The agent promises to use due diligence to find a ready, willing and able buyer under the exact terms of the listing contract, and the seller promises to pay a commission when the agent fulfills the contract.

At some point, either the listing agent or an agent from another brokerage will find a buyer and write an offer. There are certain items the agent must consider carefully when preparing the offer to purchase (also known as a deposit receipt or purchase contract).

The following list of items that must be included in the offer apply only to the most common aspects of a residential purchase. Commercial, industrial, vacant land, farm or ranch development and other types of properties require different treatment by a real estate agent.

Offers to purchase residential property must address the following:

1. The Date and Place contract is signed by buyer

2. Correct name and address of the buyer

3. Form of the buyer's deposit: cash, check, cashier's check, promissory note, money order, or other

4. Designee to hold the deposit: broker, seller or escrow

5. Purchase price of the property

6. Terms under which the property will be purchased: all cash, refinance, loan assumption or taking title "subject to" the existing loan. Do any of the existing loans contain acceleration clauses or prepayment penalties? If so, has the buyer approved the terms?

7. Amount of time to be allowed for the seller to consider the buyer's offer to purchase, and to complete the transaction. Is time of the essence?

8. Definite termination date stated in the contract

9. Covenants, Conditions and Restrictions; easements; rights or other conditions of record that affect the property: Are they acceptable to the buyer?

10. Deed of conveyance: Is it to be executed by the seller to contain any exceptions or reservations? Has the buyer approved of this?

11. Are there any stipulations or agreements regarding any tenancies or rights of persons in possession of the property?

12. Roof and electrical wiring inspections: Who pays for inspections and work, and who orders reports?

13. Are there any stipulations or agreements regarding facts a survey would reveal, such as the existence of a common wall, other encroachments, or easements?

14. Are there any special or unusual costs or charges to be adjusted through escrow? Who will pay for the title policy, escrow services, and other customary charges? Who pays for any unusual charges?

15. Who will select the escrow holder? The parties should reach a mutual agreement on this.

16. Are there any special documents to be drawn in the transaction, and if so, who will prepare them?

17. If prorations are not to be made as of the date escrow closes, what date is to be used?

18. If possession is granted prior to the close of escrow, what type of agreement must be prepared to cover this occupancy and who will prepare it?

19. If structural pest control inspection report and certification are to be furnished, who pays?

20. Are other brokers involved in this transaction? What are their names, addresses, and telephone numbers?

21. Determine the sales commission and when it will be paid if the deposit receipt initially establishes that a commission will be paid, it must contain the commission negotiability statement, which declares that by law all commissions are negotiable.

22. All parties must sign the contract. Check signatures of all buyers, all sellers, and agents. Certain documents require *in-person* and notarized signatures. Electronic signatures such as on a fax, email, or voicemail giving authorization are not allowed on most recorded documents.

23. Every purchase contract prepared or signed by a real estate salesperson must be reviewed, initialed, and dated by salesperson's broker within five working days after preparation or signing by the salesperson or before the close of escrow, whichever occurs first.

24. If the transaction is a residential sale of four-or-fewer units and involves seller-assisted financing, and a licensee is the arranger of such credit, a financing disclosure statement must be prepared and provided to both buyer and seller.

25. A specific written disclosure must be made to prospective buyers of one-to-four dwelling units with facts about the particular piece of property that could materially affect the property's value and desirability.

26. Licensees acting as listing and selling brokers in certain residential real estate transactions must make informational written and oral disclosures concerning who is representing whom.

27. A real estate licensee who acts as the agent for either the buyer or the seller in the sale or transfer of real property, including manufactured housing, must disclose to both parties the form, amount and source of any compensation received or expected to be received from a lender involved in financing related to the transaction.

As soon as possible following the opening of escrow, the seller should furnish escrow with the following items.

Seller Provides:

1. Escrow instructions signed by all Sellers.

2. The latest available tax and assessment bills, and any other statements or bills that are to be prorated through escrow.

3. Seller's loan payment books and records.

4. Seller's fire, liability and other insurance policies, if they are to be assigned to the buyer.

5. A beneficiary statement, demand, certificate, or offset statement from the holder of any mortgage or trust deed of record on the property; any items showing the amount due on any loan of record; the payment date; the date to which interest is paid; and other important information. Consent to the transfer from lenders of record must be given.

6. Any subordination or other agreement required by the purchase contract, to be approved by the parties through escrow.

7. Certificates or releases showing satisfaction of mechanic's liens, security agreements (chattel mortgages), judgments, or mortgages that are to be paid off through escrow.

8. List of tenants' names and the apartments they occupy, together with the amount of rent paid and unpaid, the dates when rents are due, and, if required, an assignment to the buyer of any unpaid rent, as well as details on advance security deposits, if any.

Seller Provides:

9. Assignment to buyer of all leases affecting the property.

10. Letters from the seller to tenants instructing them to pay all subsequent rent to the buyer and reaffirming the conditions of the tenancy, including notice of the transfer of the security deposit, if any, to the buyer.

11. The seller's executed and acknowledged deed of conveyance to the buyer or a valid authority to execute the deed of the seller by the seller's attorney-in-fact if the seller is acting through an agent.

12. An executed bill of sale covering any personal property to be conveyed to the buyer, together with an inventory of the items for the buyer's approval.

13. A security agreement (chattel mortgage) for execution by the buyer covering any personal property included in the purchase price but not paid for by the buyer in cash.

14. The deed by which the seller acquired title to the property and the seller's policy of title insurance.

15. Any unrecorded instruments affecting the title.

16. Any other documents or instruments that the seller is to prepare or deliver.

17. Any approvals required for documents that the seller is to receive at closing.

18. Information required to be disclosed to the buyer under the seller financing disclosure, if necessary.

As soon as possible after opening escrow, the buyer should furnish the escrow holder with certain documents and information, and should review or inspect personally all of the following items.

Buyer Provides:

1. Review of signed escrow instructions by all purchasers.

2. Review the preliminary title report for the subject property to make sure that there are no items of record affecting the property that have not already been approved by the buyer.

3. Review any Conditions, Covenants, and Restrictions affecting the property, whether of record or not.

4. Confirm terms of any mortgages or deeds of trust to be assumed by the buyer, or that will remain an encumbrance on the property.

5. Examine any beneficiary statements, fire insurance or liability policies if they are to be assigned to the buyer.

6. Examine offset statements on loans to be assumed, or those under which the buyer is taking title to the property "subject to" existing loan terms; verify the unpaid principal balances owed, the interest rates, dates to which interest is paid and other vital information.

7. Review and approve structural pest control and other reports to be delivered through escrow.

8. Carefully review all new loan documents prior to signing.

9. Compare the terms of the purchase contract, escrow instructions, title report, and deed to make sure there are no discrepancies in the transaction documents.

10. If tenancies are involved, review the names, addresses and telephone numbers of tenants; the rent amounts, rent due dates, copies of rent agreements or leases, letters from the seller to the tenants verifying the terms of occupancy and notifying the tenants of change of ownership, the assignments of any unpaid rent and leases, details on security deposits if any.

11. Examine the bill of sale and inventory covering the items of personal property to be conveyed to the purchaser.

12. Review copies of any bills to be prorated in escrow.

13. Verify all amounts and prorations on the estimated escrow settlement sheet.

14. Reinspect the property to determine that it is in the same condition as it was when the buyer made the purchase offer. Recheck for any undisclosed items that might affect the use of the property, such as party walls, access roads to other properties, irrigation canals or ditches, common drives or persons in occupancy or possession of the property, which the county records would not disclose.

15. Deposit sufficient cash or clear funds to cover any balance owed on the purchase contract plus buyer's closing costs and expenses, and approvals as required. The parties should always keep copies of any documents and instruments they sign, deliver to, or receive from any party in the real estate transaction.

Requirements for an Escrow

There must be a binding contract between the parties to an escrow. The binding contract can be a deposit receipt, agreement of sale, exchange agreement, an option, or mutual escrow instructions of the buyer and seller.

The signed instructions become an enforceable contract, binding all parties to the escrow. When there is a conflict between the signed instructions and the original agreement of the principals, the original contract will prevail.

Amendments to the escrow instructions can change the original agreement if all parties agree. When all instructions are completed, escrow closes, the buyer gets a deed, and the seller gets the money.

The Clarks put their home on the market, listing it with a local broker. It was competitively priced, and the broker said it would take about two weeks to sell. An agent from another real estate company showed the house to the Lee, and they loved it. After writing up an offer and presenting it to the Clarks, the buyers' agent called them with the news that the sellers had accepted.

*The next day, the agent took the buyer's **earnest money** (usually about one percent of the purchase price) to the escrow office, gave it to the escrow agent, and got a receipt. The escrow holder immediately cashed the check and deposited it in a trust account. The escrow holder then drew up escrow instructions to reflect the terms and conditions of* *the sale. The sellers signed their copy, the buyers signed theirs, and both were returned to the escrow company. The escrow was now open*

The second requirement of a valid escrow is a conditional delivery of transfer documents and funds, and means the seller will deliver a signed grant deed that conveys title to the buyer. The buyer and/or the lender will deliver to escrow the funds that are required to complete the sale.

The escrow agent holds the security for any loan (trust deed) conditionally until directed by the terms of the escrow. The escrow agent keeps all documents and funds until all other terms of the escrow are completed. Then the agent distributes or disburses the money according to the expressed conditions of the escrow.

Sometime before escrow closes, the seller will be asked to sign a grant deed conveying title to the buyer. Because the

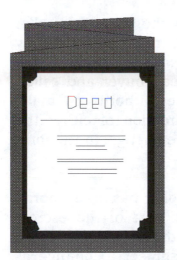

seller will sign over ownership to the buyer before getting any money, the escrow holder is instructed to hold the signed deed until funds from the buyer are deposited in escrow and all other terms of the escrow have been met. Conditional delivery of the grant deed has been made by the seller.

Toward the end of the escrow period, the buyer will sign a note and trust deed for the loan in the presence of a notary. The buyer is promising to pay back the money, using the property as security for the loan. Escrow has not closed, and the buyer does not yet own the property. Nor, has the seller received the promised money, but the note and trust deed are signed and deposited into escrow, conditionally, until all other terms have been met. Only then will escrow request loan funds.

To be Valid, an Escrow Must Include the Following:

• Binding contract between buyer and seller

• Conditional delivery of transfer documents to a third party

---

The escrow is closed when all the terms and conditions of the escrow are met. Upon close of escrow, the buyer gets the grant deed, after it has been recorded, and the seller gets the money.

Escrow Principles and Rules

Once instructions have been signed by the buyer and seller and returned to the escrow holder, neither party may unilaterally change escrow instructions. Any changes must be made by mutual agreement between buyer and seller. The escrow agent does not have the authority to make changes in the contract upon the direction of either the buyer or seller, unless both agree to the change, in the form of an amendment.

In addition, it should be noted, the broker has no authority whatsoever to amend or change any part of the escrow instructions without the knowledge of the principals. Often, terms of the loan for the buyer are subject to change as complications may appear and include credit problems, liens, or there may be a cloud on the title.

In addition, time is of the essence when a buyer tries to lock in a certain interest rate on a mortgage or home loan. These issues can delay and create obstacles for the escrow officer to close the transaction. The obstructions may require an amendment. The written consent of both buyer and seller, in the form of an amendment to the original instructions, must be given before any dates or changes are made.

The Clarks and the Lees signed escrow instructions on June 9. The agreement reflected a sales price of $450,000, with $90,000 as a down payment. After signing the instructions, however, the buyers decided they only wanted to put $80,000 down, and told the escrow officer to change the instructions. An amendment was written for them to sign, and a copy sent to the sellers to sign.

The buyers were disappointed when the Clarks did not want to change the contract and refused to sign the amendment. When the Lees wanted to back out, the escrow officer reminded them that they had a mutually binding legal agreement with the sellers. Neither side could change any part of the agreement, including terminating it, without the written agreement of the other.

As agent for both parties to an escrow, the escrow agent is placed in a position of trust. By operating as a dual agent, the escrow holder sits between the buyer and seller as a stakeholder with an obligation to both sides to act as a neutral third party.

Escrow Officers must observe these rules:

➢ Escrow instructions must be understood by the principals to the escrow and must be mutually binding. Instructions must be carefully written to be very clear about the agreement between the buyer and seller. Each party must understand his or her obligation to carry out the terms of the contract without assuming the escrow holder has any power to force compliance. The escrow holder may not act unless directed by the principals.

➢ The escrow holder does not get personally involved in disagreements between the buyer and seller, nor act as a negotiator for the principals. Escrow instructions make each party's obligations and agreements clear, and it is up to the buyer and seller to keep the promises they each made in their agreement with the other. All parties must know that the escrow agent is not an attorney, and must advise anyone seeking legal advice to get counsel from a professional.

➢ An escrow agent has a limited capacity as agent for buyer and seller, and may only perform acts described in the contents of escrow instructions. While acting as a dual agent, the escrow officer must operate in the best interest of both parties, without special preference to either. The escrow agent serves each principal after escrow closes, in providing them with the documents and/or funds to which they are entitled.

➢ All parties must sign escrow instructions for the contract to be binding. An escrow is officially open when both buyer and seller have signed instructions.

➢ Escrow instructions must be clear and certain in their language.

➢ All documents to be recorded must be sent to the title company in a timely manner (as quickly as possible), and all interested parties should receive copies of recorded documents.

➢ Escrow instructions should specify which documents or funds the escrow holder may accept.

➢ Overdrawn trust accounts (debit balances) are prohibited by law.

> Information regarding any transaction is held in trust by the escrow officer and may not be released to anyone without written permission of the principals.

> An escrow holder has a duty to disclose to the principals any previously undisclosed information that might affect them. An amendment would be drawn at the direction of the buyer and seller to reflect any change as a result of new disclosures.

> A high degree of trust along with good customer service and relations must be provided by an escrow holder.

> An escrow holder must remain strictly neutral regarding the buyer's and the seller's interests.

> Escrow records and files must be maintained daily. A systematic review of open escrow files will make sure no procedure has been overlooked, or time limit ignored.

> Before closing an escrow, all files must be audited carefully.

> All checks or drafts must have cleared before any funds may be released to the seller. Escrow must close in a timely manner, according to the agreement between buyer and seller. A prompt settlement must be made to all principals.

Escrow Procedures

Escrow procedures may vary according to local custom. In some areas, escrow companies or banks conduct escrows. In other areas, title companies or attorneys do the job. However, there are certain procedures that are followed during the regular course of all escrows.

Open Escrow

The person, who opens escrow, if there is a real estate agent involved, is the selling agent. That person usually has an earnest money check that must be deposited into escrow or some other trust account no more than one business day after buyer and seller have signed the deposit receipt. So, at the first opportunity, the real estate agent must take the buyer's check to the escrow officer to put in a trust account. The agent then gives the  escrow officer all the information needed to prepare escrow instructions. Usually within a day or two, computer-generated instructions are ready for buyer and seller to sign. The escrow instructions reflect the agreement between the buyer and seller as seen in the offer to purchase (deposit receipt) and usually include all disclosures required by law. Only the seller's set of escrow instructions include the amount of commission to be paid to the broker, unless, as in some cases, the buyer is paying a commission also.

Direct Escrow

If no real estate agent is involved, the principals may go to escrow   directly, and tell the escrow officer to prepare instructions according to their agreement.

Prepare Escrow Instructions

Usually the escrow holder prepares the instructions on a computer-generated form, with details of the particular transaction completed in the blank spaces on the form. All parties sign identical instructions, with the exception of the  commission agreement that is prepared for the seller to sign--if the seller is in fact paying the commission. Buyer and seller sign the instructions, which are then returned to the escrow holder who follows the directions in the agreement to complete the escrow. Imagine you are selling your home. The following probably would be included in your escrow instructions:

1. *Purchase Price*: This is the amount of money the buyer and seller have agreed upon for the sale of the property.

2. *Terms*: The buyer and seller agree on how the buyer will purchase the property: cash, new loan, loan assumption, V.A., or FHA loan, seller to carry a trust deed, trade, or any other special agreements provided in the contract between buyer and seller. This section describes the amount of the down payment and the terms of any loans for which the buyer will apply.

3. *Vesting*: The buyer will take title in one of the following ways: sole ownership, joint tenancy, tenants in common, or tenancy in partnership. How the buyer will take title may be important for tax or inheritance purposes and the escrow holder must be directed how to draw the deed to reflect the wishes of the buyer, but may not give advice regarding vesting.

4. *Matters of Record*: Buyer and seller may disagree on a matter of record--some circumstance affecting the property--that is recorded. It may be an easement, an existing street bond, or a trust deed which must be resolved.

5. *Closing*: Buyer and seller will agree on how long they want the escrow to last. They will mention a specific length of time for the escrow and instruct accordingly.

6. *Inspections*: Buyer and seller will agree on whether or not to have certain inspections of the property before the close of escrow, such as a pest control inspection; property inspection to identify any plumbing, electrical, or structural problems; a soil inspection to check for slippage or unstable compaction. The buyer's approval of the reports will be a contingency of the sale and must be mentioned in the escrow instructions.

7. *Prorations*: The division of expenses and income between the buyer and seller as of the date of closing is known as proration. Some items that are prorated are taxes, rental deposits or income, insurance premiums. The reason for prorations is that some payments may have been made

by the seller for a time period beyond the agreed-upon date for escrow to close. Or the seller may be in arrears on taxes. The escrow holder debits or credits the seller or buyer, depending on the escrow closing date.

8. *Possession*: The buyer and seller will have agreed on when the buyer can move into the house, and the escrow instructions must reflect their agreement on the date the buyer will take possession of the property. The close of escrow could be the date of possession, or sometimes the seller will rent the property back from the buyer after the close of escrow. In that case, a lease agreement should be signed and handled by the parties outside of escrow.

9. *Documents*: The escrow holder will need to know which documents to prepare, have signed by the proper party, and record at the close of escrow. Usually, these will be a grant deed and a trust deed.

10. *Disbursements*: The escrow holder must settle the accounts of the buyer and seller according to the escrow instructions. Also, the escrow holder must provide a closing statement of costs and charges to each party and a final distribution of funds at the close of escrow.

Order Title Search

At the time the buyer and seller reach an agreement about the sale of the property, they also select a title company. One of the jobs of the escrow officer, after escrow has been opened, is to order a title search of the subject property.

The title company prepares a preliminary title report, and searches the records for any encumbrances or liens against the property. The company checks to make sure the seller is the owner of record, and inspects the history of ownership, or chain of title, in the preliminary title search.

The purpose is to ensure all transfers of ownership have been recorded correctly, and that there are no unexplained gaps.

The buyer is allowed a certain number of days to approve this preliminary title report. Buyer approval is important to eliminate surprises regarding the title as the escrow progresses. The escrow holder should notify the buyer and seller if there is any difference in the preliminary report and the escrow instruction, by way of an addendum "for information only."

As you recall, the escrow agent is a neutral party and only has the authority to do what is described in the escrow instructions. The escrow officer must wait for instructions about what to do next. The preliminary title report is the foundation for the title insurance policy on the buyer's title as instructed by the buyer and seller in the escrow instructions.

The Clarks and the Lees had instructed their escrow officer to order a preliminary title search. The Lees had three days to approve the report, as a contingency of the sale. When they examined it, however, they found there was a bond against the property for street repairs. They had not been aware of it.

The bond was a lien in the amount of $3,500. The buyers could not approve the preliminary title report until the issue was cleared up. An agreement about who would pay the bond had to be reached by the buyers and sellers, then new instructions given to the escrow officer, who would prepare an amendment for both parties' signatures.

Request for Payoff Demands and/or Beneficiary Statements

The escrow officer must also see that existing loans are paid off, or assumed, depending on the agreement of the buyer and seller.

If the existing loan, or the seller's debt, is going to be paid off with proceeds from the sale, a demand from the lender holding the note and trust deed is needed, along with the unpaid principal balance and any other amounts that are due.

The escrow officer requests a demand for payoff of a loan from the lender who holds a loan against the subject property. The exact amount of loans that are to be paid off must be known so the escrow officer's accounting will be correct at the close of escrow.

If an existing loan is going to be assumed, or taken "subject to," a beneficiary statement is requested by the escrow holder from the lender.

A statement of the unpaid balance of a loan, the beneficiary statement also describes the condition of the debt. The escrow agent follows instructions about financing the property, and prepares any documents necessary for completing the escrow at the close. These might be a note and trust deed, or assumption papers.

The buyers are obtaining an adjustable loan in the amount of $360,000. The down payment will be $90,000, to make the purchase price of $450,000. The existing $250,000 loan on the property is held by Union Bank. The existing loan will be paid off when the buyer's new loan is funded, and the seller will get the balance of the purchase price, $200,000, less the seller's costs of selling (commissions, termite work, escrow and title fees, etc.).

Union Bank is notified of the expected payoff and asked by the escrow officer to send a statement of the unpaid balance and condition of the existing loan. This is known as a request for demand for payoff.

Other Reports

The parties to an escrow may request any number of reports about the condition of the property. The escrow holder is asked in the instructions to accept any reports submitted into escrow. These may include a structural pest control report (termite report), property inspection report, soil condition report, or environmental report. Any approval from the buyer or seller about a report is held in escrow until needed, or given to the appropriate party at the close of escrow.

New Loan Instructions and Documents

Escrow accepts loan documents or instructions about financing the subject property and completes them as directed. The escrow agent gets the buyer's approval of and signature on loan documents, and receives and disburses loan funds as instructed.

Fire Insurance Policies

The parties to an escrow will have agreed on fire insurance policies and will instruct the escrow officer accordingly. The escrow holder will accept, hold and deliver any policies and will follow instructions about transferring them. A lender will require fire insurance, and will expect the escrow holder and the buyer to be accountable for either a new policy or the transfer of an existing one.

Settlement

The escrow holder will be instructed by the buyer and seller about prorations and other accounting to be done at the close of escrow.

> ### Prorations Normally Include:
>
> • Interest
>
> • Premiums on fire insurance
>
> • Security deposits and rents (if the property is a rental)
>
> • Seller's current property taxes

The buyer and seller will have agreed on impound accounts, and the escrow holder will be guided on how to handle the credit and debit. After the escrow agent completes the accounting, the agent tells the buyer to deliver the down payment (usually in the form of a cashier's check), plus other escrow costs, to the escrow office.

At this time, the principals sign the loan documents, and complete any other paperwork required for the financing. If all is in order, the loan is funded and the money sent to the title company to pay off all encumbrances of record. Then the escrow may close.

Audit File

At the close of escrow, the escrow officer must examine each file to make sure all accounting has been accurate, and that escrow instructions have been followed. A cash reconciliation statement is completed by the escrow holder and closing statements are prepared for all principals.

Recording

The escrow holder orders the title company to record all transaction documents as instructed by the buyer and seller. This occurs after a final check of the title company records to be sure nothing has changed since the preliminary title search was done. Then the title company issues a policy of title insurance to insure the buyer's title. Documents that might require recording are the grant deed, trust deed, contract of sale or option.

Balancing the File

The last job of the escrow holder is to close the escrow. The escrow officer gives closing statements to buyer and seller,

disburses all money, and delivers all documents to the proper parties after making sure all documents have been recorded by the title company.

The seller gets a check for the proceeds of the sale minus escrow fees, real estate commissions, or any other costs of selling, and any pertinent documents; and the buyer gets a grant deed.

Termination of an Escrow

The authority to conduct an escrow is given mutually by the buyer and seller in the escrow instructions. Neither party may end the escrow without the agreement of the other, in writing. Also, the escrow officer may not return any funds or documents to either party without agreement from all parties.

During the escrow, the escrow officer is an agent for both buyer and seller, as you recall, and must operate from the original escrow instructions. When they instruct the escrow agent to prepare an amendment canceling the escrow, a buyer and seller mutually end their agreement after they both sign the amendment.

Rights and Obligations of the Parties

A buyer and a seller are known as principals in an escrow. The escrow holder is a neutral third party who is a dual agent for buyer and seller. A real estate agent is not a party to an escrow unless he or she is the buyer or the seller.

A buyer is the party purchasing the property and the one who will receive a deed conveying the title.

A seller is the owner of record who must deliver the title agreed upon in the contract.
An escrow agent is an impartial third party who collects all documents and money, through the escrow, and transfers them to the proper parties at the close of escrow.

An escrow agent may be a bank, savings and loan, title insurance company, attorney, real estate broker or an escrow company. A real estate broker may act as an escrow agent in the course of a regular transaction for which a real estate license is necessary. The broker conducts the escrow as a service only if he or she is the listing or selling broker to the subject sale.

Escrow Companies Incorporated

The Commissioner of Corporations licenses escrow companies, but does not allow individuals to apply. Only a corporation is qualified and must make an application. A $25,000 bond, or more, based upon predicted yearly average transactions and trust fund use must be furnished by an applicant for an escrow office license. A bond must be posted by all parties (officers, directors, trustees and employees) having access to money or securities being held by the escrow company as safety against loss.

Audit

An escrow company must keep accounts and records which can be examined by the Commissioner of Corporations. A yearly inspection prepared by an independent certified public accountant, describing operations, must be delivered to the Commissioner.

Prohibitions

• Referral fees may not be paid by an escrow company to anyone as a reward for sending business to them.

• Commissions may not be paid to a real estate broker until the closing of an escrow.

• Blank escrow instructions to be filled in after signing are not acceptable. Initials must be placed wherever there is a change or deletion.

• Information regarding an escrow may only be provided to parties to the escrow.

• Copies of escrow instructions must be provided to anyone signing them.

Agency

An escrow agent holds a limited agency, or authority. Any duties to be conducted must be mentioned specifically in escrow instructions or they are not authorized by the buyer and seller. The escrow holder must remain neutral, as the agent of both the buyer and seller, during the course of the escrow. After all conditions of the escrow have been met, the escrow officer is the agent of each of the parties in dealing with their individual needs.

Relationship of the Escrow Agent and the Real Estate Broker

No transaction can be completed without a good relationship between a broker and an escrow agent. The good will, positive guidance and technical knowledge of an escrow officer have helped many brokers get through an escrow, especially those new to the business.

After the real estate broker negotiates the sale, it is the job of the escrow agent to see that the agreements made by the parties are carried out. The broker and the escrow agent must check with each other regularly to make sure information is correct and to inform each other of how the escrow is progressing.

Designating the Escrow Holder

The choice of an escrow agent is always that of the buyer and seller. However, they probably do not have a relationship with an escrow agent, and may rely on the advice of their real estate broker.

Post Test

The following self test repeats the one you took at the beginning of this chapter. Now take the exam again--since you have read all the material-- and check your knowledge of parties, documents and real estate basics.

True/False

1. An escrow is a short-lived trust arrangement.

2. When there is a conflict between signed instructions and the original agreement between the principals, the original contract will prevail.

3. Escrow holds documents, conditionally, until all terms of the escrow are met.

4. A buyer or a seller can change escrow instructions unilaterally.

5. A real estate broker has authority to amend escrow instructions.

6. An escrow agent operates as a dual agent.

7. A beneficiary statement is requested if an existing loan is going to be assumed.

8. Prorations usually include principal and interest.

9. The escrow holder gives closing statements to the buyer and seller at the end of the escrow.

10. The escrow holder must return any funds to buyer or seller if requested to do so by either.

chapter 2

PARTIES, DOCUMENTS, REAL ESTATE BASICS

Focus

- **Introduction**
- **Parties**
- **Types of deeds**
- **Other documents**
- **Real estate basics**
- **Recording system**

Pre-Test

The following is a self test to determine how much you know about parties, documents, and real estate basics before reading this chapter. Take it without studying, then read the material presented in the text. At the end of the chapter you will find a repeat of this exam. Test your knowledge by answering the questions again, then check your improvement. (The answers are found at the end of the book.) Good luck.

True/False

1. A third party who carries out the written provisions of an escrow agreement is known as an escrow holder.

2. Property is usually transferred with a grant deed.

3. A request for notice of default is a way anyone interested in a particular trust deed can make sure of being informed if a notice of default has been recorded.

4. A preliminary change of ownership gives a buyer temporary title.

5. Ownership in severalty is the same as concurrent ownership.

6. An encumbrance is a limitation on ownership to real property.

7. A mechanic's lien is an example of a non-money encumbrance.

8. Property acquired by a husband and wife during a marriage, except for certain separate property, is owned by the wife.

9. An encumbrance that creates a legal obligation to pay is known as a lien.

10. A lis pendens indicates pending litigation on a property.

Introduction

The business of escrow, like many other professions, has a language all its own, as well as sharing much of the vocabulary of the real estate industry. This chapter will introduce and define the terms you will use to open, complete and close an escrow. You also will be introduced to the buyers and the sellers, the borrowers and the lenders, and others, as you journey through this introduction to escrow.

Parties

As an escrow agent, you must be knowledgeable about the parties with whom you are dealing. Following is a list of the likely entitities you will meet as you become a practiced escrow professional.

Administrator/Administratrix
A person appointed by the court to handle the affairs of a deceased person when there is no one named in a will to do so

Assignee
The person to whom a claim, benefit or right in property is made

Assignor
The person transferring a claim, benefit or right in property to another

Beneficiary
The lender under a deed of trust

Escrow Holder
An independent third party legally bound to carry out the written provisions of an escrow agreement; a neutral,

bonded third party who is a dual agent for the principals; sometimes called an escrow agent

Executor/Executrix
A person named in a will to handle the affairs of a deceased person

Grantee
The person receiving real property because it has been granted in a deed by another individual

Grantor
The person who executes or signs a document giving title or ownership of real property to another party. A grantor might sign a grant deed, a quitclaim deed or a gift deed

Lessee
Tenant, renter

Lessor
Landlord, owner

Principal
The main party to a transaction

Trustee
Holds bare legal title to property as a neutral third party where there is a deed trust. Only duties are to foreclose or reconvey after a pay-off on a loan

Trustor
The borrower under a trust deed

Types of Deeds

Grant Deed

When property is transferred by private grant the instrument generally used is a grant deed. The parties involved are the grantor, or the person conveying the property, and the grantee, the person or group receiving the property.

A grant deed contains two implied warranties by the grantor. One is that the grantor has not already conveyed title to any other person, and the other is that the estate is free from encumbrances other than those disclosed by the grantor.

The grantor also promises to deed any rights he or she might acquire to the property after conveying it to the grantee. For example, oil or mineral rights might revert to the property at some time in the future, after the present owner has sold the property. "After acquired title" means any benefits that come to the property after a sale must follow the sale and accrue to the new owner. A grant deed must contain certain basics in order to be legally binding.

Requirements for a Valid Grant Deed

- In writing: according to the Statute of Frauds

- Parties identified: the parties to the transfer (grantor and grantee) sufficiently described

- Competent to convey: the grantor must be competent to convey the property (not a minor or incompetent)

Requirements for a Valid Grant Deed (continued)

- Capable of holding title: the grantee must be capable of holding title (must be a real living person, not fictitious)
- Adequately described: the property being conveyed must be adequately described
- Words of granting: words to indicate the act of granting (grant, convey) must be included

- Signed: the deed must be signed by the grantor

- Delivered: the deed must be delivered to and accepted by the grantee

A grant deed is not effective until it is delivered. It must be the intention of the grantor that the deed be delivered during his or her lifetime. For example, a deed would not be valid if signed and put in a safe place until the death of the grantor, and then recorded. Recording a deed is considered the same as delivery.

After a deed has been acknowledged by the grantor, it may be filed with the county recorder, giving constructive notice of the sale. An acknowledgment is a signed statement, made before a notary public, by a named person confirming that the signature on a document is valid and that it was made of free will. A deed does not have to be acknowledged to be valid, but must be acknowledged to be recorded.

The purpose of recording a deed is to protect the chain of title, which is a sequential record of changes in ownership showing the connection from one owner to the next. A complete chain of title is desirable whenever property is transferred and required by title insurance companies if they are writing a policy on a property.

> *Fermina Daza, a single woman, owned the house in which she lived. After marrying Fernando Ariza , she decided to sell the house. Because the chain of title showed that Fermina owned it under her maiden name, she had to sign the deed as "Fermina Ariza (who acquired title as Fermina Daza)" when she sold it.*

The priority of a deed is determined by the date it is recorded. In other words, recording establishes a claim of ownership which has priority over any deeds recorded after it. The first to record a deed is the first in right.

> *Calvin sells his house to Margaret, and--without telling Margaret--also sells it to Anita. Anita records her deed before Margaret has a chance to record hers. Anita is the owner of record and gets the house. Margaret has a definite cause for a lawsuit against Calvin.*

> *Anna sells her house to Victor, who moves in without recording the deed. Anna also sells the house to Alex, telling him to record the deed quickly, making him aware that Victor also has an interest in the property. In this case, Victor gets the house because of Alex's knowledge of the prior sale and also because of Victor's possession of the property (he had moved in), which established his right of ownership.*

41

A grantee must accept a deed before it is considered effective. Acceptance is automatic if the grantee is an infant or incompetent person. Acceptance may be shown by the acts of the grantee, such as moving onto the property.

The grant deed need not be signed by the grantee. An undated, unrecorded and unacknowledged grant deed may be valid as long as it contains the essential items noted below.

Not Necessary for Valid Grant Deed

- Acknowledgment
- Competent grantee; may be a minor, felon or incompetent
- Date
- Legal description
- Mention of the consideration
- Recording
- Signature of grantee

RECORDING REQUESTED BY
New Land Title Company
AND WHEN RECORDED MAIL
TO:

Name: Robert R. Mullins
Street Address: 2185 Memory Lane
City, State: Costa Mesa, CA 92626
Zip

Order No. 56748932-SMS

| REC |
| RCF |
| MICRO |
| RTCF |
| LIEN |
| SMPF |
| PCOR |

Space Above This Line for Recorder's Use

GRANT DEED

THE UNDERSIGNED GRANTOR(S) DECLARE(S)

City of : __Costa Mesa__

Conveyance tax is $_____
Parcel No. 123-45-6789

DOCUMENTARY TRANSFER TAX $_____

□Computed on full value of interest of property conveyed
□Full value less value of liens or encumbrances remaining at the time of sale

FOR A VALUABLE CONSIDERATION,
receipt of which is hereby acknowledged,
Michael L. Horton and Lisa M. Horton,
Husband and Wife as Joint Tenants do (does)
hereby GRANTS to Robert R. Mullins and
Margie M. Mullins, Husband and Wife as Joint
Tenants

the following real property in the city of
Costa Mesa
county of Orange, state of California

Lot 12 in Tract 2316 as recorded in Book 42 pages 5-10 inclusive of Miscellaneous Maps in the office of the County Recorder of the County of Orange State of California and described as follows: commencing at a point on the Southerly line thereof 450.8 feet West of the Southeast corner thereof, thence North 68 degrees 58 minutes West 100 fee, thence North 23 degrees 02 minutes East 60 feet, thence South 66 degrees 58 minutes East one hundred feet, thence South 23 degrees 02 minutes West 60 feet to the point of beginning..

Dated:_____

STATE OF CALIFORNIA
COUNTY OF_____

On_____before me.

Michael M. Horton
_____

Linda L. Horton
_____

a Notary Public in and for said County and State, personally appeared:

_____

_____

Personally known to me (or providedto me on the basis of satisfactory evidence whose name(s) is/are subscribed to the within instrument and acknowledged to me that he/she/they executed the same in his/her/their authorized capacity(ies) and that by his/her/their signature(s) on the instrument the person(s) or the entity upon behalf of which the person(s) acted, executed the instrument.

WITNESS my hand and official seal.

Signature_____   (This area for official notorial seal)

Quitclaim Deed

Another type of deed used to transfer property is a quitclaim deed. This type of deed was commonly used to transfer real property interests between husband and wife.

However, an interspousal grant deed is now used between spouses instead of a quitclaim deed.

A quitclaim deed is often used to clear a cloud on the title; there might be a minor defect in the chain of title which needs to be removed. They may also be used to terminate an easement.

A quitclaim deed is a deed conveyance that operates as a release of whatever interest the grantor has in the property, sometimes called a release of a deed. The quitclaim deed contains similar language to a deed, with the important exception that rather than using the words *grant and release*, it contains language such as *remise, release and quitclaim*. Grantors therefore do not warrant title or possession. Grantors only pass on whatever interest they may have, if any. In effect, a grantor forever quits whatever claim he or she had, if in fact any existed.

The quitclaim deed transfers only whatever right, title and interest the grantor had in the land at the time of the execution of the deed and does not pass to the grantee any title or interest subsequently acquired by the grantor. Thus the grantee cannot claim a right to any "after-acquired title."

Although a quitclaim deed may or may not vest any title in the grantee, it is not inferior to the other types of deeds in what it actually conveys. For example, if a grantor executes and delivers a warranty deed to one person and subsequently executes and delivers a quitclaim deed to the same property to another person, the grantee under the quitclaim deed will prevail over the grantee under the warranty deed, assuming the holder of the quitclaim is first to record the deed.

Depending on local custom, ordinarily a warranty or bargain and sale deed will be used to transfer a fee simple interest (not in California). A quitclaim deed is not commonly used to convey a fee, but is usually restricted to releasing or conveying minor interests in real estate for the purpose of clearing title defects or clouds on title. It may also be used to convey lesser interests such as life estates and to release such interests as a remainder or reversion.

A title searcher will regard a quitclaim deed in the chain of title as a red flag, and most title companies will not guarantee titles derived out of a quitclaim, at least not without further clarification.

Quitclaim deeds also are often used between close relatives, such as when one heir is buying out the other, or where a seller's finances are so troubled that it is inconsequential to the buyer whether he or she is getting any warranties or not.

Executing a quitclaim deed does not carry even an implied warranty as regards ownership, liens, encumbrances or that the grantor has not previously signed a deed to someone else. It does convey ownership of the property to another person.

RECORDING REQUESTED BY
New Land Title Company
AND WHEN RECORDED MAIL
TO:

Name: Robert R. Mullins
Street Address: 2185 Memory Lane
City, State: Costa Mesa, CA 92626
Zip

Order No. 56748932-SMS

| REC |
| RCF |
| MICRO |
| RTCF |
| LIEN |
| SMPF |
| PCOR |

Space Above This Line for Recorder's Use

QUITCLAIM DEED

THE UNDERSIGNED GRANTOR(S) DECLARE(S)

City of : _Costa Mesa_

Conveyance tax is $_____
Parcel No. 123-45-6789

FOR A VALUABLE CONSIDERATION, receipt of which is hereby acknowledged, Michael L. Horton and Lisa M. Horton, Husband and Wife as Joint Tenants do (does) hereby REMISE, RELEASE AND FOREVER QUITCLAIM to Robert R. Mullins and Margie M. Mullins, Husband and Wife as Joint Tenants the following real property in the city of Costa Mesa, County of Orange, State of California

DOCUMENTARY TRANSFER TAX $_____

☐Computed on full value of interest of property conveyed

☐Full value less value of liens or encumbrances remaining at the time of sale

Lot 12 in Tract 2316 as recorded in Book 42 pages 5-10 inclusive of Miscellaneous Maps in the office of the County Recorder of the County of Orange State of California and described as follows: commencing at a point on the Southerly line thereof 450.8 feet West of the Southeast corner thereof, thence North 68 degrees 58 minutes West 100 fee, thence North 23 degrees 02 minutes East 60 feet, thence South 66 degrees 58 minutes East one hundred feet, thence South 23 degrees 02 minutes West 60 feet to the point of beginning..

Dated:_____

STATE OF CALIFORNIA
COUNTY OF_____

On_____before me.

a Notary Public in and for said County and State, personally appeared:

_____

_____

Personally known to me (or providedto me on the basis of satisfactory evidence whose name(s) is/are subscribed to the within instrument and acknowledged to me that he/she/they executed the same in his/her/their authorized capacity(ies) and that by his/her/their signature(s) on the instrument the person(s) or the entity upon behalf of which the person(s) acted, executed the instrument.

WITNESS my hand and official seal.

Signature_____

_____
Michael M. Horton

_____
Linda L. Horton

(This area for official notorial seal)

Warranty Deed

A warranty deed is one which contains express covenants of title. In other words, the seller who uses a warranty deed to transfer the property title to a buyer is guaranteeing clear title as well as the right to transfer it. Rarely is it used in California because title companies have taken over the role of insuring title to property.

Trust Deed

A trust deed is a security instrument that conveys title to a trustee to hold as security for the payment of a debt. There are three parties to a trust deed: the borrower (trustor), lender (beneficiary) and a neutral third party called a trustee. The only interest conveyed to the trustee is bare legal title, and the trustee's only obligation is to foreclose if there is a default on the loan, or reconvey the trust deed to the borrower when it is paid in full.

RECORDING REQUESTED BY
SMS SETTLEMENT SERVICES
AND WHEN RECORDED MAIL
TO:

| REC |
| RCF |
| MICRO |
| RTCF |
| LIEN |
| SMPF |
| PCOR |

Name: Robert Trabuco
Street Address: 21128 Rose
City, State: Mission Viejo, CA
Zip: 92691

Order No. 004860-DW

Recorder's Use

Space Above This Line for

DEED OF TRUST WITH ASSIGNMENT OF RENTS

This DEED OF TRUST, made **January 1, 1999**, between **Robert Trabuco and Amelia Trabuco** herein called TRUSTOR,
whose address is **542 Paramount Drive, Chino Hills, CA**

SMS SETTLEMENT SERVICES, a California Corporation, herein called TRUSTEE and **Jim Getz, An Unmarried Man and Mary Anne Getz**, herein called BENEFICIARY, Trustor irrevocably grants, transfers and assigns to Trustee in Trust, with Power of Sale, that property in City of **Mission Viejo,** County of **Los Angeles**, California, described as:

All that tract and parcel of land located on the northwest corner of the subdivision more commonly known as Rainbow Ridge and being more fully described in Deed Book 123, page 891.

Together with the rents, issues and profits thereof, subject, however, to the right, power and authority hereinafter given to and conferred upon Beneficiary to collect and apply such rents, issues and profits. For the Purpose of Securing (1) payment of the sum of $180,000.00 with interest thereon according to the terms of a promissory note or notes of even date herewith made by Trustor, payable to order of Benficiary, and extensions or renewals thereof; (2) the performance of each agreement of Trustor incorporated by reference or contained herein or reciting it is so secured; (3) Payment of additional sums and interest thereon which may hereafter be loaned to Trustor, or his successors or assigns, when evidenced by a promissory note or notes reciting that they are secured by this Deed of Trust.

To protect the security of this Deed of Trust, and with respect to the property above described, Trustor expressly makes each and all of the agreements, and adopts and agrees to perform and be bound by each and all of the terms and provisions set forth in subdivision A of that certain Fictitious Deed of Trust reference herein, and it is mutually agreed that all of the provisions set forth in subdivision B of that certain Fictitious Deed of Trust recorded in the book and page of Official Records in the office of the county recorder of the county where said property is located, noted below opposite the name of such county:

Said agreements, terms and provisions contained in said Subdivision A and B, (identical in all counties are printed on the reverse side hereof) are by the within reference thereto, incorporated herein and made a part of this Deed of Trust for all purposes as fully as if set forth at length herein and Beneficiary may charge for a statement regarding the obligation secured hereby, provided the charge therefor does not exceed the maximum allowed by laws.

The foregoing assignment of rents is absolute unless initiated here, in which case, the assignment serves as additional security.

The undersigned Trustor, requests that a copy of any notice of default and any notice of sale hereunder be mailed to him at this address hereinbefore set forth.

Dated: **January 1, 1999**

STATE OF CALIFORNIA   _____
COUNTY   **Robert Trabuco**
OF_____   _____

                                      Amelia Trabuco
On_____before
me.

a Notary Public in and for said County and State, personally appeared:
_____

_____
Personally known to me (or proved to me on the basis of satisfactory evidence whose name(s) is/are subscribed to the within instrument and acknowledged to me that he/she/they executed the same in his/her/their authorized capacity(ies) and that by his/her/their signature(s) on the instrument the person(s) or the entity upon behalf of which the person(s) acted, executed the instrument.

WITNESS my hand and official seal.

Signature_____   **(This area for official notorial seal)**

**TO: SMS
SETTLEMENT
SERVICES
COMPANY
TRUSTEE**

REQUEST FOR FULL RECONVEYANCE

The undersigned is the legal owner and holder of the note or notes, and of all other indebtedness secured by the foregoing Deed of Trust. Said note or notes, together with all other indebtedness secured by said Deed of Trust, have been fully paid and satisfied, and you are hereby requested and directed, on payment to you of any sums owing to you under the terms of said Deed of Trust, to cancel said note or notes above mentioned, and all other evidences of indebtedness secured by said Deed of Trust delivered to you herewith, together with the said Deed of Trust, and to reconvey, withour warranty, to the parties designated by the terms of said Deed of Trust, all the estate now held by you under the same.

Dated_____   _____

                                      _____
                                      _____

SIGNATURE MUST BE NOTARIZED

Please mail Deed of Trust,
Note and Reconveyance to_____

Do not lose or destroy this Deed of Trust OR THE NOTE which it secures. Both must be delivered to the Trustee for cancellation before reconveyance will be made.

Reconveyance Deed

A reconveyance deed conveys title to property from a trustee back to the borrower (trustor) upon payment in full of the debt secured by the trust deed. When the trustor pays off a loan, a request for full reconveyance or a request for partial reconveyance is executed by the beneficiary and given to the trustor along with the original note and deed of trust.

The trustor gives these documents to the trustee, who then issues the deed of reconveyance. Upon recording, it is evidence that the loan has been fully paid and the lien on the trust deed is extinguished.

Following are copies of a request for full reconveyance, the full reconveyance forms, the request for partial reconveyance and the partial reconveyance form. Usually, a partial reconveyance is used with large parcels of property when a portion of the note has been paid and release clauses are part of the trust deed.

The request for full reconveyance generally is found on the back side of a deed of trust (see preceding form). The only time a separate form should be necessary is if the original deed of trust has been lost and a copy is used for reconveyance.

Sheriff's Deed

A sheriff's deed is given to a buyer when property is sold through court action in order to satisfy a judgment for money or foreclosure of a mortgage.

Gift Deed

A gift deed is used to make a gift of property to a grantee, usually a close friend or relative. The consideration in a gift deed is called love and affection.

<u>Deeds</u>

- Grant Deed
- Quitclaim Deed
- Warranty Deed
- Trust Deed
- Reconveyance Deed
- Sheriff's Deed
- Gift Deed

Other Documents

Request for Notice of Default

A request for notice, as it is sometimes called, is a way anyone interested in a particular trust deed can make sure of being informed if a borrower is not making timely payments and a notice of default is recorded. The request for notice must be recorded with the county recorder. Any parties with an interest in knowing whether or not the property is about to be sold at a trustee's sale, if they are on file as requesting notice of an upcoming foreclosure, may then act for their own benefit to protect their interest in the property. The most likely candidate to be harmed by a surprise foreclosure is the holder of a lien junior to the one being foreclosed.

Junior Shrewdmoney sold his home for $200,000 and carried back a second trust deed. At the time of the sale, Junior asked escrow to record a request for notice of default on the first trust deed.

Five years went by before the buyer stopped making payments on the first trust deed. A notice of default was recorded by the holder of the first trust deed, starting foreclosure procedings. During the five years, however, the value of the property had decreased to an amount less than the buyer paid for the property, and in fact, the property was now worth little more than the amount of the first trust deed.

If Junior had not been notified in a timely manner of the trustee's sale, his interest in the property would have been canceled by the sale, with any proceeds going to the foreclosing lender of the first loan. Junior can now file his own notice of default

53

and protect his trust deed by becoming the new owner, subject to bringing current the first trust deed.

A request for notice must contain the recording data applying to the deed of trust and the name and address of the person who wants the information. The recorder will enter this on the record of the deed of trust or mortgage, and if subsequently any notice of default or sale is recorded, the person named in the request will have to be notified. Some trust deeds have the request printed on the deed and it is not necessary to record a separate request for notice.

Substitution of Trustee

The trustee under a deed of trust does not need to formally accept the position of trustee. Forms used by most escrow holders usually name a title company or their own escrow company. Anyone can be a trustee, with the only restriction on naming a trustee under a deed of trust being that it cannot be the borrower (trustor).

Because anyone can be a trustee, it is very easy for a named trustee under a deed of trust to be out of business or out of the state. Who then will start foreclosure, and who will reconvey the property to the trustor when the loan is paid off if the trustee is nowhere to be found?

The beneficiary under a deed of trust has the power to change the trustee of his deed of trust at any time by completing a "substitution of trustee" which deletes the current trustee and names a new one instead.

Request for Notice of Delinquency

Even though a request for notice of default may be filed by the holder of a junior lien (1st, 2nd, 3rd, etc.) , by the time a lender gets around to foreclosure, the borrower may be many months behind in payments. Anyone acquiring the property at a foreclosure sale must bring current all payments and fees for existing senior loans on the property.

By recording a request for notice of delinquency, the junior lien holder filing the request will be notified of the delinquency of four payments and then can decide whether to bring pressure on the borrower in default on the senior loan before the amount becomes unmanageable, or pay the amount in arrears.

Statement of Information

Buyers and sellers must complete a statement of personal information as a necessary and essential part of each escrow opened. The title company needs the correct information regarding places of employment, former residences, former marriages and social security numbers to identify each party to the escrow as just that party and no other.

SMS

Statement of Information

FILL OUT COMPLETELY AND RETURN TO STRATEGIC MORTGAGE SERVICES

ESCROW # 00020-SMS   **TRACT#**   **LOT #**

Name_____   Social Security   Driver's
                                                    #_____   License#_____

Date of birth_____   Place of birth_____   Bus. phone_____   Home phone_____

Resided in USA since_____   Resided in California since_____

If you are married, please complete the following: Date Married_____at_____

Name of Spouse_____   Social Security #_____Driver's License #_____

Resided in USA since_____   Resided in California since_____

Previous Marriage or Marriages (if no previous marriage, write "None"):
Name of former spouse_____   Deceased___Divorced__Where___When____

Name of former spouse_____   Deceased___Divorced____Where___When___

Children by current or previous Marriages:
Name_____   Born_____   Name_____   Born_____
Name_____   Born_____   Name_____   Born_____

Information covering past 10 years:
Residence: _____

Number/Street	City	From	To
Number/Street	City	From	To

Employment _____

Firm Name	Location
Firm Name	Location

Spouse Employment: _____

Firm Name	Location
Firm Name	Location

Have you or your spouse owned or operated a business?

☐Yes   ☐No   If so please list
                                              names_____

I have never been adjudged, bankrupt, nor are there any unsatisfied judgments or other matters
pending against me which might affect my title to this property except as follows:

_____

The undersigned declare, under penalty of perjury, that the foregoing is true and correct.
Executedon_____   at_____
               date   city
                                          Signature

Preliminary Change of Ownership

This document gives information to the county tax assessor about the property and who now owns it. The assessor can then determine from the sales price the method used to finance the purchase and the reason for the change in ownership, whether or not a change in property tax is required. The following preliminary change of ownership report allows the assessor to place the appropriate tax on the property, starting on the date of conveyance to the next assessment date. The form must be completed before the close of escrow by the buyer, or the county recorder will impose an extra fee for recording the grant deed.

Even then, the buyer must submit the completed form within 60 days after closing escrow or other penalties will be accrued. The tax assessor then gets to revalue the property and increase the taxes due for the time from the close of escrow to when the next tax bill is issued.

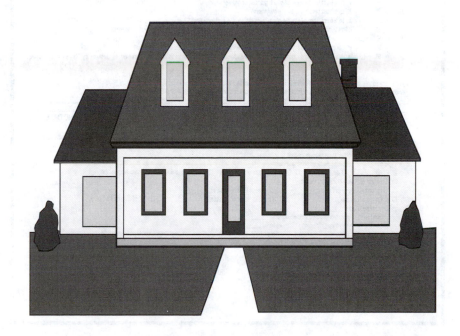

PRELIMINARY CHANGE OF OWNERSHIP REPORT

To be completed by transferee (buyer) prior to transfer of subject property in accordance with Section 480.03 of the Revenue and Taxation Code. A Preliminary Change of Ownership Report must be filed with each conveyance in the County Recorder's office for the county where the property is located; this particular form may be used in all 58 counties of California.

THIS REPORT IS NOT A PUBLIC DOCUMENT

FOR RECORDER'S USE ONLY

SELLER/TRANSFEROR: Michael M. Horton and Linda L. Horton
BUYER/TRANSFEREE: Robert R. Mullins and Margie M. Mullins
ASSESSOR'S PARCEL NUMBER(S) 123-45-6789
PROPERTY ADDRESS OR LOCATION:

      2165 Memory Lane
      Santa Ana, CA 92705

MAIL TAX INFORMATION TO:

      Name   Robert R. Mullins
      Address 2165 Memory Lane

      Costa Mesa, CA 92626

NOTICE: A lien for property taxes applies to your property on March 1 of each year for the taxes owing in the following fiscal year, July 1 through June 30. One-half of these taxes is due November 1, and one-half is due February 1. The first installment becomes delinquent on December 10, and the second installment becomes delinquent on April 10. One tax bill is mailed before November 1 to the owner of record. **IF THIS TRANSFER OCCURS AFTER MARCH 1 AND ON OR BEFORE DECEMBER 31, YOU MAY BE RESPONSIBLE FOR THE SECOND INSTALLMENT OF TAXES DUE FEBRUARY 1.**

The property which you acquired may be subject to a supplemental assessment in an amount to be determined by the Orange County Assessor. For further information on your supplemental roll obligation, please call the Orange County Assessor at 714-834-2727.

PART I: TRANSFER INFORMATION   Please answer all questions.

YES	NO		
☐	☑	A.	Is this transfer solely between husband and wife (Addition of a spouse, death of a spouse, divorce settlement, etc.)?
☐	☑	B.	Is this transaction only a correction of the name(s) of the person(s) holding title to the property (For example, a name change upon marriage)?
☐	☑	C.	Is this document recorded to create, terminate, or reconvey a lender's interest in the property?
☐	☑	D.	Is this transaction recorded only to create, terminate, or reconvey a security interest (e.g. cosigner)?
☐	☑	E.	Is this document recorded to substitute a trustee under a deed of trust, mortgage, or other similar document?
☐	☑	F.	Did this transfer result in the creation of a joint tenancy in which the seller (transferor) remains as one of the joint tenants?
☐	☑	G.	Does this transfer return property to the person who created the joint tenancy (original transferor)?
		H.	Is this transfer of property:
☐	☑		1. to a trust for the benefit of the grantor, or grantor's spouse?
☐	☑		2. to a trust revocable by the transferor?
☐	☑		3. to a trust from which the property reverts to the grantor within 12 years?
☐	☑	I.	If this property is subject to a lease, is the remaining lease term 35 years or more including written options?
☐	☑	J.	Is this a transfer from parents to children or from children to parents?
☐	☑	K.	Is this transaction to replace a principal residence by a person 55 years of age or older?
☐	☑	L.	Is this transaction to replace a principal residence by a person who is severely disabled as defined by Revenue and Code Section 69.5?

If you checked yes to J, K, or L, an applicable claim form must be filed with the County Assessor.
Please provide any other information that would help the Assessors to understand the nature of the transfer.

IF YOU HAVE ANSWERED "YES" TO ANY OF THE ABOVE QUESTIONS EXCEPT J, K, OR L, PLEASE SIGN AND DATE, OTHERWISE COMPLETE BALANCE OF THE FORM.

PART II: OTHER TRANSFER INFORMATION
A. Date of transfer if other than recording date _____ .
B. Type of transfer. Please check appropriate box.

    ☑ Purchase   ☐ Foreclosure   ☐ Gift   ☐ Trade or Exchange   ☐ Merger, Stock, or Partnership Acquisition
    ☐ Contract of Sale - Date of Contract _____
    ☐ Inheritance - Date of Death _____   ☐ Other: Please explain: _____
    ☐ Creation of Lease   ☐ Assignment of a Lease   ☐ Termination of a Lease
      Date lease began _____
      Original term in years (including written options) _____
      Remaining term in years (including written options) _____
C. Was only a partial interest in the property transferred? ☐ Yes ☑ No   If yes, indicate the percentage transferred _____%

PRELIMINARY CHANGE OF OWNERSHIP REPORT

Please answer, to the best of your knowledge, all applicable questions, sign and date. If a question does not apply, indicate with "N/A."

PART III: PURCHASE PRICE AND TERMS OF SALE

A. CASH DOWN PAYMENT OR Value of Trade or Exchange (excluding closing costs)   Amount **$5,000.00**

B. FIRST DEED OF TRUST @ **7.57**% interest for **30** years. Pymts/Mo.= **$857.00** (Prin. & Int. only)   Amount **$80,000.00**

☐ FHA   ☑ Fixed Rate   ☑ New Loan
☑ Conventional   ☐ Variable Rate   ☐ Assumed Existing Loan Balance
☐ VA   ☐ All inclusive D.T. ($ _____ Wrapped)   ☑ Bank or Savings & Loan
☐ Cal-Vet   ☐ Loan Carried by Seller   ☐ Finance Company
Balloon Payment   ☐ Yes   ☑ No   Due Date _____ Amount $ _____

C. SECOND DEED OF TRUST @ _____% interest for _____ years. Pymts/Mo.=$_____ (Prin. & Int. only)   Amount $_____

☐ Bank or Savings & Loan   ☐ Fixed Rate   ☐ New Loan
☐ Loan Carried by Seller   ☐ Variable Rate   ☐ Assumed Existing Loan Balance
Balloon Payment   ☐ Yes   ☐ No   Due Date _____ Amount $ _____

D. OTHER FINANCING: Is other financing involved not covered in (b) or (c) above? ☐ Yes ☑ No   Amount $_____
Type _____ @ _____% interest for _____ years. Pymts./Mo.=$_____ (Prin. & Int. only)
☐ Bank or Savings & Loan   ☐ Fixed Rate   ☐ New Loan
☐ Loan Carried by Seller   ☐ Variable Rate   ☐ Assumed Existing Loan Balance
Balloon Payment   ☐ Yes   ☑ No   Due Date _____ Amount $ _____

E. IMPROVEMENT BOND   ☐ Yes   ☑ No   Outstanding Balance: Amount $_____

F. TOTAL PURCHASE PRICE (or acquisition price, if traded or exchanged, include real estate commission if paid.)
Total Items A through E $ **100,000.00**

G. PROPERTY PURCHASED   ☑ Through a broker   ☐ Direct from seller   ☐ Other (explain) _____

If purchased through a broker, provide broker's name and phone number: **Century One Real Estate (714) 555-7676**
_____

Please explain any special terms or financing and any other information that would help the Assessor understand the purchase price and terms of sale.
_____
_____
_____

PART IV: PROPERTY INFORMATION

A. IS PERSONAL PROPERTY INCLUDED IN PURCHASE PRICE
(other than a mobilehome subject to local property tax)? ☐ Yes   ☑ No
If yes, enter the value of the personal property included in the purchase price $_____ (Attach itemized list of personal property).

B. IS THIS PROPERTY INTENDED AS YOUR PRINCIPAL RESIDENCE?   ☑ Yes   ☐ No
If yes, enter date of occupancy _____/_____/_____ ,or intended occupancy **02/01/1995**
     Month   Day   Year   Month Day Year

C. TYPE OF PROPERTY TRANSFERRED:
☑ Single-family residence   ☐ Agricultural   ☐ Timeshare
☐ Multiple-family residence (no. of units: _____)   ☐ Co-op/Own-your-own   ☐ Mobilehome
☐ Commercial/Industrial   ☐ Condominium   ☐ Unimproved lot
☐ Other (Description: _____)

D. DOES THE PROPERTY PRODUCE INCOME?   ☐ Yes   ☑ No

E. IF THE ANSWER TO QUESTION D IS YES, IS THE INCOME FROM:
☐ Lease/Rent   ☐ Contract   ☐ Mineral Rights   ☐ Other - Explain: _____

F. WHAT WAS THE CONDITION OF PROPERTY AT THE TIME OF SALE?
☑ Good   ☐ Average   ☐ Fair   ☐ Poor
Enter here, or on an attached sheet, any other information that would assist the Assessor in determining the value of the property such as the physical condition of the property, restrictions, etc.
_____
_____
_____

I certify that the foregoing is true, correct and complete to the best of my knowledge and belief.

Signed _____ Dated _____
     NEW OWNER/CORPORATE OFFICER

Please Print Name of New Owner/Corporate Officer **Robert R. Mullins and Margie M. Mullins**

Phone Number where you are available from 8:00 a.m. - 5:00 p.m. **(714) 555-2323**
     (NOTE: The Assessor may contact you for further information)

If a document evidencing a change of ownership is presented to the recorder for recordation without the concurrent filing of a preliminary change of ownership report, the recorder may charge an additional recording fee of twenty dollars ($20).

Power of Attorney

A power of attorney is used when a principal is not available to sign documents necessary for the conveyance of real property or some other legal act. It is valid for the party named in executing documents, both buying and selling, and has the same force and effect as the principal granting the power would have if he or she signed. The power of attorney must be recorded in the county in which the real property is located.

There are two types of power of attorney you will become familiar with as an escrow officer: specific and general. The specific power is used for a specific function such as the sale of real property. It lists the purpose precisely for what it is intended. The purpose of the general power of attorney is broad and may be used by the person empowered to sign anything the principal giving the power would sign or do.

Some lenders, however, will not allow a person with a power of attorney to sign loan documents or grant deeds, so it may be necessary to check with the title company and the lender to see what is accepted.

Notary Public Jurats

A notary jurat is the form attached (when documents are notarized) that states the person appeared before the notary and proved identity. The form makes a notary responsible for identifying the party whose name is to be notarized, and also makes the notary accountable for that determination. The notary does not necessarily need to see the person sign the document, but simply notarizes the document on the basis of the party appearing in person and acknowledging the signatures. A notary public jurat is not, as many believe, affirmation of the truth of a document, but of the truth that this person appearing has signed the document.

Real Estate Basics

Ownership of Real Property

All property has an owner--either the government or a private institution or an individual. Title is the evidence that the owner of land is in lawful possession. It is the proof of ownership. Separate ownership and concurrent ownership are the two ways real estate may be owned.

Escrow agents can never tell people how to take title. Parties must consult with their attorney, accountant or anyone they choose and then give the escrow agent instructions regarding vesting.

Separate Ownership

Property owned by one person or entity is known as sole and separate, or ownership in severalty. A corporation is known to hold title in severalty, because it is a sole entity.

Concurrent Ownership

When property is owned by two or more persons or entities at the same time, it is known as concurrent ownership, or co-ownership.

Concurrent ownership comes in several forms such as joint tenancy, tenancy in common, community property and tenancy in partnership.

Four Types of Concurrent Ownership:

- Joint Tenancy
- Tenancy in Common
- Community Property
- Tenancy in Partnership

Joint Tenancy: When two or more parties own

real property as co-owners, with the right of survivorship, it is called joint tenancy. The right of survivorship means that if one of the joint tenants dies, the surviving partner automatically becomes sole owner of the property.

The deceased's share does not go to his or her estate or heirs, but becomes the property of the co-tenant without becoming involved in probate. Also, the surviving joint tenant is not liable to creditors of the deceased who hold liens on the joint tenancy property.

> *John, Paul, George and Edward are joint tenants. Edward dies and his interest automatically goes to John, Paul and George as joint tenants with equal one-third interests.*
>
> **************
>
> *Kelly and Roger own a house as joint tenants. Roger dies and Kelly now owns the house as her sole and separate property without probate. Roger's heirs are not entitled to his share because of the right of survivorship.*

In order to have a joint tenancy, there are four things that must be in agreement: time, title, interest and possession.

The Four Unities of Joint Tenancy:

- **Time**
All parties must become joint tenants at the same time

- Title
All parties must take title on the same deed

- Interest
All parties must have an equal interest in the property

- Possession
All parties have equal right of possession, known as an undivided interest

All four items must occur to have a joint tenancy. If any one of the unities is broken, the joint tenancy is dissolved. Co-owners may sell their interest, give it away or borrow money against it, without consent of the other joint tenants. Because of the right of survivorship, a joint tenant may not will his or her share.

Tenancy in Common: When two or more persons, whose interests are not necessarily equal, are owners of undivided interests in a single estate, a tenancy in common exists. Whenever some other form of ownership or vesting is not mentioned specifically, and there are co-owners, title is assumed to be a tenancy in common.

The only requirement of unity for tenants in common is the equal right of possession or undivided interest--as it is called. That means each owner has a certain equitable interest in the property (such as one-half interest, or one-fourth interest), but has the right to use the whole property. None of the owners may exclude any co-owner from the property, nor claim any portion of the property for exclusive use.

The Four Requirements of Tenants in Common:

- Tenants in common may take title at different times
- Tenants in common may take title on separate deeds
- Tenants in common may have unequal interests
- Tenants in common have an undivided interest or equal right of possession

---

Any tenant in common may sell, encumber or will his or her interest, with heirs simply becoming a tenant in common among the others. A tenant in common must pay a proportionate share of any expenses incurred on the property, including money spent for repairs, taxes, loan payments and insurance. When tenants in common do not agree on matters pertaining to the property, any of the co-owners may file a partition action which asks the court to decide the fate of the investment.

Stacey, Steven, Catherine and Dan are joint tenants. Dan sells his interest to Eva. The joint tenancy has been broken regarding the interest Dan had in the property. The new vesting, after the sale of Dan's interest, is Stacey, Steven and Catherine as joint tenants with equal interests, and the right of survivorship, with Eva as a tenant in common.

Stacey, Steven, Catherine and Eva, in the above property, wish to restore a joint tenancy with each of the four having the right of survivorship. Eva holds a tenancy in common, so she will have to be added to the joint tenancy. Since all joint tenants must take title at the same time, on the same document, Stacey, Steven, Catherine and Eva must sign a new deed that lists Stacey, Steven and Catherine as joint tenants and Eva as a tenant in common. Then the property can be deeded to all four parties as joint tenants. All requirements for a joint tenancy--time, title, interest and possession-- will then be fulfilled.

Community Property: All property acquired by a husband and wife during a valid marriage--except for certain separate property--is called community property. Separate property includes: all property owned before marriage; all property acquired by either of the parties during marriage by gift or inheritance; all income derived from separate property.

If spouses want to maintain the status of their separate property, they must be very careful not to co-mingle it with their community property. Separate property (such as an apartment building with a negative cash flow) may not be supported with community property funds, nor can the income of either spouse  be used in any way to maintain separate property. Any income, including wages from either spouse, is considered community property.

Community property can not be sold or encumbered by only one of the partners. Either spouse may <u>buy</u> real or personal property without the consent of the other; both are bound by the contract made by either one, unless the new property is bought specifically as separate property, with funds from a separate property account.

Either party may will one-half of the community property. If there is no will, the surviving spouse inherits all community property. This is important to know, particularly with multiple marriages, for estate planning.

Property may be owned with the intention that it go to one's children, only to learn after the parent's death that children of the first marriage are no longer natural heirs. If there is a subsequent husband or wife and no will has been made, the new spouse will become the natural heir to the real property.

Regarding separate property, if there is no will, the surviving spouse gets one-half and one child gets one-half. If there is more than one child, the surviving spouse gets one-third and the children get two-thirds.

Tenancy in Partnership: Ownership by two or more persons who form a partnership for business purposes is known as tenancy in partnership. Each partner has an equal right of possession for partnership.

Limitations On Real Property

An encumbrance is an interest in real property that is held by someone who is not the owner. Anything that

affects the title or the use of the property is an encumbrance. A property is encumbered when it is burdened with legal obligations against the title. Encumbrances fall into two categories: those that affect the title, known as money encumbrances, and those that affect the use of the property, known as non-money encumbrances. The encumbrances that create a legal obligation to pay are known as liens. A lien uses real property as security for the payment of a debt.

Common types of liens are trust deeds and mortgages; mechanic's liens; tax liens; and special assessments, attachments and judgments. Those types of encumbrances that affect the physical use of the property are easements, building restrictions, and zoning requirements and encroachments.

Money Encumbrances (Liens)

A lien is an obligation to pay a money encumbrance that may be voluntary or involuntary. An owner may choose to borrow money, using the property as security for the loan, creating a voluntary lien.

On the other hand, if the owner doesn't pay taxes or the debt owed, a lien may be placed against his or her property without permission, creating an involuntary lien.

A lien may be specific or general. A specific lien is one that is placed against a certain property, while a general lien affects all property of the owner.

Trust deeds and mortgages are both instruments used in real estate financing to create voluntary, specific liens against real property. They will be discussed in detail later.

Tax Liens and Special Assessments: If any government taxes, such as income or property taxes are not paid, they become a lien against the property. Special assessments are levied against property owners to pay for local improvements, such as underground utilities, street repair, or water projects. Payment for the projects is secured by a special assessment which becomes a lien against real property.

Attachments and Judgments: An attachment is the process by which the court holds the property of a defendant pending outcome of a lawsuit. An attachment lien is valid for three years and may be extended in certain cases.

A judgment is the final determination of the rights of parties in a lawsuit by the court. A judgment does not automatically create a lien. A summary of the court decision, known as an abstract of judgment, must be filed with the county recorder. When the abstract is filed, the judgment becomes a general lien on all property owned or acquired by the judgment debtor for 10 years, in the county in which the abstract is filed.

Lis Pendens: A Lis Pendens is recorded notice that indicates pending litigation on a property. It clouds the title preventing the sale or transfer of the property until removed.

<u>Non-Money Encumbrances</u>

A non-money encumbrance is one that affects the use of property such as an easement, a building restriction or an encroachment.

Easements: An easement is the right to use another's land for a specified purpose, sometimes known as a right-of-way.   An interest in an easement is non-possessory.   That means the holder of an easement can use it only for the purpose intended and may not exclude anyone else from using it.

Easements are created in various ways--commonly by express grant or reservation in a grant deed or by a written agreement between owners of adjoining land.   An

easement always should be recorded to assure its continued existence.   It is recorded by the party benefiting from the easement as the "dominant tenement."

Five Ways to Create an Easement:

1. Express Grant: The "servient tenement," or the giver of the easement, grants the easement by deed or express agreement.

2. Express Reservation: The seller of a parcel who owns adjoining land reserves an easement or right-of-way over the former property. It is created at the time of the sale with a deed or express agreement.

3. Implied Grant or Reservation: The existence of an easement is obvious and necessary at the time a property is conveyed, even though no mention is made of it in the deed.

4. Necessity: An easement created when a parcel is completely landlocked and has no access. It is automatically terminated when another way to enter and leave the property becomes available.

5. Prescription: An easement by prescription may be created continuous and uninterrupted use, by a single party, for a period of five years. The owner must know about the use, and the use must be against the owner's wishes (open and notorious). The party wishing to obtain the prescriptive easement must have some reasonable claim to the use of the property.

Easements May be Terminated or Extinguished by:

1. Express Release: The only one who can release an easement is the dominant tenement

2. Legal Proceedings: Quiet title action to terminate the easement brought by the servient tenement against the dominant tenement

3. Merger: This joins the dominant tenement and the servient tenement

4. Non- Use: When applied to a prescriptive easement for a period of five years, this terminates the easement

5. Abandonment: Obvious and intentional surrender of the easement

6. Destruction of the Servient Tenement: If the government takes the servient tenement for its use, as in eminent domain, the easement is terminated

7. Adverse Possessions: The owner of the servient tenement may, by his or her own use, prevent the dominant tenement from using the easement for a period of five years, thus terminating the easement

Restrictions: Another type of encumbrance is a restriction, which is a limitation placed on the use of property. It may be placed by a private owner, a developer or the government. It is usually placed on property to assure that land use is consistent and uniform within a certain area.

Restrictions are created in the deed at the time of sale or in the general plan of a subdivision by the developer. For example, a developer may use a height restriction to ensure views from each parcel in a subdivision.

Private restrictions are placed by a present or past owner and affect only a specific property or development, while zoning is an example of government restrictions that benefit the general public.

Restrictions are commonly known as C.C.&R.'s or Covenants, Conditions and Restrictions. A covenant is a promise to do or not do certain things. The penalty for a breach of a covenant is usually money damages. An example of a covenant might be that the tenant agrees to make some

repairs, or that a property may be used only for a specific purpose, such as a church or homeless shelter.

A condition is much the same as a covenant, a promise to do or not do something, except the penalty for breaking a condition is return of the property to the grantor. A condition subsequent is a restriction placed in a deed at the time of conveyance on future use of the property. Upon breach of the condition subsequent, the grantor may take back the property. A condition precedent requires that a certain event, or condition, occur before title can pass to the new owner.

Encroachments: The placement of permanent improvements on adjacent property owned by another is known as an encroachment.

Recording System

County Recorders

Each county in the state has a County Recorder's office where documents may be recorded. As you recall, a deed does not have to be recorded to be valid. However, recordation maintains the chain of title necessary to create a history of ownership of real property

Background of Land Title in California

Ownership of land in California began with Spanish explorers who claimed it for the king of Spain in the early 16th Century. Since the king technically owned everything, all land was granted to private parties by the military representatives of Spanish rule. Ownership and transfer of land and property rights were determined by local authorities operating under a strict set of civil laws that were given to them by the Spanish king.

This continued until 1822, when Mexico began colonizing California and governing the territory. Mexican governors totally controlled who received grants of land during this time, and recorded the grants, known as expedientes, in the government archives. Even 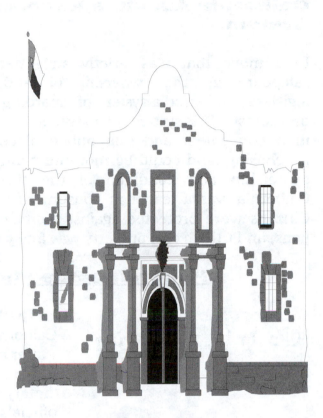 so, the land descriptions were vague and evidence of title may or may not have been in the actual possession of the owner. This led to many disputes over ownership in later years, after California became as state.

In 1848, the Treaty of Guadalupe Hidalgo ended the war with Mexico, and California became a possession of the United States. Land claims that had been granted by Mexico were honored, and confirmed with patents to the land, by the U.S. government, to those with proven ownership. Even though Spain or Mexico granted ownership, according to the Roman Civil Law they followed, the laws changed after California became a state in 1850. England's Common Law principles now governed the title of real property.

California Adopts a Recording System

In a move that was strictly an American device for safeguarding the ownership of land, the California legislature adopted a system of recording evidence of title or interest. This system meant records could be collected in a convenient and safe public place, so that those purchasing land could be more fully informed about the ownership and condition of the title. Even then, California was a leader in consumer-friendly legislation. Citizens were protected against secret conveyances and liens, and title to real property was freely transferable.

Recording Specifics

The Recording Act of California provides that, after acknowledgment or being signed before a notary or certain public officials, any instrument or judgment affecting the title to--or possession of--real property may be recorded. Recording permits, rather than requires, the filing of documents that affect title to real property.

The process consists of copying the instrument to be recorded in the proper index, and filing it in alphabetical order, under the names of the parties, without delay. The document must be recorded by the county recorder in the county within which the property is located to be valid there.

When the recorder receives a document to be filed, he or she notes the time and date of filing and at whose request it was filed. After the contents of the document are copied into the record, the original document is marked "filed for record," stamped with the proper time and date of recording, and returned to the person who requested the recording.

The Effect: Public Notice

This process gives constructive notice of the content of any instrument recorded to anyone who cares to look into the records. Recording is considered to be public notice of the information filed there. However, possession is considered constructive notice, and a buyer should always check to be sure there is no one living on the property who might have a prior claim to ownership. It is the buyer's duty to conduct proper inquiry before purchasing any property. Failure to do so does not relieve the buyer of that responsibility.

> *Ann bought a property through her broker, sight unseen. The escrow closed and the deed was recorded. When Ann tried to move into her new home, however, she found George living there. He told her he had bought the property a year ago and had not bothered to record the deed, but had moved in and considered it his home. When she consulted her attorney, Ann found that indeed George--because he was in possession of the property--had given actual notice to anyone who might inquire. Ann had a duty to see for herself, and--failing to do that, or instruct her broker to do it--lost the property.*

Priorities in Recording

As we have seen, recording laws are meant to protect citizens against fraud and to give others notification of property ownership. Other information that might influence ownership can be recorded also, such as liens and other encumbrances. To obtain priority through recording, a buyer must be a good faith purchaser, for a valuable consideration, and record the deed first.

Priority means the order in which deeds are recorded. Whether or not it is a grant deed, trust deed or some other evidence of a lien or encumbrance, the priority is determined by the date stamped in the upper right-hand corner of the document by the county recorder at the time it is recorded.

If there are several grant deeds recorded against the property, the one recorded first is valid. In a case where there are several trust deeds recorded against a property, no mention will be made about which one is the first trust deed, which is the second, and so forth.

A person inquiring about the priority of the deeds should look at the time and date the deed was recorded for that information. You will see, as we proceed in our study, the importance of the date and time of recording.

Post Test

The following self test repeats the one you took at the beginning of this chapter. Now take the exam again--since you have read all the material-- and check your knowledge of parties, documents and real estate basics.

True/False

1. A third party who carries out the written provisions of an escrow agreement is known as an escrow holder.

2. Property is usually transferred with a grant deed.

3. A request for notice of default is a way anyone interested in a particular trust deed can make sure of being informed if a notice of default has been recorded.

4. A preliminary change of ownership gives a buyer temporary title.

5. Ownership in severalty is the same as concurrent ownership.

6. An encumbrance is a limitation on ownership to real property.

7. A mechanic's lien is an example of a non-money encumbrance.

8. Property acquired by a husband and wife during a marriage, except for certain separate property, is owned by the wife.

9. An encumbrance that creates a legal obligation to pay is known as a lien.

10. A lis pendens indicates pending litigation on a property.

chapter **3**

REAL ESTATE FINANCE

Focus

- **Introduction**
- **How the process works**
- **Promissory note**
- **Trust deeds and mortgages**
- **Transfer of property by the borrower**
- **Special clauses in financing instruments**
- **Foreclosure**
- **Junior trust deeds**
- **Other types of loans secured by trust deeds**
- **Unsecured loans**
- **Alternative financing**
- **Truth-in-Lending Act (Regulation Z)**
- **Equal Credit Opportunity Act**
- **Soldiers' and Sailors' Civil Relief Act**

Pre-Test

The following is a self test to determine how much you know about real estate finance before reading this chapter. Take it without studying, then read the material presented in the text. At the end of the chapter you will find a repeat of this exam. Test your knowledge by answering the questions again, then check your improvement. (The answers are found at the end of the book.) Good luck.

True/False

1. Hypothecation is when an owner uses a property as security for a loan, but does not give up possession.

2. A trustee is a neutral third party in a trust deed.

3. In a trust deed, the borrower is the same as the beneficiary.

4. The beneficiary hold bare legal title to a property encumbered by a trust deed.

5. A reconveyance deed is used to deed a property to the trustor after the deed of trust has been paid in full.

6. An "or more" clause allows a borrower to pay off a loan early with no penalty.

7. A holder in due course is someone who buys an existing negotiable note.

8. Foreclosure is the cure for a tenant's default on monthly rental payments.

9. A trustee must sign a reconveyance deed.

10. A land contract and a contract of sale are alike.

Introduction

Imagine buying a house and being required to pay the total price in cash. The sweet pleasure of home ownership probably would belong somewhere in the next century for most of us. With the average price of a single family home being so high, buying a home would be unthinkable without the practical benefit of financing.

By allowing a home buyer to obtain a loan for the difference between the sales price and the down payment, real estate lenders have provided the solution to the problem of how property can be bought and sold without the requirement of an all-cash sale.

What started out as a simple loan by a local bank--with an agreement that the borrower pay it all back in a timely manner--is now a complex subject. Buyers and sellers need to rely on experts to explain all the choices there are on financing the purchase or sale of property. A real estate licensee is probably one of the experts to whom they will turn.

This chapter on real estate finance is organized with each part building on what you have learned in the earlier sections of the chapter. Try to master each subject--promissory notes, trust deeds, mortgages, special financing clauses, foreclosure, junior trust deeds, other security instruments, miscellaneous provisions of finance and consumer protection--as you come to it. There is a thread that connects everything you are about to study in this chapter. Read with that in mind.

Now that you know real estate finance is nothing more than lenders loaning money so people can buy property, let's start with an examination of the lending process.

How the Process Works

When a loan is made, the borrower signs a promissory note, or note--as it is called, which states that a certain amount of money has been borrowed. The note is the evidence of the debt.

When money is loaned for the purpose of financing real property, some kind of collateral is usually required as well as the promise to pay the money back. That means the lender wants some concrete assurance of getting the money back beyond the borrower's written promise to pay. The property being bought or borrowed against is commonly used as security, or collateral, for the debt. In other words, the lender feels more secure about making the loan if assured of the property ownership in case of default, or nonpayment of the loan. Then the lender can sell it to get the loan money back.

Commonly, financing is secured with a trust deed or mortgage. Under a trust deed, after signing the promissory note, the borrower is required to execute a trust deed at the same time, which is the security guaranteeing loan repayment. This is known as hypothecation, a process which allows a borrower to remain in possession of the property while using it to secure the loan. If the borrower does not make payments per the agreement, he or she then loses the rights of possession and ownership.

The lender holds the trust deed, along with the note, until the loan is repaid.

Note and Trust Deed

The promissory note is *evidence* of the debt, or the money borrowed, and the trust deed is *security* for the debt.

The trust deed allows the lender, in case of loan default, to order the trustee to sell the property described in the deed. (More explanation of this process follows later in the chapter.)

When a buyer obtains a loan to purchase property, he or she is using the lender's money to finance the sale. This is known as leverage. The use of borrowed capital to buy real estate is a process that permits the buyer to use little of one's own money and large amounts of someone else's.

There are several reasons leverage is appealing to both the home buyer and the investor. The main advantage to the home buyer is not having to amass the entire purchase price to become a home owner. The investor can use leverage to control several investments, rather than just one, each purchased with a small amount of personal funds, and a large amount of a lender's money. The investor can then

earn a return on each property, therefore increasing the amount of yield on investment dollars.

Promissory Note

A promissory note is a written promise to pay back a certain sum of money with specified terms at an agreed upon time. Sometimes it is simply called the note. Informally, it could be called an IOU. The maker is the person borrowing the money, or making the note. It is a personal obligation of the borrower and a complete contract in itself, between the borrower and lender. The holder is loaning the money, or the one holding the note.

According to the Uniform Commercial Code, to be valid or enforceable, a promissory note must meet certain requirements.

A Promissory Note is:

1. An unconditional written promise to pay a certain sum

2. Made by one person to another

3. Signed by the maker or borrower

4. Payable at a definite time

5. Paid to bearer or to order

6. Voluntarily delivered by the borrower and accepted by the lender

INSTALLMENT NOTE
(INTEREST INCLUDED)
(THIS NOTE CONTAINS AN ACCELERATION CLAUSE)

$189,000   Mission Viejo   ,California,   1/1/99

In installments and at the times hereinafter stated, for value received, Robert Trabuco and Amelia Trabuco

promise to pay to Jim Getz and Mary Anne Getz

_____ , or order

at 21128 Rose, Rancho Santa Margarita, CA 92626

the principal sum of One Hundred Eighty Thousand   dollars

with interest from January 1, 1999   on the amounts of

principal remaining from time to time unpaid, until said principal sum is paid, at the rate of   8.9   percent

per annum. Principal and interest due in monthly installments of One Thousand Five Hundred Dollars, $1,500, or more on the 15th day of each and every month, beginning on the 15th day of February, 1999.

and continuing until said principal sum has been fully paid. AT ANY TIME, THE PRIVILEGE IS RESERVED TO PAY MORE THAN THE SUM DUE. Should the interest not be so paid, it shall be added to the principal and thereafter bear like interest as the principal, but such unpaid interest so compounded shall not exceed an amount equal to simple interest on the unpaid principal at the maximum rate permitted by law. Should default be made in the payment of any of said installments when due, then the whole sum of principal and interest shall become immediately due and payable at the option of the holder of this note.

If the trustor shall sell, convey, or alienate said property, or any part thereof, or any interest therein, or shall be divested of his title or any interest therein in may manner or way, whether voluntarily or involuntarily, without the written consent of the beneficiary being first had and obtained, beneficiary shall have the right, at its option, to declare any indebtedness or obligations secured hereby, irrespective of the maturity date specified in any note evidencing the same, immediately due and payable.

Should suit be commenced to collect this note or any portion thereof, such sum as the Court may deem reasonable shall be added hereto as attorney's fees. Principal and interest payable for lawful money of the United States of America. This note is secured by a certain DEED OF TRUST to the SMS SETTLEMENT SERVICES, a California corporation, as TRUSTEE.

_____   _____
Robert Trabuco   Amelia Trabuco

A promissory note is a negotiable instrument. The most common type of negotiable instrument is an ordinary bank check. A check is an order to the bank to pay money to the person named. A promissory note is the same thing. It can be transferred by endorsement (signature), just like a check. If correctly prepared, it is the same as cash.

Types of Promissory Notes

Commonly, a promissory note is referred to as "the note." We will follow that practice as we study the basic types of notes in use with a trust deed.

<u>Straight Note</u>

Calls for payment of interest only, or no payments, during the term of the note, with all accrued money (either principal only, or principal and interest if no payments have been made) due and payable on a certain date

<u>Partially Amortized Installment Note</u>

Calls for periodic payments; such payments may or may not include interest; usually demands a balloon payment of unpaid principle and interest at the end of the term to completely pay off debt

<u>Fully Amortized Installment Note</u>

Calls for periodic payments of fixed amounts, to include both interest and principal, which will pay off the debt completely by the end of the term

> ### Adjustable note
>
> The interest rate in the note varies upward or downward over the term of the loan, depending on the money market conditions and an agreed upon index

Conflict in Terms of Note and Trust Deed

As you recall, a note is the evidence of a debt. A trust deed is only an incident of the debt. As we shall see in the next section, a trust deed must have a note to secure it, but a note does not need a trust deed to stand alone. If there is a conflict in the terms of a note and the trust deed used to secure it, the provisions of the note will prevail. If a note is unenforceable, the presence of a trust deed will not make it valid. However, if a note contains an acceleration clause (due on sale), the trust deed must mention it as well for the clause to be enforceable.

Trust Deeds and Mortgages

The term that describes the interest of a creditor (lender) in the property of a debtor (borrower) is security interest.

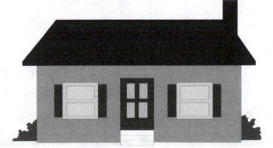

The security interest allows certain assets of a borrower to be set aside so that a creditor can sell them if the borrower defaults on the loan. Proceeds from the sale of that property can be taken to pay off the debt. The rights and duties of lenders and borrowers are described in a document called a security instrument. In some statees, trust deeds are the principal instruments used to secure loans on real property.

Mortgages accomplish the same thing as trust deeds, and are used in other states as security for real property loans. You will hear the term mortgage used loosely in trust deed states, as in mortgage company, mortgage broker and mortgage payment--but the mortgage reference here really is a trust deed.

Trust Deeds (Deeds of Trust)

As we mentioned, a trust deed is used to secure a loan on real property. It describes the property being used as security for a debt, and usually includes a power of sale and assignment of rents clause.

Trust Deeds Can Include:

- Power of Sale Clause:
  Gives trustee the right to foreclose, sell and convey ownership to a purchaser of the property if the borrower defaults on the loan

- Assignment of Rents Clause:
  Upon default by the borrower, the lender can take possession of the property and collect any rents being paid

---

The thing to remember about a trust deed is that it is the security for a loan. If the borrower fails to pay, the lender can use the proceeds from sale of the property used as collateral (or secured by the trust deed) for payment.

Foreclosure is the procedure used by the lender who must exercise the right to collect what is owed if the borrower defaults on payments. Under a deed of trust, foreclosure normally takes no more than four months. We will study foreclosure later in this chapter.

A trust deed becomes a lien on a certain described property to secure the repayment of a debt. It does not have to be recorded to be valid, but to insure safety of position and notice to all that a debt is owed. Since trust deeds, and rarely mortgages, are used to secure real property loans in certain states, we will examine the trust deed here.

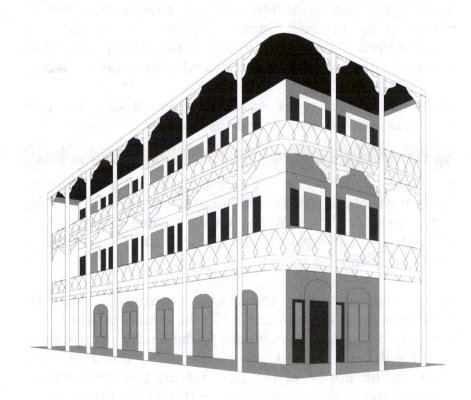

Title

The most distinguishing feature of a trust deed is the conveyance of title to a trustee by the borrower, until the

debt is paid off. When a trust deed is used to secure a loan, even though the borrower technically owns the property, bare legal title is transferred to the trustee by the deed of trust.

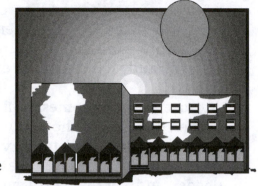

The trustee is only given the right to do what is

necessary to carry out the terms of the trust. He or she can only foreclose or reconvey, and does not have any other rights relating to the property, such as the right to use or the right to sell. Commonly, the trustee is not even notified until either foreclosure (in case of loan default) or reconveyance (when the loan is paid in full) takes place.

Think of the trustee as a neutral party, holding the title for the borrower until the loan is paid off, and foreclosing for the lender if the borrower defaults. Neither the trustor (borrower) nor the beneficiary (lender) holds the title until all terms of their agreement have been met. Upon payment of the debt in full, the trustee is notified by the beneficiary to sign the reconveyance deed, which states that clear legal title is now vested in the name of the actual property owner.

After being signed by the trustor (borrower), the trust deed--not the note--is recorded in the county where the property is located, then is sent to the lender or trustee to hold for the life of the loan. Recording of the trust deed gives public notice of the lien against the property for anyone interested in searching the title of the property.

The reconveyance deed is also recorded, after being signed by the trustee, to give public notice of the lien payment.

Parties

There are three parties to a trust deed: the trustor, the trustee and the beneficiary.

Three Parties to a Trust Deed:

- Trustor, or borrower; holds equitable title while paying off the loan; conveys bare legal title to trustee by way of the trust deed

- Trustee, or neutral third party; holds bare legal title solely for the purpose of reconveyance or foreclosure; is not involved with the property until asked to reconvey or foreclose

- Beneficiary, or lender; holds the note and trust deed until reconveyance (pay-off of the debt)

Roy and Dale bought a house. They signed a note secured by a deed of trust and were given a grant deed, as proof of conveyance, from the seller. The beneficiary, Bank of America, held the note and trust deed. Commonwealth Land Title Company was named as the trustee. When they signed the trust deed, Roy and Dale granted Commonwealth

Title bare legal title so the company could conduct duties as a trustee. Years went by, and the loan was paid off. Upon notification by Bank of America (the beneficiary), Commonwealth Title (trustee) signed a reconveyance deed, giving clear legal title to Roy and Dale.

Quentin and Kate bought their first house with a 90 percent loan from First Interstate Bank. As trustors, or borrowers, they were given a grant deed by the seller, which conveyed title to them. First Interstate, the beneficiary or lender, held the note Quentin and Kate had signed, promising to pay back the money loaned, and trust deed which secured the loan. Continental Lawyers Title Company was named as the trustee, and held bare legal title until the loan was paid off.

The payments were high, but both Quentin and Kate had good jobs, and were confident they could afford the house. After a few years, Kate was laid off, and they fell behind in their payments. They weren't getting along, and finally Kate left Quentin.

Sadly, he notified the beneficiary (First Interstate) that he could no longer make the payments, and the trustee was notified to start foreclosure procedures. A trustee's sale was held, and the house was sold, with the proceeds going to First Interstate to pay off the debt. Quentin moved to Anchorage to start over.

Statute of Limitations

The rights of the lender (beneficiary) under a deed of trust do not end when the statute has run out on the note. The trustee has title and can still sell the property to pay off the debt.

Remedy for Default

Under a deed of trust, either a trustee's sale or judicial foreclosure is permitted.

Reinstatement

When a trust deed debtor is in default on a loan, the loan may be reinstated if all delinquencies and fees are paid prior to five business days before the trustee's sale.

Redemption

Under a trust deed with a power of sale, there is no right of redemption after the trustee's sale. The sale is final.

Deficiency Judgment

A deficiency judgment is one against a borrower for the difference between the unpaid amount of the loan, plus interest, costs and fees of the sale, and the amount of the actual proceeds of the foreclosure sale. This means if the property sells for less than what is owed to the lender, the borrower will be personally responsible for repayment after the deficiency judgment is filed.

When a loan is secured by a trust deed and the lender forecloses under a power of sale (trustee's sale), a deficiency judgment is not allowed in most cases. When trust deeds, rather than mortgages, are used to secure loans, the only security for a beneficiary is the property itself. Any other personal assets of the borrower in default are protected from judgment under the trust deed.

> *Edward fell on hard times and lost his house, which was financed with a note secured by a deed of trust, to foreclosure. He owed $250,000 which included the costs of the foreclosure. However, the proceeds of the trustee's sale only amounted to $200,000. The lender lost the deficient $50,000, unable to obtain a deficiency judgment against Edward.*

Satisfaction

Satisfaction, or payment in full of a trust deed, requires that the lender deliver the original note and trust deed to the party making the request.

Benefits of a Trust Deed to a Lender

- In case of default, lender takes possession, collects rents
- Relatively short and simple foreclosure process
- Trustee holds title and can easily grant title to buyer at foreclosure sale
- No redemption after foreclosure
- A trust deed never expires

Benefits of a Trust Deed to a Borrower

- Property is the only security for a loan; no deficiency judgment allowed when loan is a purchase money loan

---

Mortgages

A mortgage is a financial instrument that is used to secure a property for the payment of a promissory note. It serves the same purpose as a trust deed by acting as the security for a debt. A mortgage is a lien against a described property until payment of the debt.

Do not get confused when you hear the word mortgage to describe some financial transaction. As mentioned earlier, even though mortgages are not commonly used in some states, you will hear reference to home mortgage, mortgage loan broker and mortgage banker. In reality, a trust deed is the instrument used.

A mortgage is held by the lender for the life of a loan, or until the borrower pays it off. There are some similarities to a trust deed, and some differences, as we shall see in the following examination of mortgages.

Parties

In a mortgage there a two parties: a mortgagor and a mortgagee. The mortgagor (borrower) receives a loan from the mortgagee (lender) and signs a promissory note and mortgage. The mortgage becomes a lien in favor of the mortgagee until the debt is paid in full.

The Two Parties to a Mortgage are:

- Mortgagor (borrower)

- Mortgagee (lender)

Title

A mortgage creates a lien on real property. Title is vested in the borrower, unlike a trust deed, where technically a deed of trust gives limited title (bare legal title) to a trustee, even though it is also spoken of as a lien. In both cases, possession of the property remains with the borrower.

Statute of Limitations

The Statute of Limitations runs out on a note secured by a mortgage in four years. This means a lender must sue after four years of nonpayment to get his or her money back, or the mortgage expires.

Remedy

The only remedy for default of a mortgage is judicial foreclosure, or a court action.

Reinstatement

Under a mortgage, a borrower in default may reinstate the loan by paying all delinquencies, plus all costs of the foreclosure action, at any time before the court approves the foreclosure.

Redemption

The right of redemption, or Equity of Redemption as it is known in those states using mortgages rather than trust deeds, allows a borrower in default to redeem the property within three months after foreclosure sale if the proceeds are sufficient to pay off all indebtedness plus any other foreclosure costs. If the sale does not bring enough money to pay off the debt, the mortgagor has one year to redeem the property by paying off the amount owed, plus costs.

Deficiency Judgment

A lender who forecloses against a defaulted mortgage may obtain a deficiency judgment against the debtor. Because a court action is required in order to foreclose against a mortgage, a deficiency judgment is allowed. As you recall, a deficiency judgment may be filed against a borrower for the difference between the unpaid amount of the loan, plus foreclosure costs, and the amount of the proceeds of the foreclosure sale. In that case, the lender may get a personal judgment against the borrower that will be effective for 10 years.

Satisfaction

Satisfaction of a mortgage, or payment in full, requires that the lender deliver the original note and mortgage to the party making the request.

Basic Differences Between Trust Deeds and Mortgages

Parties	Reinstatement
Title	Redemption
Statute of Limitations	Deficiency Judgment
Remedy	Satisfaction

Transfer of Property by the Borrower

A borrower may transfer ownership of the property and responsibility for the debt.

Loan Assumption

When a property is sold, a buyer may assume the existing loan. Usually with the approval of the lender, the buyer takes over primary liability for the loan, with the original borrower secondarily liable if there is a default.

What this means in trust deed states, is that even though the original borrower is secondarily responsible, according to the loan assumption agreement, no actual repayment of the loan may be required of that person. If the new owner defaults, the property is foreclosed, and no deficiency judgment is allowed beyond the amount received at the trustee's sale, even though the original borrower's credit is affected by the foreclosure.

Special Clauses in Financing Instruments

When a borrower signs a note promising to repay a sum, the lender usually will include some specific requirements in the note regarding repayment. These are special clauses meant to protect the lender and his or her interests.

Acceleration Clause

An acceleration clause allows a lender to call the entire note due, on occurrence of a specific event such as default in payment, taxes or insurance, or sale of the property.

Alienation Clause (Due on Sale)

Another clause, known as an
alienation or due-on-sale
clause, is a kind of
acceleration clause. A lender
may call the entire note due if
there is a transfer in property
ownership from the original
borrower to someone else.
This clause protects the lender

from an unqualified, unapproved buyer taking over a
loan. Justifiably, the lender fears possible default, with
no control over who is making the payments.

Assumption Clause

An assumption clause allows a buyer to assume
responsibility for the full payment of the loan with the
lenders knowledge and consent.

Subordination Clause

A subordination clause is used to change the priority of a
financial instrument. Remember, the priority of a trust
deed is fixed by the date it is recorded: the earlier the
date, the greater the advantage. When a note and trust
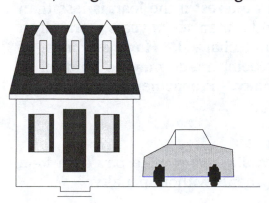
deed includes a
subordination clause, a
new, later loan may be
recorded, and because
of the subordination
clause, assume a
higher priority. This
clause is used mainly
when land is
purchased for future
construction

that will require financing. The lender on the new financing would want to be in first position to secure his or her interest, so the trust deed on the land would become subordinate to a new loan on the structure when the new loan was funded and recorded.

Prepayment Clause

Occasionally, a note will include a prepayment clause in case a borrower pays off a loan early. When lenders make loans, they calculate their return, over the term of the loan. If a loan is paid off before that time, the lender  gets less interest than planned, thus the return on investment is threatened. So the borrower is required to make it up by paying a penalty. It may not make a lot of sense to us as consumers, but that's the banking business.

Traditionally, a formula that has been used is to charge 20 percent of six month's interest if the loan is less than seven years old. If it is older than seven years, normally a prepayment penalty is not charged. However, most of the new loans currently being made may be paid off at any time without a penalty. Prepayment penalties are rare.

"Or More" Clause
An "or more" clause allows a borrower to pay off a loan early, or make higher payments without penalty.

Foreclosure

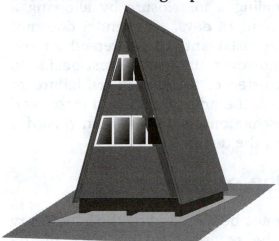

Foreclosure is a legal procedure used to terminate the rights and title of mortgagor or trustor in real property by selling the encumbered property and using the sale proceeds to pay off creditors.

Generally, a mortgage can only be foreclosed judicially, or through a court procedure. However, a trust deed containing a power of sale may be foreclosed either judicially or by trustee's sale.

Trustee's Sale

A Trustee's Sale may occur only when there is a power of sale included in the trust deed. This is commonly part of all trust deeds, and a trustee's sale is the most usual way to foreclose against a trust deed in default. In a trustee's sale, as we have seen, normally no deficiency judgments are allowed. Nor does the debtor have any rights of redemption after the sale.

During the statutory reinstatement period, however, the debtor or any other party with a junior lien may reinstate (bring current and restore) the loan in default. After the statutory reinstatement period, the debtor may still redeem the property and stop the foreclosure sale by paying off the entire debt, plus interest, costs and fees, at any time within five business days prior to the date of the sale.

The Procedure

When a borrower is behind in payments, usually a lender will work toward avoiding a foreclosure by allowing a grace period, usually 10 to 15 days. The lender does not want the property, but just wants to get repaid for the loan. At some point, however, the lender must decide to foreclose, notify the trustee of the borrower's failure to pay (default), and deliver the original note and trust deed to the trustee with instructions to prepare and record a notice of default against the debtor.

Notice of Default

The notice of default must be executed by the beneficiary or trustee and must be recorded in the office of the county recorder where the property is located at least three months before notice of sale is given. Within 10 days after recording the notice of default, a copy of the notice must be sent by certified or registered mail to all persons who have filed a request for notice. A copy must also be sent within one month after recording to the specific parties.

Notice of Default must be sent to:

- Successors in interest to the trustor
- Junior lien holders
- Vendee of any contract of sale
- State Controller if there is a tax lien against the property

---

Anyone interested in a particular deed of trust may record a request for notice of default and notice of sale with the county recorder where the property is located.

Notice of Sale

If the default is not cured by the borrower within the reinstatement period of three months, the trustee issues a notice of trustee's sale, which sets a sale date not sooner than 20 days after the recording date of the notice of trustee's sale.

The trustor and anyone else requesting notice must be notified at least 20 days before the sale, and the notice of sale must be published once a week for a period of 20 days in a local newspaper of general circulation. The notice of sale must be posted publicly in the city of the sale, as well as on a door of the property.

Foreclosure Facts

- Reinstatement period: three months
- Trustee's sale may be held 20 days after notice of sale is issued
- Notice of Sale must be published in local newspaper once weekly for 20 days prior to sale

---

The Sale

The sale is conducted at public auction by the trustee in the county where the property is located, approximately four months after the Notice of Default is recorded.

Until the auction bidding is over, the debtor or any junior lien holder may still redeem the property by paying off the defaulted loan in full, plus all fees, costs and expenses permitted by law. Reinstatement of the loan by bringing all payments up to date and paying all fees may be made at any time until five business days prior to the date of sale.

<u>Loan Reinstatement:</u>

- Loan may be made current (reinstated) up to five days prior to the foreclosure sale

---

Anyone may bid at the auction, but the first lien holder, or holder of the debt being foreclosed, is the only one who may "credit bid," or bid the amount that is owed the holder on the defaulted loan without actually having to pay the money. All other bids must be in cash or cashier's checks.

The sale is made to the highest bidder, and the buyer receives a Trustee's Deed to the property. The debtor no longer has any interest in, nor right to, redeeming the foreclosed property.

Steps in a Trustee's Sale

1. Beneficiary notifies trustee to foreclose

2. Trustee records notice of default

3. Reinstatement period (three months) is met

4. Notice of trustee's sale posted; date, time and place of sale published (three weeks)

5. Sale is held; highest cash bidder wins

6. Trustee's deed is given to buyer (sale is final, borrower has no right of redemption)

The sale is subject to certain liens of record that do not get eliminated by a foreclosure sale. That means the new buyer is responsible for payment of those liens.

Liens Not Eliminated by Foreclosure

- Federal tax liens
- Assessments and real property taxes
- Mechanic's liens

The sale of a property at a trustee's sale will extinguish the trust deed lien securing the debt to the beneficiary (lender) and will also extinguish any junior liens. That means the holder of a junior lien (a second, third or fourth trust deed), in order to protect his or her interest, had better make a bid for the property, or possibly lose the right to collect on the loan if the sale amount is not enough for a pay off.

Trustee Applies Foreclosure Sale Proceeds
in this Order:

1. Trustee's fees, costs and sale expenses
2. Beneficiary -- to satisfy the full amount of unpaid principal and interest, charges, penalties, costs and expenses
3. Junior lien holders in order of priority
4. Debtor--any money left over

Junior Trust Deeds

Another way to finance a property, either at the time of a sale, or afterward, is by using a Junior Trust Deed, which is any loan recorded after the first trust deed, secured by a second, third or subsequent trust deed. Many times in a sale, where the first trust deed loan plus the buyer's down payment are not enough to meet the purchase price, additional money is needed.

Outside Financing

One way to get the needed financing is for the buyer to obtain a secondary loan through an outside source, such as a mortgage banker, or private investor. At the same time the buyer is applying for a loan secured by a first trust deed from a conventional lender, a second--or junior--loan is arranged to complete the financing.

As you recall, any loan made at the time of a sale, as part of that sale, is known as a purchase money loan. At the close of escrow, then, the loan from the first trust deed is funded and sent to the escrow holder to be given to the seller after all necessary loan documents have been signed by the buyer.

The same is true of the new purchase money loan secured by a second trust deed. That loan is also funded and the money sent to the escrow holder to be given to the seller after all loan documents have been signed by the buyer. At the same time, the escrow holder asks the buyer to bring in the down payment. The proceeds from both the first and the second loan, plus the down payment, are then given to the seller at the close of escrow.

After several weeks of looking for the right home, Tom and Darlene found one that was exactly what they wanted. They only had 10 percent of the purchase price as a down payment, but had excellent credit and felt sure they could qualify to obtain secondary financing.

The house was priced at $200,000. They made a full price offer, with the buyer to qualify for an 80 percent first trust deed, a 10 percent second trust deed and 10 percent as a down payment. Their offer was accepted and the seller was given all cash at the close of escrow.

Tom and Darlene's Offer

New first trust deed	$160,000
New second trust deed	20,000
Down payment	20,000
Sales price	$200,000

Seller Financing

Another common source for secondary financing of a sale is the seller. If the seller is going to be the lender, he or she agrees to "carry back," or act as a banker, and make a loan to the buyer for the needed amount. That loan is secured by a trust deed, in favor of the seller, recorded after the first trust deed.

When a seller "carries the paper" on the sale of his or her home, it is also called a purchase money loan, just like the loan made by an outside lender. If a seller receives a substantial amount from the proceeds of a first loan, plus the buyer's down payment, it may be in the seller's interest to carry a second trust deed--possibly for income or to reduce tax liability by accepting installment payments.

Dominick made an offer on a house owned by Bruno, who accepted an offer of $275,000, with $27,500 as the down payment. The buyer qualified for a new first loan in the amount of $220,000, and asked Bruno to carry a second loan in the amount of $27,500 to complete the purchase price.

When the seller extends credit in the form of a loan secured by a second deed of trust, the note may be written as a straight note, with interest-only payments, or even no payments. Or it could be an installment note with a balloon payment at the end, or Fully Amortized Note with equal payments until it is paid off. The term of the loan is decided by the buyer and seller. The instructions of the buyer and seller regarding the seller financing are usually carried out through escrow.

A trust deed held by the seller may be sold by the seller to an outside party, usually a mortgage broker. The note and trust deed will be discounted, or reduced in value by the mortgage broker, but it is one way a seller can get cash out of a trust deed that was carried back.

Ben and Jerry owned a house together as investors. After several years, they put the house on the market for $350,000 and hoped to get a full-price offer so they could go their separate ways with the profit from the house. After a short time, they did get a full price offer. The buyer offered to put $70,000 down, get a $240,000 new first loan and asked Ben and Jerry to carry $40,000 for five years, as a second trust deed.

Ben and Jerry would have turned the offer down if their agent hadn't suggested they accept and sell the second trust deed after the close of escrow. Even though it would be discounted, it was one way they could get most of the cash out of their investment.

If the second trust deed was sold at a discounted 20 percent, or $8,000, Ben and Jerry would end up with $40,000, less $8,000, or $32,000. In that way they would get the cash out of the sale, though they would be netting less than they originally planned

111

because of the discount. They followed their agent's suggestion, and were satisfied with the result.

Disclosures Regarding the Borrower's Credit-Worthiness Needed in Transactions Involving:

- A purchase money loan on one-to-four units
- Seller financing to the purchaser
- "An arranger of credit" (real estate agent)

Whenever there is seller financing in a real estate transaction, the law requires the buyer and seller to complete a Seller Financing Disclosure Statement. It gives both the seller and buyer all the information needed to make an informed decision about using seller financing to complete the sale.

The seller can see from the disclosure whether or not the buyer has the ability to pay off the loan by looking at the buyer's income, and whether or not the buyer has a good credit history. The buyer can see what the existing loans are, as well as such things as due date and payments on existing loans that would be senior to the loan in question.

Generally, when there are real estate agents involved in a transaction, the agent who writes the offer (the cooperating agent), rather than the listing agent, acts as the arranger of credit. There is a place on the disclosure for the agent to sign, signifying that he or she has compiled with the law regarding the transaction.

Home Equity Loans

Another way a junior loan can be created is by a home equity loan. Assuming there is enough equity, or the difference between the value of a home and the money that is owed against it, a homeowner can apply for a cash loan for any purpose.

A lender uses strict standards about the amount of equity required in a property before loaning money, and particularly for a junior loan. The reason is simple. All a lender wants is to get his or her money back in a timely manner, along with the calculated return on the investment. Care must be taken, in case of a decrease in the value of the subject property, to make sure there is enough of a margin between the total amount owed and the value of the property. If the lender has to sell the property at a foreclosure sale, he or she will be assured of getting the money back. By only loaning up to 80 percent or 90 percent of the property value, the lender leaves some room for loss.

Michael's home was appraised at $100,000, with a $40,000 first trust deed recorded against it. Michael wants a $40,000 home equity loan. To determine whether or not to make the loan, the lender adds the amount owed to the amount desired in the loan to determine the percentage that would be

> *encumbered by the existing first trust deed, and the desired second trust deed. If the lender would only loan up to 80 percent of the appraised value of the property, would Michael get his loan?*

The priority of the loan will depend on what other instruments are recorded ahead of it, but it will be known as a hard money loan and will be secured by a deed of trust against the property. (Of course Michael does get his loan because the figures work out.)

> *Alberta, a homeowner, wanted to modernize her home. She owed $50,000 on a first trust deed, and the house was worth about $250,000. She had no trouble obtaining a home equity loan, secured by a second deed of trust, for her improvements.*

Balloon Payment Loans

Often, when a lender makes a first trust deed loan or a junior trust deed loan or when a seller takes back a junior purchase money note and trust deed, the monthly installments required do not amortize the loan over the term. The result is a large payment of principal and/or interest (balloon payment), due on the last installment.

In the interest of consumer welfare, the law requires the holder of a balloon note secured by an owner-occupied building of one-to-four units to give 90- to 150-days' warning of the balloon payment due date.

Regarding hard money junior loans negotiated by loan brokers (under $20,000), if payments are made in installments and the term is less than three years, the final payment may not be more than twice the amount of the smallest payment.

The law dealing with balloon payments is for loans other than purchase money loans extended by a seller to help a buyer finance a sale.

Hard Money Loan

- A hard money loan is one made in exchange for cash, as opposed to a loan made to finance a property

---

Other Types of Loans Secured by Trust Deeds

Blanket Loan

A trust deed that covers more than one parcel of property may be secured by a blanket loan. It usually contains a release clause that provides for the release of any particular parcel upon the repayment of a specified part of the loan. Commonly, it is used in connection with housing tracts. or construction loans.

Open-End Loan

An additional amount of money may be loaned to a borrower in the future under the same trust deed. The effect is to preserve the original loan's priority claim against the property.

All Inclusive Deed of Trust

Also known as an all-inclusive trust deed (AITD), or a wrap-around trust deed, this type of loan wraps an existing trust deed with a new trust deed, and the borrower makes one payment for both. In other words, the new trust deed (the AITD) includes the present encumbrances, such as first, second, third, or more trust deeds, plus the amount to be financed by the seller.

The AITD is subordinate to existing encumbrances because the AITD is created at a later date. This means any existing encumbrances have priority over the AITD, even though they are included, or wrapped, by the new all-inclusive trust deed. At the close of escrow the buyer receives title to the property.

Typically an AITD is used in a transaction between buyer and seller to make the financing attractive to the buyer and beneficial to the seller as well. Instead of the buyer assuming an existing loan and the seller carrying back a second trust deed, the AITD can accomplish the same purpose with greater benefit to both parties in some instances.

AITD's have been popular when interest rates are high and the underlying loans are not adjustable. When interest rates are low and a buyer can obtain a loan from an institution, it does not make sense to wrap an underlying loan, therefore paying a higher rate of interest to the seller than if an outside loan was obtained.

Benefits of an All Inclusive Trust Deed

Seller:
- Usually gets full-price offer
- Higher interest rate on amount carried

Buyer:
- Low down payment
- No qualifying for a loan or payment of loan fees

The AITD does not disturb the existing loan. The seller, as the new lender, keeps making the payments while giving a new increased loan at a higher rate of interest to the borrower. The amount of the AITD includes the unpaid principal balance of the existing (underlying) loan, plus the amount of the new loan being made by the seller. The borrower makes payment on the new larger loan to the seller, who in turn makes payment to the holder of the existing underlying loan. The new loan "wraps around" the existing loan.

A seller usually will carry back a wrap-around trust deed at a higher rate of interest than the underlying trust deed, thereby increasing the yield. The seller continues to pay off the original trust deed from the payments on the wrap-around, while  keeping the difference. This type of financing works best when the underlying interest rate is low, and the seller can then charge a higher rate on the wrapped loan.

A wrap-around loan isn't for everyone. If a seller needs to cash out, it won't work. Also, most loans contain a due-on-sale clause, and cannot be wrapped without the lender's knowledge and approval. Depending on the buyer's and seller's motivation, sometimes an AITD will be created, with full knowledge of the risk. This is how the term "creative financing" came into being.

Generally, these payments are collected by the note department of a bank or a professional collection company and sent on to the appropriate parties. This assures the maker (borrower) of the AITD that all underlying payments are being forwarded and are kept current by a neutral party.

Attila wanted to sell his house in San Francisco and return to Asia. He listed it for $100,000. The existing first trust deed was for $50,000 at 8 percent, payable at $377 monthly. He thought about carrying a second trust deed at 10 percent, counting on the income from the note. However, Bonnie, his listing agent, explained he could get a greater return by carrying an all-inclusive trust deed (AITD) instead of just a note and second trust *deed from a buyer. She also told him any offer that included an AITD should be referred to an attorney. Attila, with his attorney's approval, accepted the following offer soon after listing the house:*

<u>*Attila's Offer*</u>

Sales price

$100,000

Cash by buyer (down payment)

<u>20,000</u>

AITD in favor of Atilla

$80,000

- *Payments on new AITD of $80,000 at 10 percent to be $702 made monthly to Attila*
- *Payments on existing first trust deed of $50,000 at 8 percent, in the amount of $377 monthly, to be paid by Attila to original lender*

AITD payment to Attila

$702

Existing First Trust Deed payment

<u>377</u>

Monthly difference to Attila

$325

In some instances, a "rider" containing additional agreements between a buyer and seller will be attached to an all inclusive deed of trust.

Additions to an AITD

The note will be placed on contract collection with a bank or trust company authorized to do business. Money is collected and disbursed for current installments, payments of taxes and insurance if necessary and any amount then remaining is disbursed to the holder of the note secured by the AITD.

If the trustor (borrower) defaults, beneficiary obligations (lender) will be suspended until the default is cured. If the trustor is delinquent in making any payments due under the note, and the beneficiary incurs any penalties or other expenses on account of the underlying obligations during the period of trustor delinquency, the amount of any penalties and expenses will be added to

the amount of the note and will be payable by the trustor with the next payment due under the note.

In the event of foreclosure of the all inclusive deed of trust, the beneficiary agrees that he or she will, at the trustee's sale, bid an amount representing that due under the AITD, less the total balance due on the underlying notes, plus any advances or other disbursements which the beneficiary is allowed by law to include in the bid.

When the note secured by the AITD becomes due or the trustor requests a demand for payoff of the note, the main amount payable to the beneficiary will be reduced by the unpaid balances of the underlying obligations.

If any installment payment under the note secured by the AITD is not paid within 15 days after the due date, a late charge may be incurred by the trustor and be due and payable upon the beneficiary's demand.

Adequate funds for the payment of taxes and fire insurance will be deposited and held by the collection account holder. Monthly, an amount equal to one-twelfth of the annual tax amount and one-twelfth the amount of the annual fire insurance billing will be deposited by the trustor. Taxes and insurance reserves have been provided by the trustor to the beneficiary for the initial reserve fund.

If the trustor makes any additional payments or added increments beyond the required monthly amount, the beneficiary, upon a request by the trustor in writing, will forward any extra funds to the holders of the underlying notes for application to the unpaid principal balances.

Wrap-Around Loans (AITD's)

- Secured by a trust deed that "wraps," or includes existing financing plus the amount to be financed by the seller

---

Unsecured Loan

The lender receives a promissory note from the borrower, without any assurance of payment. The only recourse is a lengthy court action to force payment. This is truly the traditional IOU.

Alternative Financing

Alternative financing is one way lenders and borrowers can respond to the realities of today's unsteady economy. Because there are different kinds of lenders and different kinds of borrowers who are in need of credit to buy homes, there is no single type of financing that fits everyone.

The changing needs of consumers have caused lenders to respond by offering various solutions to credit demands. In the past, the only way people could buy a home was to use the fixed-rate loan. Today, any number of variable-rate loans are available to serve consumers.

After borrowers began to see the benefits of these "alphabet soup" loans, they realized this was one solution to the uncertainty of a rapidly changing marketplace. It is the job of a real estate agent to help consumers understand these new types of loans and to select the one that best suits their needs.

Graduated Payment Adjustable Mortgage

The loan known as a graduated payment adjustable mortgage (GPAM) has partially deferred payments of principal at the start of the term, increasing as the loan matures. This loan is for the buyer who expects to be earning more after a few years and can make a higher payment at that time. It is also known as a flexible rate mortgage.

Variable or Adjustable Rate Mortgage

The variable rate mortgage (VRM) or adjustable rate mortgage (ARM) loan provides for adjustment of its interest rate as market interest rates change. The interest rate is tied to some reference index that reflects changes in market rates of interest. Changes in the interest rate may be reflected in the changing payment, the term of the loan, or a combination of both.

Shared Appreciation Mortgage

Under a shared appreciation mortgage (SAM), the lender and the borrower agree to share a certain percentage of the appreciation in the market value of the property which is security for the loan. In return for the shared equity, the borrower is offered beneficial loan terms.

Rollover Mortgage

The rollover mortgage (ROM) is a loan where the interest rate and monthly payment are renegotiated, typically every five years.

Reverse Annuity Mortgage

This type of loan--the reverse annuity mortgage (RAM)--is used by older homeowners who have owned their homes for a long time and have a large amount of equity but not much of a monthly income. This loan uses their built-up equity to pay the borrower a fixed annuity, based on a percentage of the property value.

The borrower is not required to repay the loan until a specified event such as death or sale of the property, at which time the loan is paid off. A retired couple can draw on their home equity by increasing their loan balance each month.

Truth-in-Lending Act (Regulation Z)

The Truth-in-Lending Act, known as Regulation Z, requires a lender to inform the borrower how much he or she is paying for credit. The lender must reflect all financing costs as a percentage, called the Annual Percentage Rate (APR).

Equal Credit Opportunity Act

This federal law, the Equal Credit Opportunity Act, protects borrowers from discrimination based on race, sex, color, religion, national origin, age or marital status.

Soldiers' and Sailors' Civil Relief Act

Persons in the military, under this law known as the Soldiers' and Sailors' Civil Relief Act, are protected from foreclosure on their homes while serving time in the military service.

Post Test

The following self test repeats the one you took at the beginning of this chapter. Now take the exam again--since you have read all the material-- and check your knowledge of real estate finance.

True/False

1. Hypothecation is when an owner uses a property as security for a loan, but does not give up possession.

2. A trustee is a neutral third party in a trust deed.

3. In a trust deed, the borrower is the same as the beneficiary.

4. The beneficiary hold bare legal title to a property encumbered by a trust deed.

5. A reconveyance deed is used to deed a property to the trustor after the deed of trust has been paid in full.

6. An "or more" clause allows a borrower to pay off a loan early with no penalty.

7. A holder in due course is someone who buys an existing negotiable note.

8. Foreclosure is the cure for a tenant's default on monthly rental payments.

9. A trustee must sign a reconveyance deed.

10. A land contract and a contract of sale are alike.

chapter 4

ESCROW, TITLE & OTHER PROFESSIONALS

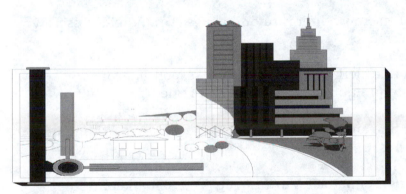

Focus

- **Introduction**
- **Escrow professionals**
- **Title insurance professionals**
- **Escrow associations**
- **Insurers**
- **Real estate brokers**
- **Builders**
- **Attorneys**
- **Independent escrow companies**

Pre-Test

The following is a self test to determine how much you know about escrow and other professionals before reading this chapter. Take it without studying, then read the material presented in the text. At the end of the chapter you will find a repeat of this exam. Test your knowledge by answering the questions again, then check your improvement. (The answers are found at the end of the book.) Good luck.

True/False

1. The job of escrow clerk requires a four year college degree.

2. Mathematical ability is an essential requirement of an escrow officer.

3. A loan escrow officer specializes in loan escrows.

4. An escrow administrator manages a multi-office escrow business.

5. A title clerk is the main person responsible for interpretation of the condition of title.

6. A title analyst might deal with tidelands and submerged lands.

7. Another name for a "title rep" is title marketer.

8. In order to conduct escrows, a real estate broker must be licensed by the Real Estate Commissioner.

9. A real estate broker must keep all escrow funds in a personal account.

10. The Corporations Commissioner monitors the escrow activities of lawyers.

Introduction

The jobs of escrow and title officer have developed throughout the years into professions requiring much more than simply searching a title or gathering documents. Both have grown into independent industries, with special designations and codes of ethics which guide their professional conduct, just like those followed by other real estate professionals.

Escrow Professionals

Escrow professionals provide service either as a separate company, as part of a title company, or as a department within banks or other financial institutions. An escrow career track can emphasize sale escrows, loan escrows or a combination of both. Learning the business of escrow requires a personality suited to details, some instructional escrow classes and, most important of all, practical hands-on experience.

Clerk

As an entry level position, the job of clerk, whether it is known as secretary, receptionist or general office worker, is where most escrow professionals start their career. An awareness of office functions as well as word and data processing are basic to being successful. Also, for a beginner in the escrow business, a background in finance or real estate is a valuable asset.

After working in an escrow office for some time, an ambitious escrow secretary may eventually function as a junior escrow officer or escrow officer in training.

Escrow Officer

Escrow officer is the next natural progression after working with escrows and becoming familiar with the many tasks required to complete an escrow.

Duties of an Escrow Officer:

- Gathering information, examining and organizing it into accurate escrow instructions

- Preparing documents for various escrows

- Being aware of aspects which are parallel to escrow, such as title and legal requirements

- Having knowledge of real estate financing to the extent of being able to answer clients' questions and prepare financing documents appropriate to the acquisition and sale of real property

- Being aware of the productivity and its relationship to the cost of doing business as an escrow holder

---

An escrow officer must possess certain personal talents and gifts in order to be successful in the complicated, fast-paced world of escrow. Efficiency, organization and a systematic approach are primary skills an escrow officer must exercise during the orderly process of each unique escrow, to be thorough in processing all details.

Qualifications of an Escrow Officer

Organization is essential in coordinating documents and other instruments. A systematic and logical perception of all processes, as well as the ability to gather information and to produce properly drawn instructions--is a primary qualification.

Because of an escrow's many complicated legal requirements, a background in law is an extra, welcome, qualification. Laws affecting real estate transfers are constantly changing and an escrow officer must be aware of their impact on current escrows.

A competent escrow officer rarely wastes time or money. Mistakes usually cost someone, and an efficient officer can save time and money by conducting business in an orderly, capable manner.

Prorations, closing statements, computation of demands, financial statements and balancing all require mathematical proficiency. An escrow officer must be skillfulwith numbers and have the ability to calculate accurately.

A serene, patient personality is well suited to the career of escrow officer. Good judgment and a sense of humor under difficult conditions are basic requirements for a successful career in escrow.

Loan Escrow Officer

A loan escrow professional specializes in closing loan escrows or as a loan underwriter.

An escrow officer and a loan escrow officer have many of the same duties.

Duties of a Loan Escrow Officer

- Supervise the process of closing a loan, from the beginning when the loan committee gives the loan file to the loan officer through the final funding of the loan

- Follow lender directions for supplying support documents, credit requirements, title provisions and other information

- Act as a go-between for lenders and borrowers

- Acknowledge differences in requirements of lenders for loan processing

- Know how loans are structured, from technical provisions of consumer protection laws and requirements of the many regulatory agencies, to the complications of construction loans and income property loans. The loan officer must work closely with the escrow officer to assure all legal aspects are in order for the closing.

Personal Attributes of a Loan Escrow Officer

A loan escrow officer must be capable of adjusting to more changes and having more contact with the customer than a general escrow officer who primarily closes sale escrows.

Outstanding communication skills are necessary when explaining the various steps in the loan escrow process because of the complexities of the lending process. Because of the greater possibility of conflict and surprise in the lending process, a loan officer must be adept at coping with upset and emotional customers.

A loan officer must be skilled at mathematics in order to calculate loan payoffs and payment schedules.

All escrow officers must be efficient and organized, and a loan escrow officer is no different. The use of computer technology has speeded up loan processing and allowed the loan officer greater flexibility and organization in less time than in the past.

Training

Generally, a loan officer has worked in some part of the loan industry before coming to escrow as a professional. Former employment often includes savings banks, commercial banks, mortgage bankers, insurance companies, mortgage brokers, credit unions and finance companies. Formal training is available from professional groups and private schools.

Manager

As an escrow manager, a career professional must possess greater technical knowledge and have more practical experience than an escrow officer.

A manager must be able to coordinate the various concurrent jobs in a timely and efficient way in an escrow office. He or she must balance technical competence with knowledge of how to make a profit for the company. The manager must be profit oriented as well as service oriented.

A successful manager must be able to communicate ideas both written and verbal . The effectiveness of management will be impaired if communication is not free flowing within the organization and between the organization and other real estate professionals. As always, when dealing with fellow workers , respect for their ideas and position is basic to good relations.

The ability to train new escrow professionals is a necessary quality for an escrow manager. Communicating ideas and concepts as well as guiding new workers through the confusing maze of balancing existing escrows while opening new ones is a challenging task for a manager. As we have mentioned before, escrow is learned through doing, and a manager must be able to teach the practical lessons of the business as well as supervise the office.

Another important task for the escrow manager is marketing the business. Customers are necessary if there  is to be a business, and constant, aggressive representation in the community of the escrow company is the only way to assure a large market share of the customers.

Finally, an ongoing, objective evaluation of staff workers will allow a manager to identify problemareas and develop training to strengthen weaknesses in the product.

Administrator

All the relationships in a multi-office escrow business are the responsibility of the escrow administrator. The position does require a highly developed technical knowledge of escrow, but most importantly requires excellent management skills.

A complete understanding of the contribution of human resources and how they may be used is basic to the profitability of the company. The administrator is responsible for recognizing the staff's potential and how that potential can be used for a greater return on the company dollar. The major qualification of an administrator is to be skilled at problem solving. Ultimately, all problems will end up with the administrator, whose ability to resolve uncertainty and to settle disputes is essential.

Desirable Traits of an Administrator:

- Exceptional communication skills

- Personal organization

- Ability to delegate tasks

- Fair and unprejudiced dealings with personnel

- Skilled coordination of all aspects of escrow

Title Insurance Professionals

Job descriptions in the business of title insurance go from research and interpretation of title information, to underwriting insurance, to administering and marketing the title company's services.

Searcher

The beginner job position in the title business is as a title searcher. When a title order is opened, the searcher must evaluate the instructions for the type of search required. Normally, tracing the chain of title or history of sales on the property is included in the search. There may also be a request in the instructions for information on loans, ownership of minerals, easements, reversionary rights under a recorded deed restriction, leasehold interest or special title requirements. Particular policy coverages like condemnation, trust deed foreclosure, subdivision and litigation guarantees require special searches. Maps or copies of documents are ordered as requested.

After reviewing the instructions for the title order, the searcher prepares a chain of title, starting from the policy date of the latest title policy issued on the property under search, to the present time. The chain of title includes the types of documents, parties involved and other recorded data on the property in question.

A general index search is the next order of business for the searcher. After the chain of title has been prepared and the title search completed, a search of recorded documents by alphabetical index is done to discover any judgments, divorces, tax liens, bankruptcies, probates, incompetencies and other general matters affecting the parties involved with the property.

Researched documents such as deeds, reconveyances, judgments and other liens are placed on microfilm or microfiche and copies are made for the title search. The job of the searcher is easier in sparsely populated counties where the recordings are few and is more complicated in areas like Los Angeles County where thousands of documents are recorded daily.

Historically, the searcher has had to look through lot books in which documents have been posted by hand and classified by legal description. Today, however, the general index or name search has been automated along with the lot  book. Information is now searched from computerized files in a title plant.

After all recorded documents have been found and assembled by date order into a non-interrupted chain of title, the searcher submits the package to the opinion department for legal review. If all is in order, the search is returned to the title department.

Before a sale is recorded, but after the initial or preliminary title search, new documents on the property in question may be recorded. The searcher must complete a final screening by computer or manually before the title order is closed.

The title searcher has a high degree of responsibility for accuracy. Missed documents in the chain of title can cause significant damage to the title company which is guaranteeing that all past title matters have been researched and exposed for examination. It is desirable for a searcher to be detail oriented and to have a high degree of skill in clerical matters.

As the searcher compiles a history of property ownership , decisions must be made about whether a document in the chain should be included and whether, in fact, the document even affects the property. An orderly and logical method must be used to sift through the myriad data found and present it for the issuance of the policy of title insurance.

After entering the title business as a searcher, a capable worker can advance to the position of senior searcher, or long-order searcher. This position requires knowledge and skill in dealing with such complex matters as property resurveys, street abandonments, railroad title reversions, tideland and wetland matters and oil searches.

Examiner

A policy of title insurance is written based upon interpretation. The main person responsible for the interpretation is the title examiner or title officer. The title examiner orders the search and examines the information compiled from the search.

During the course of the title examination, the title officer works closely with the escrow officer who has placed the title order, based on instructions for the transaction in question.

As a result of examination and inquiry, the title examiner submits a written opinion about the clear title of the property, known as a preliminary title report. Also known as an interim binder, this report is a commitment to issue title insurance on the property.

If there is a question about interpretation of the condition of the title of the property in question, the examiner may seek the advice of a title advisor, attorney or reference sources.

Another job of the examiner is to check the accuracy of the preliminary title report regarding the legal description, vesting of title and encumbrances on the land.

All legal documents required by the transaction must be examined by the title officer prior to recording to make sure escrow instructions have been followed and the documentation is adequate for closing.

The most skilled and capable title officers in the company are asked to deal with specialized and complicated title matters where the greatest degree of risk exists for title insurers.

Advisory Title Officers

Many times senior title examiners operate in the capacity of advisor title officers. They solve complicated issues and make underwriting decisions about whether a property is an acceptable insurance risk for the company. A separately staffed underwriting department may exist in the larger title companies.

Title Analyst

The job of title analyst involves research and development, particularly on complex projects. When title insurers are asked to deal with complicated underwriting tasks, the title research analyst complements the work of advisory title officers. The title analyst might deal with questions of Native American lands, tidelands and submerged lands, lake and river boundaries or land resurvey problems.

Also, a title analyst might develop new underwriting procedures for the company or expand procedures already in place.

Title Marketer

Title companies rely on "title reps" to market their product in specific geographical areas, much like any other sales oriented company. Title representatives call on existing customers and new prospects to promote their title company.

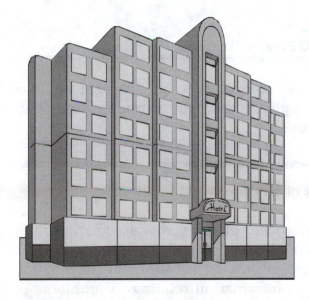

The high tech end of title marketing is usually handled by experienced marketers with technical background in the various fields. Wholesale customers of title insurance might be developers, franchisers or hotel chains.

Branch Manager

The duties of a title company branch manager include staff selection, setting an example, training and development, expanding market share, reporting results and personnel assessment. A manager must be skilled at interviewing, leadership, teaching, sales and communication.

Executive Management

As financial services companies combine their offerings to bring greater opportunity to the public, more administrators are required to manage various locations and to deal with newly developed duties. The title industry requires its executives to develop and understand the big picture as far as planning, market share, future growth and profit.

An executive administrator must possess superior communication skills and be able to project and promote the company image both internally and to the outside business community.

Escrow Associations

The escrow industry, dedicated to professionalism, has advanced various goals through various local and national organizations.

<u>Goals of an escrow association:</u>

"The objects and purposes of an escrow association shall be to promote sound and ethical business practices among its members; to provide for the collection, study and dissemination of information relating to problems of and improvements in land title evidence; to promote and encourage sound legislation affecting land titles; to encourage practices which will best serve the public interest; to educate and inform the public of the integrity and stability of its members and the advantages and desirability of their services."

Under the education arm of state organizations, training programs and continuing education are offered. Seminars, workshops and annual educational conferences are designed to bring escrow professionals current information regarding changes in the industry.

Local and state organizations publish newsletters outlining trends, new legislation, timely topics and recent court decisions. New education opportunities for escrow professionals are provided by *Escrow Update* and *A.E.A. News* (American Escrow Association).

Public recognition and ethical standards of the escrow industry are enhanced by professional organizations. By monitoring laws which impact the industry and advocating legislation which will benefit the industry and the public, escrow organizations educate and strengthen the growth of the industry.

The escrow industry is also empowered by the establishment of career designations for escrow professionals by the CEA, as well as a Code of Ethics.

Professional Escrow Designations:

- Certified Escrow Officer (CEO)

- Certified Senior Escrow Officer (CSEO)

Insurers

Title Companies

Escrow holders use both title insurers and general insurance companies in conducting their business.

There are two kinds of title companies: those directly responsible for their own financial risk, or underwriting, and those indirectly responsible for underwriting policies.

The Insurance Commissioner is the supervisor for title insurers in the state where the home office is located, and is aided by insurance commissioners in states where branch offices are used. The criteria for financial responsibility (bonding and reserve requirements) are regulated by the Insurance Code and are different from those fixed by the Corporations Commissioner, Banking Commissioner and the Real Estate Commissioner.

In some states, many title insurers offer escrow benefits along with their title business. In Northern California most of the sale escrow work is done by title companies. Escrow holders are responsible for most of the escrows in Southern California.

Insurance Companies

In the 1920s and 1930s, insurance companies were major investors in housing. After World War II, the need for housing was so great and the capital to build was so inadequate that insurance companies from the eastern part of the country moved west to fill the need for capital.

Insurance companies became commonplace loan processors and helped maintain the housing boom.

By the 1960s, insurance companies began to move their interest from investing in single family home loans to loans on large, income producing projects. Loan underwriting and escrow practices have had to modify with the changing needs of the insurance industry.

Insurance companies are regulated by the Insurance Commissioner and must conform to the legal and financial requirements and regulations of that department. The Insurance Commissioner is also responsible for audits of financial procedures used by insurance companies.

Commonly, insurance companies make their loans through mortgage bankers or other money brokers. Some companies, however, deal directly with the public and use escrow holders to complete their loans or sales.

Because many insurance companies have large real estate portfolios, they act as principals as well as lenders with real estate as security. In this capacity, they must be very specific about their title insurance needs, usually requiring extended coverage.

Real Estate Brokers

Depending on each situation, real estate brokers can be escrow holders themselves, or customers of escrow services.

A real estate broker operating in the capacity of escrow holder is exempt from the requirements of the Corporations Commissioner and is not under supervision of the Department of Corporations. Any company, broker or agent licensed by the Real Estate Commissioner, while performing acts in the course of or incidental to the real estate business, may hold escrows in connection with any transaction. A broker, however, may not hold escrows for separate individuals or entities, for compensation, unless he or she is representing the buyer or seller or both in a particular transaction.

In order for a broker to advertise escrow services, it must be mentioned in any promotion that the services are only in connection with real estate brokerage. Because the escrow business is so unpredictable, many broker-owned escrows have been converted to independent escrow companies so those businesses can expand their possible markets.

When a broker does act as an escrow holder, he or she must maintain all escrow funds in a trust account. That account, along with all required records, remains subject to inspection by the Real Estate Commissioner's investigative staff and auditors.

The business of escrow holder cannot be taken up as a second job, or sideline. The broker is responsible for accurate record keeping and detailed organization of all aspects of escrow, even though only in-house brokerage transactions are being handled.

As the primary practitioners of the residential resale industry, real estate brokers are the main source of business for escrow holders. One of the jobs of escrow companies is marketing their product. By cooperating and offering special services such as pick up and delivery of documents an escrow company can count certain real estate brokers as steady customers. Other real estate professionals, such as title companies, seek business from brokers directly because of the broker's close association with the escrow company. Hopefully, then, when a title order on a particular transaction is opened, the title company will get the order.

Builders

Many large developers and builders have established their own escrow companies in an effort to control the various parts of their business, and to get a greater return on their investment dollar. These escrow companies are licensed by the Corporations Commissioner, and fall under the guidelines and requirements of that department.

Subdivision escrows are highly specialized and require knowledge of the many different legal requirements. The escrow holder must know about the correct creation of protective restrictions for a development, must make sure that the preliminary public report has been delivered to all prospective purchasers, must be knowledgeable about the formation of homeowners' associations, and must be aware that a legal percentage of parcels in the new development be

147

sold before the first one can close--per legal requirements for subdivisions.

In some states, builders are licensed by the State Contractors Licensing Board, in addition to the Corporations Commissioner overseeing their escrow procedures. Builders are also lightly supervised by the Federal Housing Administration or Veterans Administration or other secondary lenders if they build under government sponsored programs. Developers then may use an escrow company of their choice for the loan processing in connection with their sales.

Many title insurance companies have developed special subdivision departments which have trained personnel to quicken the submission of subdivisions' paperwork throughout the Department of Real Estate. Designated title professionals work specifically with builders and developers to meet their special needs.

Attorneys

The escrow activities of lawyers are monitored by the State Bar Association. Attorneys have the authority to hold escrows for their clients and are exempted from licensing and other requirements as long as the escrow is held in connection with the business of law. Money must be deposited in trust accounts and must be separated by individual files.

Independent Escrow Companies

Closing sale and loan transactions are the principal means of business for independent escrow companies. Additionally, an independent escrow company may act as a corporate trustee on outstanding deeds of trust or as a collection service for customer's accounts as a special service.

Independent escrows are tightly supervised and regulated by the Corporations Commissioner to assure consumer protection. The Commissioner's rules require someone at each escrow company location to have at least five years experience in the escrow field whenever the company is open for business.

An auditing and liaison staff is maintained by the Corporations Commissioner who oversees financial responsibility, ethics and bonding requirements. Frequent audits are held, with the escrow company under examination responsible for the cost of the audit. Each escrow company must maintain orderly files and records in accordance with the Commissioner's rules.

In California, the Escrow Fidelity Corporation (created by the state legislature, governed by industry members and a casualty insurance administrator) provides employee fidelity bonds for independent escrow holders. An annual assessment of $2,250 for each location must be paid by each company as a required member of the fund. The Escrow Fidelity Corporation holds a fidelity bond equal to 1% of the total escrow trust funds on deposit by independent escrows within California. In addition, a trust balance is required of each member escrow company, depending on the amounts of trust funds held.

Post Test

The following self test repeats the one you took at the beginning of this chapter. Now take the exam again--since you have read all the material-- and check your knowledge of escrow and title professionals..

True/False

1. The job of escrow clerk requires a four year college degree.

2. Mathematical ability is a primary requirement of an escrow officer.

3. A loan escrow officer specializes in loan escrows.

4. An escrow administrator manages a multi-office escrow business.

5. A title clerk is the main person respsonsible for interpretation of the condition of title.

6. A title analyst might deal with tidelands and submerged lands.

7. Another name for a "title rep" is title marketer.

8. In order to conduct escrows, a real estate broker must be licensed by the Real Estate Commissioner.

9. A real estate broker must keep all escrow funds in a personal account.

10. The Corporations Commissioner monitors the escrow activities of lawyers.

chapter 5

CONTRACTS

Focus

- Introduction
- Contracts in general
- Essential elements of a contract
- Statute of Frauds
- Performance of contracts
- Discharge of contracts
- Statute of Limitations
- Remedies for breach of contract
- Real estate contracts
- Liquidated damages
- Option

Pre-Test

The following is a self test to determine how much you know about contracts before reading this chapter. Take it without studying, then read the material presented in the text. At the end of the chapter you will find a repeat of this exam. Test your knowledge by answering the questions again, then check your improvement. (The answers are found at the end of the book.) Good luck.

True/False

1. An option is an example of a unilateral contract.

2. A written contract does not take precedence over oral agreements.

3. A contract is an agreement to do or not to do a certain act.

4. A promise given by one party with the expectation of performance by the other party is known as a bilateral contract.

5. A contract that has been approved is said to be rescinded.

6. Another name for mutual consent is implied agreement.

7. Parties to a contract may be unimancipated minors.

8. Mutual consent is sometimes called a meeting of the minds.

9. In an option, the buyer must perform.

10. The failure to perform a contract is called breach of contract.

Introduction

So far, we have studied the nature of escrow, who needs an escrow, the documents needed with some real estate basics, finance and who the professionals are that carry out escrows. This chapter explains what a contract is and how contracts are used to assure the understanding and approval of all parties to an agreement.

In every real estate transaction, some kind of contract that transfers or indicates an interest in the property is used. It is important that you, as a student of escrow, understand the nature of legal agreements so you are able to prepare instructions which accurately and legally reflect the agreement between the principals.

Contracts in General

A contract is an agreement, enforceable by law, to do or not to do a certain thing. It may be an express contract, where the parties declare the terms and put their intentions in words, either oral or written. A lease or rental agreement, for example, is an express contract. The landlord agrees to allow the tenant to live in the dwelling and the renter agrees to pay rent in return.

An implied contract is one where agreement is shown by act and conduct rather than words. This type of contract is found every day when we go into a restaurant and order food, go to a movie or have a daily newspaper delivered. By showing a desire to use a service, we imply that we will pay for it.

Contracts may be bilateral or unilateral. A bilateral contract is one in which the promise of one party is given in exchange for the promise of the other party. In other words, both parties must keep their agreement for the contract to be completed. An example might be a promise from a would-be aviatrix to pay $2,500 for flying lessons, and a return promise from the instructor to teach her to fly.

A unilateral contract is one where a promise is given by one party with the expectation of performance by the other party. The second party is not bound to act, but if he or she does, the first party is obligated to keep the promise. An example would be an option (see page 171).

A contract may be executory or executed. In an executory contract, something remains to be done by one or both parties. An escrow that is not yet closed or a contract not signed by the parties are examples of an executory contract. In an executed contract, all parties have performed completely.

One of the meanings of execute is to sign, or complete in some way. An executed contract may be a sales agreement that has been signed by all parties.

Also, contracts may be void, voidable, unenforceable, or valid.

Types of Contracts

Void contract
No contract at all; lacks legal effect (*example: due to lack of capacity or illegal subject matter*)

Voidable contract
One which is valid and enforceable on its face, but may be rejected by one or more of the parties (*example: induced by fraud, menace or duress, elderly party no longer competent*)

Unenforceable contract
Valid, but for some reason cannot be proved by one or both of the parties (*example: an oral agreement which should be in writing because of Statute of Frauds*)

Valid contract
Binding and enforceable; has all the basic elements required by law

---

Essential Elements of a Contract

For a contract to be legally binding and enforceable, the following requirements must be met:

Essential Elements of a Contract

- Legally competent parties
- Mutual consent
- Lawful objective
- Sufficient consideration
- Contract in writing (when required by law)

Legally Competent Parties

Parties entering into a contract must have legal capacity to do so. Almost anyone is capable, with a few exceptions. A person must be at least 18 years of age, unless married, in the military or emancipated.

A minor is not capable of appointing an agent, or entering into an agency agreement with a broker to buy or sell. A broker could represent an informed adult in dealing with a minor, but the client must be willing to take a chance that the contract may be voidable. Brokers dealing with minors should proceed cautiously and should seek an attorney's advice.

When it has been determined judicially that a person is not of sound mind, no contract can be made with that incompetent person. Also, if it is obvious that a person is completely without understanding, even without declaration, there can be no contract. In the case of an incompetent, a court appointed guardian would have legal capacity to contract.

Both minors and incompetents may acquire title to real property by gift or inheritance. Any conveyance of acquired property, however, must be court approved. A contract made by a person who is intoxicated or under the influence of legal or illegal drugs may be canceled when the individual sobers up. But it also may be ratified or approved, depending on the parties.

Any person may give another the authority to act on his or her behalf. The document that does this is called a Power of Attorney. The person holding the power of attorney is called an Attorney-in-Fact. When dealing with real property, a power of attorney must be recorded to be valid, and is good for as long as the principal is competent. A power of attorney can be canceled by the principal at any time by recording a revocation and a title company will only honor a power of attorney for one year. After that time, a new one must be signed and recorded. A power of attorney is useful, for example, when a buyer or seller is out of town and has full trust in that agent to operate in his or her behalf.

Mutual Consent

In a valid contract, all parties must mutually agree. Mutual consent, or mutual assent, is sometimes called a meeting of the minds. It is an offer by one party and acceptance by the other party.

Offer

One party must offer and another accept, without condition. An offer shows the contractual intent of the offeror, or the person making the offer, to enter into a contract. That offer must be communicated to the offeree, or the person to whom the offer is being made. Unconditional acceptance of the offer is necessary for all parties to be legally bound. The offer must be definite and certain in its terms, and the agreement must be genuine or the contract may be voidable by one or both parties.

Acceptance

An acceptance is an unqualified agreement to the terms of an offer. The offeree must agree to every item of the offer for the acceptance to be complete. If the original terms are changed in any way in the acceptance, the offer becomes a counteroffer, and the first offer is terminated. The person making the original offer is no longer bound by that offer, and may accept the counteroffer or not. The counteroffer becomes a new offer, made by the original offeree.

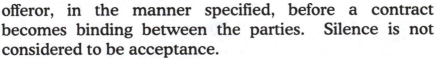

Acceptance of an offer must be communicat-ed to the offeror, in the manner specified, before a contract becomes binding between the parties. Silence is not considered to be acceptance.

Termination

An offeror is hopeful that his or her offer will be accepted in a timely manner and a contract will be formed. An offer is specific, however, and an offeror does not have to wait indefinitely for an answer. An offer may be terminated by the following acts.

Termination of an Offer

- Lapse of time: an offer is revoked if the offeree fails to accept it within a prescribed period

- Communication of notice of revocation: this can be done by the offeror anytime before the other party has communicated acceptance

- Failure of offeree to fulfill a condition of acceptance prescribed by the offeror

- A qualified acceptance, or counteroffer by the offeree

- Rejection by the offeree

- Death or insanity of the offeror or offeree

- Unlawful object of the proposed contract

Genuine Assent

A final requirement for mutual consent is that the offer and acceptance be genuine and freely made by all parties. Genuine assent does not exist if there is *fraud, misrepresentation, mistake, duress, menace or undue influence* involved in reaching an agreement.

Fraud is an act meant to deceive in order to get someone to part with something of value. An outright lie, or making a promise with no intention of carrying it out, can be fraud. Lack of disclosure--causing someone to make or accept an offer--is also fraud. For example, failure to tell a prospective buyer who makes an offer to purchase on a sunny day that the roof leaks is fraud. It can make the contract voidable.

Innocent misrepresentation occurs when the person providing the wrong information is not doing it to deceive, but for the purpose of reaching an agreement. Even though no dishonesty is involved, a contract may be rescinded or revoked by the party who feels misled.

Mistake, in contract law, means negotiations were clouded or there was a misunderstanding in the material facts. It does not include ignorance, inability or poor judgment. For example, if you accepted an offer to purchase your home based on what you thought was an all cash offer, and later found that you had agreed to carry a second trust deed, you would be expected to carry through with the agreement. Even though you made a "mistake" in reading the sales contract, you now have a binding agreement.

There are times when you could be credited with a misunderstanding, and ultimately get out of the contract. For instance, what if you were given directions to a friend's beach house, went there on your own and fell in love with it. You immediately made an offer, which was accepted, only to discover you had gone to the wrong house. Because you thought you were purchasing a different property than the one the seller was selling, this could be considered a "major misunderstanding of a material fact," and there would be no mutual agreement, voiding any contract that was signed.

Use of force, known as duress, or menace, which is the threat of violence, may not be used to get agreement. Undue influence or using unfair advantage is also unacceptable. All can cause a contract to be voidable by the injured party.

No Genuine Assent if:

- Fraud
- Misrepresentation
- Mistake
- Duress
- Menace
- Undue Influence

Lawful Objective

Even though the parties are capable, and mutually agreeable, the object of the contract must be lawful. A contract requiring the performance of an illegal act would not be valid, nor would one where the consideration was stolen.

The contract also must be legal in its formation and operation. For example, a note bearing an interest rate in excess of that allowed by law would be void. Contracts contrary to good morals and general public policy are also unenforceable.

Sufficient Consideration

All contracts require consideration. There are several types of consideration in a contract. Generally, it is something of value such as a promise of future payment, money, property or personal services. For example, there can be an exchange of a promise for a promise, money for a promise, money for property, or goods for services.

Forbearance, or forgiving a debt or obligation, also qualifies as consideration. As a group, the above qualify as valuable consideration. Gifts such as real property based solely on love and affection are considered to be good consideration. They meet the legal requirement that consideration be present in a contract.

In an option, the promise of the offeror is the consideration for the forbearance desired from the offeree. In other words, the person wanting the option promises to give something of value in return for being able to exercise the option to purchase at some specifically named time in the future.

In a bilateral contract, a promise of one party is consideration for the promise of another. For example, in the sale of real property, the buyer promises to pay a certain amount and the seller promises to transfer title. It should be noted that the earnest money given at the time of an offer is *not*

the consideration for the sale. It is simply an indication of the buyer's intent to perform the contract, and may be used for damages, even if the buyer backs out of the sale.

Contract In Writing

In California, the Statute of Frauds requires that certain contracts be in writing to prevent fraud in the sale of land, or an interest in land. Included in this are offers, acceptances, loan assumptions, land contracts, deeds, escrows, and options to purchase. Trust deeds, promissory notes, and leases for more than one year also must be in writing to be enforceable.

Statute of Frauds

Most contracts required by law to be in writing are found under the Statute of Frauds. The statute was first adopted in England in 1677, and became part of English common law. Later it was introduced to this country, and is now part of California's law.

The statute's primary purpose is to prevent forgery, perjury and dishonest conduct on the part of scoundrels and crooks against citizens. Thus, it improves the existence and terms of certain important types of contracts.

The law provides that certain contracts are invalid unless they are in writing and signed by either the parties involved or their agents.

Statute of Frauds

- Any agreement where the terms are not to be performed within a year from making the contract

- A special promise to answer for the debt, default or non-performance of another, except in cases covered by the Civil Code

- An agreement made upon the consideration of marriage, other than a mutual promise to marry

- An agreement to lease real property for a period longer than one year, or to sell real property or an interest therein; also, any agreement authorizing an agent to perform the above acts

- An agreement employing an agent, broker or any other person to purchase, sell or lease real estate for one year; or find a buyer, seller, lessee or lessor for more than one year in return for compensation

- An agreement, which by its terms is not to be performed during the lifetime of the promisor, or an agreement that devises or bequeaths any property, or makes provisions for any reason by will

- An agreement by a purchaser of real estate to pay a debt secured by a trust deed or mortgage on the property purchased, unless assumption of that debt by the purchaser is specifically designated in the conveyance of such property

Personal property is also affected by the Statute of Frauds. The sale of personal property with a value of more than $500 must be accompanied by a bill of sale in writing.

Parol Evidence Rule

When two parties make oral promises to each other, and then write and sign a contract promising something different, the written contract will be considered the valid one. When prior oral or written negotiations or agreements of the parties enter into a dispute about a contract, the parol evidence rule is used to settle the disagreement.

This rule prohibits introducing outside evidence to vary or add to the terms of deeds, contracts or other writings once they have been executed. Under the parol evidence rule, when a contract is intended to be the parties' complete and final agreement, no further oral promises are allowed. Occasionally a contract is ambiguous or vague. Then the courts will allow use of prior agreements to clarify an existing disputed contract.

One of a real estate agent's major duties is to make sure all contract language conveys the parties' wishes and agreements. Oral agreements have caused much confusion and bad feelings over the years, particularly in real estate. Even a lease for less than one year should be in writing, though it is not required by the Statute of Frauds. It is easy to forget verbal agreements. A written contract is the most reasonable way to ensure mutual assent.

What about using and changing preprinted real estate forms such as a deposit receipt or a counter offer form? If the parties involved want to make handwritten changes and initial them, those changes control the document.

However, escrow instructions reflect the real estate contract between the parties. If changes are made, they should be in the form of amendments to the escrow instructions after opening the escrow.

Performance of Contracts

A principal has several choices when considering the performance of a contract. One is by the assignment of the contract to an assignee. The effect of assignment is to transfer to the assignee all the interests of the assignor, with the assignee taking over the assignor's rights, remedies, benefits and duties.

For example, the original renter assigns rental interest to a new tenant, who is then responsible for the lease. The assignor is still liable in case the assignee does not perform, but the assignee is now primarily responsible for the contract.

If the assignor wants to be released entirely from any obligation for the contract, it may be done by novation. That is the substitution, by agreement, of a new obligation for an existing one, with the intent to extinguish the original contract. For example, novation occurs when a buyer assumes a seller's loan, and the lender releases the seller from the loan contract by substituting the buyer's name on the loan.

Time is often significant in a contract; indeed, its performance may be measured by the passage of time. Real estate contract and escrow instructions must have closing dates, or they are unenforceable.

Discharge of Contracts

The discharge of a contract occurs when the contract has been terminated. Most contracts are discharged by full performance on the part of the contracting parties in accordance with the agreed-upon terms. Occasionally, the end result is a breach of contract, where someone does not fulfill part of the agreement. In that case, the injured party has several remedies available. Specifically, the following methods may discharge a contract.

Discharge of Contracts

- Acceptance of a breach of the contract
- Agreement between the parties
- Impossibility of performance
- Operation of law
- Part performance
- Release of one or all of the parties
- Substantial performance

Statute of Limitations

Under California law, any person seeking relief for a breach of contract must do so within the guidelines of the Statute of Limitations. This set of laws determines that civil actions can be started only within the time periods prescribed by law. Lawsuits must be brought within the allowed time or the right to do so will expire. Here are some actions of special interest to real estate agents, with the time frames required.

Actions Which Must Be Brought Within 90 Days: Civil actions to recover personal property such as suitcases, clothing or jewelry alleged to have been left at a hotel or in an apartment; must begin within 90 days after the owners depart from the personal property.

Actions Which Must Be Brought Within Six Months: An action against an officer to recover property seized in an official capacity--such as by a tax collector.

Actions Which Must Be Brought Within One Year: Libel or slander, injury or death caused by wrongful act, or loss to depositor against a bank for the payment of a forged check.

Actions Which Must Be Brought Within Two Years: Action on a contract, not in writing; action based on a policy of title insurance.

Actions Which Must Be Brought Within Three Years: Action on a liability created by statute; action for trespass on or injury to real property, such as encroachment; action for relief on the grounds of fraud or mistake; attachment.

Actions Which Must Be Brought Within Four Years: An action on any written contract; includes most real estate contracts.

Actions Which Must Be Brought Within 10 Years: Action on a judgment or decree of any court in the United States.

Remedies for Breach of Contract

A breach of contract is a failure to perform on part or all of the terms and conditions of a contract. A person harmed by non-performance can accept the failure to perform, or has a choice of three remedies.

Unilateral rescission is available to a person who enters a contract without genuine assent because of fraud, mistake, duress, menace, undue influence or faulty consideration. Rescission may be used as a means of discharging a contract by agreement, as we have mentioned.

However, once escrow is opened, rescission is not available--no unilateral instruction is acceptable. Once in a while, a buyer may call right after the close of escrow and order the escrow agent to "rescind" the sale. This is not possible except through court order. Some buyers think it's like buying a car where you can change your mind within three days. This is not the case once escrow instructions have been signed, and certainly not so after the escrow closes.

If one of the parties has been wronged by a breach of contract, however, that innocent party can stop performing all obligations as well, therefore unilaterally rescinding the contract. It must be done promptly, restoring to the other party everything of value received as a result of the breached contract, on condition that the other party shall do the same.

When a party is a breach-of-contract victim, a second remedy is a lawsuit for money damages. If damages to an injured party can be reasonably expressed in a dollar amount, the innocent party could sue for money damages to include: the price paid by the buyer, the difference between the contract price and the value of the  property, title and document expenses, consequential damages and interest.

A third remedy for breach of contract is a lawsuit for specific performance. This is an action in court by the injured party to force the breaching party to carry out the remainder of the contract according to the precise terms, price and conditions agreed upon. Generally, this remedy is used when money cannot restore an injured party's position. This is often the case in real estate because of the difficulty in finding a similar property.

Real Estate Contracts

Of course, all *real estate contracts* must be in writing, according to the Statute of Frauds, and must be signed by the parties.

Real Estate Contracts Include:

- Contracts for the sale of real property, or of an interest therein

- Agreements authorizing or employing an agent or broker to buy or sell real estate for compensation or commission

- Agreements for leasing realty for more than a year

Liquidated Damages

Parties to a contract may decide in advance the amount of damages to be paid, should either party breach the contract. In fact, the offer to purchase, or sales contract, contains a printed clause that says the seller may keep the deposit as liquidated damages if the buyer backs out without good reason.

Option

An option is a right, given for consideration, to a party (optionee) by a property owner (optionor), to purchase or lease property within a specified time at a specified price and terms. It is a written agreement between the owner of real property and a prospective buyer, stating the right to purchase, a fixed price and time frame. The price and all other terms should be stated clearly, as the option will become the sales agreement when the optionee exercises the right to purchase.

The optionee is the only one who has a choice, once the contract is signed and the consideration given. The option does not bind the optionee to any performance. It merely provides the right to demand performance from the optionor, who must sell if the optionee decides to buy the property during the course of the option. If the optionee decides not to buy the property during the term of the option, the consideration remains with the optionor.

The option may be assigned or sold without permission of the optionor during the course of the term, or the optionee may find another buyer for the property to exercise the option.

Normally, a real estate agent earns commission on an option only when it is exercised.

Post Test

The following self test repeats the one you took at the beginning of this chapter. Now take the exam again--since you have read all the material-- and check your knowledge of contracts.

True/False

1. An option is an example of a unilateral contract.

2. A written contract does not take precedence over oral agreements.

3. A contract is an agreement to do or not to do a certain act.

4. A promise given by one party with the expectation of performance by the other party is known as a bilateral contract.

5. A contract that has been approved is said to be rescinded.

6. Another name for mutual consent is implied agreement.

7. Parties to a contract may be unimancipated minors.

8. Mutual consent is sometimes called a meeting of the minds.

9. In an option, the buyer must perform.

10. The failure to perform a contract is called breach of contract.

chapter 6

LOCAL VARIATIONS

Focus

- **Introduction**
- **Basic regional differences**
- **General principles**
- **Southern California escrows**
- **Northern California escrows**

Pre-Test

The following is a self test to determine how much you know about local escrow variations before reading this chapter. Take it without studying, then read the material presented in the text. At the end of the chapter you will find a repeat of this exam. Test your knowledge by answering the questions again, then check your improvement. (The answers are found at the end of the book.) Good luck.

True/False

1. The format for escrow instructions is set by law.

2. Escrow instructions can be bilateral or unilateral.

3. With bilateral instructions, the buyer and seller sign the same set of instructions.

4. Unilateral instructions are used in Northern California.

5. Instructions are drawn at the beginning of the escrow period in Northern California.

6. In Southern California, both parties sign the same set of instructions.

7. One of the main differences between Northern and Southern California escrows is the way duties and responsibilities between the broker and escrow officer are divided.

8. The title insurance process is more closely connected to the escrow procedure in Southern California.

9. In Northern California, the escrow agent begins the escrow process.

10. Unilateral instructions are more complex than bilateral instructions.

Introduction

Every real estate transaction is unique. As a result, escrow instructions differ greatly from transaction to transaction. They all result, however, from the escrow officer's gathering together the purchase agreement and other important information and drawing up instructions in detail to describe how the transaction will be completed. The instructions are the written authorization to the escrow holder or title company to carry out the directions of the parties involved in the transaction. In California the purchase agreement becomes the escrow instructions.

All conditions which must be met before the close of escrow are specifically mentioned in the escrow instructions. Who will pay for what costs, how money is to be disbursed and what documents are to be recorded at the close of escrow are included in the instructions. When an escrow is opened it remains open until it is terminated according to the agreement of the parties.

The escrow instructions or purchase agreement must be in writing and signed by all parties involved as principals in the transaction. The instructions are legally binding and are revocable only by mutual consent.

Most escrow companies have standard, computer-generated forms for escrow instructions which the escrow officer uses to serve individual transactions. The forms can be altered for different kinds of transactions such as a simple sale of real property or a more complex exchange. If there is an attorney involved, he or she may want to draw up specific escrow instructions to reflect a more complicated transaction.

The format for escrow instructions is not set by law, and as long as all parties approve, escrow officers may receive and follow specially drawn instructions from a qualified outside party just as if they were drawn on their own company forms.

The escrow officer must know all facts of the purchase in order to carry out the expectations of all the parties to the transaction. All agreements between the principals should be made *before* signing escrow instructions, and those agreements must be reflected in the instructions exactly. All information given to the escrow officer should reflect the agreement by the principals in the purchase contract.

Escrow Instructions Should Give the Escrow Holder the Following Information:

- A list of all documents, money or any other items of value to be deposited into escrow and by whom they are to be deposited
- Conditions to be met before the close of escrow, such as financing, pest control work, property inspections or repairs
- A list of all items to be prorated, such as rents, deposits, insurance, interest and property taxes
- An explanation of all fees to be paid by the principals to the escrow

---

If any changes in the original instructions are required, the escrow officer must draw up an amendment or addendum to the purchase agreement for each change. Maybe the seller wants to close later than the original date agreed upon, or maybe the buyer wants to get an adjustable loan rather than a fixed rate as previously stated in the offer to purchase. No matter how small the detail, if it differs from the original agreement, *all* parties to the escrow must agree to the change by signing an amendment or addendum.

Escrow instructions are divided into two types. They can be unilateral, where the buyer signs one set of instructions and the seller signs another, or bilateral, where the buyer and seller sign the same set of instructions.

Generally, custom dictates which type is used. In areas which use unilateral instructions, the real estate agent is generally responsible for getting information to the escrow company and makes sure requirements of the escrow are met where the principal is involved. The instructions are usually drawn after all the information has been given to the escrow officer, just before the escrow is to close.

When the instructions are bilateral, the escrow instructions generally are drawn up and signed when escrow is first opened.

<u>Escrow Instructions Can Be:</u>

Unilateral
Buyer signs one set of instructions and the seller signs another

Bilateral
Buyer and seller sign the same set of instructions

Basic Regional Differences

The forms used for escrow instructions vary almost as much as the number of escrow holders. Each escrow holder (escrow officer) uses the type of instructions that he or she prefers, according to custom. Also, instructions vary widely from one part of the country to another. In California the purchase agreement becomes the escrow instructions.

However, regardless of geographical area, escrow is interested in gathering the required information and carrying out the closing process in order to transfer real property and provide the accounting to the principals.

General Principles

There are some basic principles that all escrow officers follow, whether they are in Southern, Central or Northern California, or in some other state, in order to complete an escrow.

Prepare Escrow Instruction

The contractual intent and agreement of the parties is stated here. Since escrow is a limited agency, the escrow officer may only perform those duties identified as being necessary to the well being of the escrow and delegated by the parties to the transaction.

An escrow officer is only responsible for carrying out the duties specified in the escrow instructions and is not obligated to fulfill the full disclosure requirement of a general agency.

Gather Documentation

Grant deeds, trust deeds, quitclaim deeds, notes, bills of sale, security agreements, Uniform Commercial Code forms (financing statements, information requests, termination statements, assignments) must all be collected and prepared.

Order Title Report

The title report gives the escrow holder information about liens such as existing trust deeds, unpaid taxes, judgments or tax liens.   Generally, the buyer has the right to approve or disapprove the preliminary title report as a contingency of the sale.   The preliminary title report gives all the information included in the final title report which is usually insured in favor of the buyer, seller and/or lender.

Complete Escrow Instructions

Escrow instructions are for the purpose of communicating the intentions of the principals in a transaction to the escrow officer. The escrow officer has a stated time period to accomplish all the necessary tasks delegated by the instructions so the escrow will close in a timely manner according to the wishes of the parties. Commissions must be calculated if there is a broker involved, charges must be listed and made to the correct party and all contingencies must be completed.

In Southern California, instructions are likely to be prepared as soon as escrow is opened and amended as ordered by the parties during the escrow. These are known as bilateral instructions.

Unilateral instructions are used in Northern California, with the instructions drawn at the end of the escrow period.

Prepare to Record

Upon completion of all terms of the agreement between the parties, the escrow officer will authorize the recording of documents necessary to the transfer. All documents, signed instructions and amendments have been deposited and are in the possession of the escrow holder. Good funds have been received and are in the possession of the escrow holder. All conditions of the contract have been satisfied.

Recordation

Upon recordation of grant deed, trust deed or other documents required for the transfer, the sale is complete. The seller gets the money, the broker gets the commission and the buyer gets the property, with the grant deed to follow as soon as it is mailed to him or her by the county recorder. Information about the transfer of ownership is forwarded to the fire insurance company and existing lenders or any other interested parties. A closing statement summarizing the disbursement of funds and costs of the escrow is prepared by the escrow officer and given to each of the parties.

The major differences in escrow procedures between Northern and Southern California are the way duties and responsibilities between the real estate agent and the escrow officer are divided, the form of the escrow instructions, the role of bank or title company and the apportionment of fees.

Joint (Bilateral) Escrow Instructions

In Southern California the escrow officer gets involved at the very beginning of the transaction, or immediately after the buyer and seller have reached an agreement and signed the offer to purchase.

A connection with the lender begins at the same time as other early stages of the escrow.

The joint or bilateral escrow instructions are more complex than in those drawn in Northern California and are likely to be laden with statements absolving all parties of any innocent wrongdoing or negligent failure to disclose all issues.

Sometimes when instructions are *prepared at the beginning of escrow,* they may be amended frequently. As we have seen, there are basic steps to be taken by the escrow officer. They are taken in somewhat different order than in the north, however. The following looks mainly at the differences between Northern and Southern California.

Draw Instructions

The bilateral escrow instructions, along with required deeds, purchase money encumbrances and notes are prepared and delivered to the appropriate parties for signatures as soon as possible after opening escrow. Copies of the same document are sent to both buyer and seller (bilateral instructions) or may be delivered by their respective real estate agents. Once the instructions are signed by both sides a valid contract exists and the escrow officer starts preparing the title for closing and following financing instructions.

Review Title

A preliminary title report is ordered from the title company agreed upon by the buyer and seller in the offer to purchase. After reviewing the preliminary report to discover items which must be made to conform with the conditions of the transfer, the escrow officer proceeds to follow the instructions regarding loan payoffs, liens or any other matters necessary to present the title at the closing as agreed upon by the parties.

From the preliminary title report the escrow agent examines any existing liens and reviews taxes to make sure both conform to the agreement of the parties. If instructed to pay off any liens, the escrow agent requests a demand for payment and supportive documents from the holder of the lien. If a new lender has specific requirements regarding taxes, the escrow agent must satisfy those conditions.

When the escrow agent receives any demands for payoff of loans, he or she puts the demands into the open escrow file to be paid at the closing. The payoff amounts shown in the demands must match with the understanding of the parties. Any amounts that seem unreasonable or out of the ordinary, such as a large prepayment penalty, extreme late charges or a surprise principal balance owed, should be questioned by the escrow agent and approved by the party responsible for payment, usually the seller, before the closing.

Financing

At the same time the title review is going on, the escrow agent prepares documents for any assumption of an existing loan on the property or any other special financing, such as an all-inclusive trust deed, contract of sale or any trust deeds required by the escrow. Some of the necessary documents may need to be prepared by an attorney and submitted to the escrow.

If the buyer is to assume an existing loan, a formal agreement, which might change the existing loan terms, must be prepared by the escrow agent and signed by the parties as part of the closing.

In order for a loan to be assumed, the escrow officer requests a beneficiary statement from the lender describing the condition of the loan. Principal, interest rate payment amount, payment status, and any special terms of the loan are specified. If there is a "due on sale" clause in the loan, this request for a beneficiary statement will notify the existing lender of the pending sale, who will then demand the loan be paid in full upon the closing of the escrow. If the loan is assumable, the lender will submit documents and most likely a credit application for the buyer to complete.

The escrow agent will determine, from the information provided, if the lender's prior approval of the loan assumption is required before recording the sale. If the lender requests documentation on the sale, the escrow officer will provide what is needed as instructed in the escrow instructions.

While the escrow holder is getting information about existing liens, new financing is being processed. The lender will require cooperation and complete information from the escrow officer in order to give loan approval and fund the loan without unnecessary delays.

If the buyer is applying for a new conventional loan, chances are he or she will complete a Federal Home Loan Mortgage Corporation (Freddie Mac/Fannie Mae) loan application form. VA and FHA forms ask for similar information from the buyer.

After the buyer completes the loan application, the credit history is verified and the property appraised, the loan package is ready to be approved by the loan committee. Once the loan, along with the preliminary title report, is approved, the lender issues a loan commitment letter.

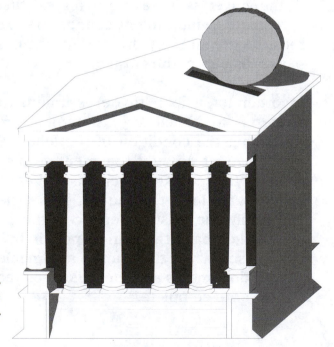

After receiving the lender's approval or qualified

approval, the escrow officer will review the loan terms to make sure they conform with the desires of the buyer as expressed in the escrow instructions. The escrow agent then must get the buyer's approval and acceptance of the terms of the loan, including any lender-required changes in the original terms of the loan.

> *Kenny and Judi applied for a loan of $250,000 at an interest rate not to exceed 8%, due in 30 years, with points not to exceed 2%. They might be offered only $225,000 because the property did not appraise as high as the buyer expected. At this point they must decide whether to accept the reduced loan and put a larger amount down, renegotiate with the seller or simply cancel the sale because the loan contingency was not met according to the agreement in the offer to purchase.*

Review Before Closing

When all conditions of the escrow have been met, all documents have been drawn, are correct and ready for signing by the parties, the escrow officer calculates prorations and other costs as per the closing date.

The required documents such as the grant deed, any trust deeds or other matters to be recorded are sent to the title company for review and recording upon further instructions.

The escrow officer than calls the buyer and asks him or her to come to the escrow office and bring the down payment and other funds necessary to close the escrow.

The buyer signs the loan documents and any disclosures not already signed, and the items are returned to the lender. The signed trust deed is sent with the other documents to the title company to be recorded.

Funds Requested by Escrow Officer

If all goes smoothly during the review and signing of documents, the escrow agent requests the loan funds from the lender. When the money is received by the escrow holder or the title company the transaction is ready to record.

The differences between the type of escrow instructions used in Southern California and Northern California are few from here on. Procedures for auditing, recording, disbursement of funds and closing are conducted by escrow officers in a similar fashion. Any differences have to do with the fact that procedures in the north combine with the title insurance process to a greater degree, and the escrow officer might perform certain title company functions that would not be required in the south.

Both Regions conduct competent escrows; and neither method is superior to the other. Bilateral instructions used in Southern California reduce the possibility of disputes between the parties about the terms of the escrow. In the north, since escrow instructions are not drawn until the end of the escrow period, the need for unending amendments is reduced.

Joint Escrow Instructions

Broker opens escrow

Prepare escrow instructions and required documents
Obtain signatures of all parties

Order title search
Receive and review preliminary report
Request demands
Request explanation of liens
Review taxes as reported
Receive demands and enter into file

Process financing
Request beneficiary statement
Review terms of transfer and
current payment status
Request copy of new loan application
Obtain loan approval
Request loan documents

Review escrow file for:
Completion of all requirements of escrow
Documents correct and ready for signature
Good funds received

Figure prorations and all other costs as of the closing

Request signatures on all remaining documents

Forward documents to title company

Obtain funds from buyer

Return loan documents

Request loan funds sent to title company

Order recording

Close file, prepare statements, disburse funds

Close file

Unilateral Escrows

In Northern California where unilateral escrow procedures are prevalent, there are three major differences.

1. The title insurance process is connected to the escrow procedure much more closely.

2. The escrow agent relies on the real estate broker far more than in joint (bilateral) escrows.

3. Escrow instructions are prepared by the escrow agent *at the end* of the escrow period. Joint instructions precede the escrow process and are often amended.

Opening the Order

With unilateral instructions, it is the real estate broker who starts the escrow process. After a buyer and seller have reached an agreement, the title company chosen by the principals is contacted by the real estate broker who orders a preliminary title report.

This is done through the escrow department of the title company.

Before the escrow officer can ask the title department to conduct a title search on the subject property, certain information must be on hand.

Information Required for Title Search:

- Legal description--usually assessor's block and parcel number

- Buyers and sellers complete an identity statement so the title company can obtain complete information about who currently owns the property in question and how title is currently held

- The type of title insurance desired-a standard policy or extended policy

- Name and address of new lender if any

- Any particular information required about copies of C,C&R,s, any special endorsements or inspections requested in the original offer to purchase between the buyer and seller

---

Preliminary Title Report

After receiving a copy of the preliminary title report, the real estate broker carefully reviews it to make sure the title is in the condition it is believed to be in by the buyer and seller as shown in the offer to purchase.

Title/Interests Held

The broker looks at how title is held (joint tenants, community property, tenants in common, and so on), or whether any life estates, leaseholds, easements or other interests affecting title exist.

Current Ownership

Vesting must match the name of the seller on the original offer to purchase. If not, the real estate broker must determine if there has been a misrepresentation by the seller or if some other mistake has occurred. In any case, at this early point vesting must be researched and any discrepancy discovered and corrected.

Parcel Description

The legal description must match the description of the subject property as described in the original offer to purchase document. Measurements of the parcel as shown in the preliminary report are compared with those on the listing to make sure they are accurate. The parcel is usually referred by an **APN** number or "Assessor's Parcel Number," on the tax record.

Exceptions or Encumbrances

The preliminary report will show any money liens, judgments, easements, taxes owed, or any restrictions affecting title or use of the property in question. The lender will then give loan approval based on his or her evaluation of the report. Some items may be named as exceptions to getting the loan, or as items that must be paid prior to the closing.

If an existing loan is to be paid off, a demand for payoff must be sent to the holder of the loan. If the present loan is to be assumed, a beneficiary statement is required from the current lien holder. The real estate broker relays information to the escrow agent regarding financing as agreed upon in the offer to purchase.

Statement of Information

All parties in a transaction are asked by the title company to complete a statement relating to information that might affect their capacity to close the escrow. There are certain matters that might be found in the general index

of the recorder's office that must be researched by the escrow officer such as judgments, tax liens, insanities, paroles, attorneys in fact, guardianship proceedings, bankruptcies, probates or other legal matters relating to the financial responsibility of the principals. Since guarding against forgery is one of the assurances given by the title policy, a signature is required from each of the principals.

Demand

A demand states the balance owed on an existing loan. It is sent to the escrow holder by the lender after a written request is made, asking for a letter disclosing the total amount owed and any supportive documents necessary for the payoff.

After receiving the demand from the lender of record, the escrow officer must verify the payoff information with the

seller to determine its accuracy according to the seller's records. Occasionally, a prepayment penalty of six months' interest on the unpaid balance will be part of the payoff, and the seller must be made aware of the amount and be in agreement.

If there is an alienation (due-on-sale) clause in the existing note, the lender will be notified of the pending sale by the demand for payoff.

Beneficiary Statement

When the buyer wants to assume or take "subject to" an existing loan, a written request for the current status of the loan is made to the lender (beneficiary). Information about the balance of the loan, the terms of payment, any insurance data and requirements of the lender for loan assumption are included in the request.

Some notes simply state that the note is assumable but the lender has the right to approve the buyer, who must submit a loan assumption application. The lender usually has the right to adjust the terms of the loan to the new borrower after giving approval of the assumption.

Neutral Depository

The escrow holder is a neutral party for the forwarding of any bills accumulated as a result of work done to complete the terms of the escrow. Pest controllers, roofers, property inspectors, or any other professionals who have completed work on the property may submit bills to the escrow holder, who will pay them at the closing from the proceeds of the sale, as directed by the principals.

Opening of Escrow

The actual opening of escrow is the main difference between unilateral and bilateral escrow instructions. After receiving loan approval and the terms of the loan being approved by the buyer, the documentation is sent to the escrow officer who holds them for the buyer's signature just prior to the closing. Then escrow instructions are drawn and the closing process starts.

Escrow Instructions

Unilateral instructions are prepared for the buyer and seller to sign. Any other documents required by the escrow are prepared at this time also. The seller's instructions show money received and a deed being given. In the buyer's instructions, money is given in return for the deed. Prorations and other fees are charged to the appropriate party and specific terms of the transaction are carried out to close the escrow.

Just prior to recording, the escrow officer conducts a final review of the escrow file to make sure all documents have been properly signed and notarized, and good funds received.

If the file is complete, documents are sent to the title officer who holds them until instructed to record. At the same time, loan funds are requested if there is a new loan involved.

Collecting Funds

The final act of the escrow officer is to collect funds from the buyer and the lender, if a new loan is involved. The buyer is contacted and asked to bring in the remainder of the down payment and the amount needed to close the escrow. After all money is deposited with the escrow officer, including closing costs, the escrow file is reconciled one more time to make sure all conditions have been met.

Closing

After the final audit, documents are ordered to be recorded and final settlement begins. Buyer and seller receive closing statements describing their costs. The buyer gets a deed and the seller gets a check.

Unilateral Escrow Instructions

Broker opens escrow

Request preliminary title report from title department

Receive and review	Order statements of
preliminary report	buyer/seller identity

Order demands	**Order beneficiary statement**
Review, inform client	Review terms, inform client

Collect bills from pest control company, property inspection, home warranty, contractors, and any other special demands to be paid at closing

Receive loan documents from lender
Prepare buyer/seller instructions and all other required documents
Execute and return buyer/seller instructions and documents

Review escrow file for:
Completion of all requirments of escrow
Documents correctly executed and notarized
Good funds received

Request loan funds from lender

**Forward documents to recording desk in title department
to be held until recording is ordered**

Complete title policy write-up

Receive loan funds

Order recording	Closing statements
Audit escrow	Disburse funds

Close file

Post Test

The following self test repeats the one you took at the beginning of this chapter. Now take the exam again -- since you have read all the material -- and check your knowledge of escrow closing procedures.

True/False

1. The format for escrow instructions is set by law.

2. Escrow instructions can be bilateral or unilateral.

3. With bilateral instructions, the buyer and seller sign the same set of instructions.

4. Unilateral instructions are revocable by either party.

5. Instructions are drawn at the beginning of the escrow period with unilateral instructions.

6. With bilateral instructions, both parties sign the same set of instructions.

7. One of the main differences between unilateral and bilateral instructions is the way duties and responsibilities between the broker and escrow officer are divided.

8. The title insurance process is more closely connected to the escrow procedure with bilateral instructions.

9. With unilateral instructions, the escrow agent begins the escrow process.

10. Unilateral instructions are more complex than bilateral instructions.

ESCROW INSTRUCTIONS

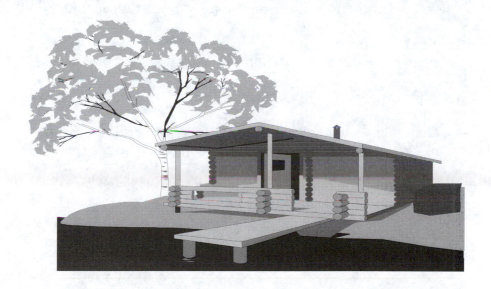

Focus

- **Introduction**
- **Collecting information**
- **Preparing for the instructions**
- **Escrow instructions**
- **Local variations**

Pre-Test

The following is a self test to determine how much you know about escrow instructions before reading this chapter. Take it without studying, then read the material presented in the text. At the end of the chapter you will find a repeat of this exam. Test your knowledge by answering the questions again, then check your improvement. (The answers are found at the end of the book.) Good luck.

True/False

1. A "take sheet" is the framework for the escrow instructions.

2. Collecting the information needed to provide complete escrow instructions is the first step for an escrow agent.

3. The three documents that serve as the heart of a sale escrow are the grant deed, promissory note and bill of sale.

4. A promissory note is the security for a debt.

5. General instructions authorize the escrow holder to carry out general procedures needed to complete the escrow.

6. General instructions are special instructions given by a buyer or seller to the escrow holder.

7. Third party instructions may include a demand or claim from a person not involved in the escrow as a principal.

8. The escrow holder's obligation to the parties starts as soon as escrow instructions are written.

9. Prorations are made on the basis of a 25-day month.

10. If rents are to be prorated, escrow holder should prorate and charge seller and credit buyer with any deposits paid in advance to the seller by tenants.

Introduction

A buyer and seller have come to an agreement and want to complete the sale of real property. To make sure all the items they have agreed upon are carried out or executed, they need a neutral third party to conduct an escrow to carry out their wishes. An escrow agent will probably conduct the escrow.

Escrow instructions may be written, as we have seen, from the agreement between the principals. The escrow agent does not direct the transaction; the principals

do. The escrow agent reacts to instructions which represent the mutual agreement of the parties.

The instructions are carefully drawn after the escrow agent gathers all the necessary information from the original agreement and the parties connected with the transaction. It is the escrow instructions that reflect, exactly, the intention of the parties to complete the transaction and describe in detail how that will be accomplished. Once the instructions are prepared, the buyer, seller and real estate agent all get copies either to sign and return to the closing agent, or to be filed and kept as required by law. We shall see here how escrow instructions are assembled.

Collecting Information

Most of the time it is the real estate agent who brings the deposit check from the buyer and is the initial contact for the escrow holder. The process of information gathering takes place before the escrow agent prepares the instructions for the parties to sign.

Deposit receipt

At the first contact with the real estate agent who is opening the escrow, the escrow holder makes a copy of the deposit receipt to keep in the transaction file. It may be used for reference if confusion or conflict arises as the escrow progresses.

Take Sheet

The escrow agent will use a "take sheet" as the framework for the instructions, making sure the escrow contract accurately reflects the understanding and intent of the parties as stated in the original deposit receipt.

This information sheet is used to list the important data without itemizing the terms of the transaction. Each of the conditions of this transaction must be evaluated correctly so the escrow or title agent can reduce them to instructions that satisfy all parties.

Take Sheet

Escrow #_____

Date opened_____

Deposit receipt on file ( )_____

Seller/Lender_____
Mailing address_____
Home address_____
Telephone (home)_____
     (work)_____
Address after close of escrow_____
_____

Buyer/Borrower_____
Mailing address_____
Home address_____
Telephone(home)_____
     (work)_____
Address after close of escrow_____
_____

Property address_____
_____

Legal description_____
_____

Buyer will deposit_____
Deposit by buyer_____
Cash to be added_____
1st Trust Deed_____
2nd Trust Deed_____
Total consideration_____

Proration as of close of escrow or:_____
     Property taxes ( )
     Homeowners dues ( )
     Rents ( )
     Interest-1st trust deed ( )
     Impound account ( )

_____ARM/fixed_____Yearss
Commission_____%_____Split
Seller's agent_____
Real estate company_____
Address_____
_____
Telephone_____Fax_____

Points_____
Close of escrow_____
Buyer's agent_____
Real estate company_____
Address_____
_____
Telephone_____Fax_____

Title Compnay_____
Address_____
Telephone_____
Title order #_____

Credit_____
Payoff_____
Address_____
Loan #_____
Payoff_____
Address_____
Loan #_____

Subject to buyer/property qualifying for:
( ) All cash
( ) Preliminary title_____days
( ) Homeowner's Protection Plan/seller
( ) Homeowner's Protection plan/buyer
( ) Homeowner's Protection-broker to pay from
     commission
( ) Supplemental taxes
( ) Bonds paid current
( ) HOA transfer paid-buyer/seller
( )Memo items
( )Property inspestion_____days
( ) Condo unit#___Space___Dues____Days_____

( )Escrow instructions signed_____days
( )Verbal approval_____days
( )Written loan approval_____days
( )Walk through_____days, not a contingency
( )Possession COE
( )Possession_____days after COE
( )Buyer acting as principal
( )Seller acting as principal
( )Geological_____days
( )Purchase price includes_____
_____
( ) Buyer to occupy

Gathering the Data

☑ Legal name, current address and telephone number of principals, brokers and lenders must be listed and kept on hand for use during the term of the escrow.

☑ Financial information about the transaction must be collected, such as the sales price, trust deeds to remain and those to be paid off, any new loans to be obtained, or the price of any personal property included.

☑ An accurate legal description is needed to assure that the buyer is getting the right parcel. A street address is also included if there is one.

☑ The type of property (single family residence, income property, etc.) must be noted in case there are local requirements to be met when there is a sale, such as retrofit or zoning limitations.

☑ The seller must provide existing loan information and the buyer or buyer's agent must provide the name of any new lender.

☑ The closing agent must have the proper names of the parties to the transaction (buyer/seller, borrower/lender, vendor/vendee, lessor/lessee).

☑ Exact terms of the escrow must be indicated, including any time limitations and date of closing.

☑ Prorations include such items as interest on existing loans, taxes, assessments, bonds, insurance, homeowner's association dues, maintenance fees and rental deposits. The expectations of the parties regarding prorations must be defined clearly, especially if the principals have agreed mutually on non-traditional proration time frames, such as using an actual "day month" instead of the 30-day month, or have decided not to prorate some normal items.

☑ Identification of the title company indicated by buyer and seller must be noted.

☑ Conditions of fire, liability and lender's insurance must be defined.

☑ Requirements are noted for pest control inspection, time frame for work to be done and an account of who will pay for the inspection and/or any work required.

☑ Distribution of charges is made based on the agreement of the parties to the transaction, as long as the charges are not in conflict with laws or rules regulating legal matters.

☑ Information must be collected, almost always from the listing broker, regarding how commissions are to be paid and how they are to be split between brokers.

☑ Any particular agreements made by the principals must be noted, such as leaseback instructions, an all inclusive trust deed (AITD) agreement to be drawn or instruction for attorney involvement (to be sent copies of all documents, etc.).

Preparing for the Instructions

Collecting the information needed to provide accurate and complete instructions is the first step for an escrow agent, as we have learned. Of major importance is the need to be specific, methodical, well organized and complete in using the information gathered to produce instructions that reflect the agreement of the parties correctly.

In producing complete, error-free instructions, the escrow agent must be sure of the mechanics of the transaction, including the time frame in which the escrow is to be carried out according to the agreement of the principals, the number and types of documents needed, an inclusive description of consideration and other agreements relating to cash, and allocation of charges to the proper parties.

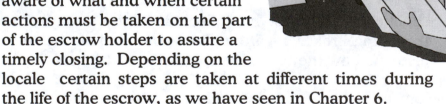

A time line is essential for the smooth progress of the escrow. The escrow holder must be aware of what and when certain actions must be taken on the part of the escrow holder to assure a timely closing. Depending on the locale certain steps are taken at different times during the life of the escrow, as we have seen in Chapter 6.

In any case, the closing agent must proceed steadily and systematically towards the end result, which is the transfer of real or personal property and the hypothecation and/or pledging of real or personal property.

Escrows are Concerned With:

- **Title:** who owns the property now and to whom and how is it being transferred?

- **Consideration:** how much is being paid, borrowed, traded or given and how is it to be allocated?

Framework of Transaction

The escrow agent must have a clear understanding of the who are the parties and what do they want to achieve?

An experienced escrow agent will create a summary of the proposed transaction before preparing or ordering any documents.

Transaction Summary

- Amount of deposit
- Balance of down payment owed
- Listing of all loan amounts
- Type of transaction
- Length of escrow
- Legal description

- Property address
- Seller's name
- Buyer's name
- Buyer's address
- Terms of financing
- Any payoffs
- Items to be prorated

Transaction Summary

Onofre and Ruby Archuleta are buying a house from Quentin and Kate Oliver for $400,000. The Archuletas are putting $160,000 down and getting a new first loan in the amount of $240,000.

$ 4,000	Good faith deposit
156,000	Balance of down payment
240,000	New first loan
$400,000	Total consideration

Type of transaction Sale

Length of escrow 45 days

Legal description Lot 6, Blk 6, tract 785
City of San Clemente
County of Orange
Map book page 36, page 12

Property address 305 Avenida Cristobal
San Clemente, CA 92672

Seller Kate/Quentin Oliver
305 Avenida Cristobal
San Clemente, CA 92672

Buyer Ruby/Onofre Archuleta
2234 Monogram Avenue
Long Beach, CA 92684

Financing $240,000 @ 8.5%-new first loan
Lender-Home Savings

Payoff Bank of America
$244,000 @ 7.5%-current balance
payable monthly @ $1,800
loan #050650

Prorations $5,000 annually-taxes
$1,200 annually-hazard insurance

Documents

An escrow holder generally is able to prepare, or order from the proper source, all documents relating to an escrow. As long as the documents don't include the shaping of a contract requiring legal judgments or other acts that would indicate the escrow holder is practicing law, the services of an attorney usually are not necessary in normal transactions.

There are three documents that serve as the heart of a sale or loan escrow: the grant deed, promissory note and deed of trust. Other documents, such as a quit claim deed, security agreement, financing statement, bill of sale and additional disclosure forms, also may be required by the escrow.

Grant Deed

Deeds may be used to convey any type of interest, burden or encumbrance, as well as fee simple transfers in property.

Deeds Conveying Special Interests

- Rights reserved by the grantor
- General plan restrictions (covenants, conditions and restrictions)
- Rights incidental or appurtenant to the parcel being transferred
- Riparian rights
- Mineral rights
- Stock rights in a mutually owned water company
- Leasehold rights of the grantor created by prior arrangement

---

When property is transferred by private grant, or by one private party to another, the instrument generally used is a grant deed. The parties involved are the grantor, or the person conveying the property, and the grantee, the person or group receiving the property. At the closing, the buyer gets the grant deed, which has been signed by the seller, as evidence of the transfer of ownership. Each time the property transfers from one party to another, a new grant deed must be prepared by the escrow officer.

A Valid Grant Deed Must

- Be In writing , according to the Statute of Frauds

- Have the parties to the transfer (grantor and grantee) sufficiently described

- Have a grantor who is competent to convey the property (not a minor or incompetent)

- Have a grantee who is capable of holding title (a real living person, not fictitious)

- Be adequately described

- Have the "granting clause" the act of granting (grant, convey) must be included

- Be signed by the grantor

- Be delivered to and accepted by the grantee

A grant deed carries with it two specific warrantees: that the grantor has not previously conveyed the same property or an interest in it to someone else, and that the estate is free from encumbrances that have not been disclosed by the grantor.

Also, if a grantor subsequently acquires any title or interest in the property which he or she has granted as a fee simple estate, that after-acquired title passes to the grantee.

A grant deed does not have to be recorded to be valid. In order for the parties' rights to be protected, however, the deed must be recorded. The deed must be acknowledged before it can be recorded.

Each county, upon the transfer of property, may charge a documentary transfer tax. The amount of the transfer tax is stamped in the upper right-hand corner of a recorded deed and sent to the buyer after the closing. The amount of the tax is based on $1.10 per $1,000 or $.55 per $500 of transferred value. The deed is sent to the buyer after the closing by the County Recorder.

How to Calculate Documentary Transfer Tax

- When a sale is all cash, or a new loan is obtained by the buyer, the tax is calculated on the entire sales price.

- When an existing loan is assumed by a buyer, the tax is calculated on the difference between the assumed loan and the sales price.

Promissory Note

A promissory note is a written promise to pay back a certain sum of money with specified terms at an agreed upon time. It is a personal obligation of the borrower and a complete contract in itself, between the borrower and lender.

According to the Uniform Commercial Code, to be valid or enforceable, a promissory note must meet certain requirements.

A Promissory Note is:

- An unconditional written promise to pay a certain sum

- Made by one person to another

- Signed by the maker or borrower

- Payable at a definite time

- Paid to bearer or to order

- Voluntarily delivered by the borrower

Normally, in a transaction where the buyer is financing the sale (borrowing money) through an institutional lender, loan documents which include a promissory note are signed by the buyer/borrower in the presence of the closing agent just before the closing. If the sale is being financed by the seller, loan documents would not be available or necessary and a promissory note is prepared by the closing agent, according to the instructions of the principals.

Types of Promissory Notes

It is useful for a closing agent to be knowledgeable about the types of promissory notes.

Straight Note: Calls for payment of interest only, or no payments, during the term of the note, with all accrued money (either principal only, or principal and interest if no payments have been made) due and payable on a certain date.

Partially Amortized Installment Note: Calls for periodic payments; such payments may or may not include interest; usually demands a balloon payment of unpaid principle and interest at the end of the term to completely pay off debt.

Fully Amortized Installment Note: Calls for periodic payments of fixed amounts, to include both interest and principal, which will pay off the debt completely by the end of the term.

Adjustable Note: The interest rate in the note varies upward or downward over the term of the loan, depending on the money market conditions and an agreed upon index. The escrow holder may not draw this type of note, but must refer the drawing to an attorney.

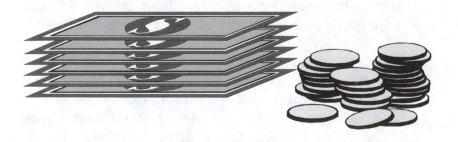

Preparing the Note

There are certain items regarding the note of which a closing agent must be aware and must include in preparing the escrow instructions.

Lender

- Name of lender?

- Institution or individual?

- Is it a loan regulated by the Business and Professions Code involving real estate licensees?

- Is it a loan regulated by the state usury law or is it a purchase money loan to a seller or other private-party loan?

Terms

- Amount borrowed?

- How many notes are required for the principal amount?

- What is the interest rate?

- Is the interest rate fixed or variable? If variable, what is the index, time period for rate changes, how is interest to be treated (deferred or added to principal payment)? Any unusual interest terms?

- How are payments to be made? Are they fixed or variable or a combination of both (graduated payment loans)? If payment does not cover monthly interest, how is deferred interest to be accrued and how are future payments to be applied.

- Is there a balloon payment? Note should be made if the loan is arranged under the Business and Professions Code sections applying to licensee-arranged loans. The regulations specify that no balloon payment is allowed until the 73rd month on a single-family, owner-occupied residence. Holders of notes containing a balloon payment must remind borrowers no sooner than 150 days nor later than 90 days from maturity of when the loan is due.

- Where will payment be made or sent? If the location is outside California, usury laws of that state may apply.

- Will there be late charges?

- Is there a pre-payment penalty?

- If there is a due-on-sale clause it must be contained in both the note and trust deed. The make-up of the acceleration clause usually will be supplied by the lender.

- What type of note is it? Payment should reflect whether the note is a straight note (interest only), installment note (principal amortized) or some other type of note.

- What is the collateral for the note? If more than one property is being used to secure the loan (blanket mortgage), it should be noted that two trust deeds are being utilized for the note.

<u>Special Requirements of the Note:</u>

- Are there restrictions on principal reductions?

- Is there a pre-payment penalty?

- If the transaction deals with a subdivision, is there a partial release clause? Is the subdivision regulated by the Subdivision Map Act and have the proper steps been taken to comply with laws regarding creation of a trust deed dividing an existing lot?

- Will the note specify whether there can be loan advances, extension of the loan, future subordination, renegotiation of rate at any time?

Deed of Trust

As we have mentioned, a trust deed is used to secure a loan on real property. It describes the property being used as security, or collateral, for a debt, and usually includes a power of sale and assignment of rents clause.

<u>Trust Deeds Usually Include:</u>

Power of Sale Clause:
Gives trustee the right to foreclose, sell and convey ownership to a purchaser of the property if the borrower defaults on the loan

Assignment of Rents Clause:
Upon default by the borrower, the lender can take possession of the property and collect any rents being paid

The process of borrowing money, secured by a trust deed, where the buyer remains in possession of the property during the payoff of the loan or note, is called hypothecation.

A certain uniformity is required by FNMA/FHLMC in trust deeds securing loans bought by those agencies. The following is a list of inclusions necessary to describe the rights and obligations of parties to a trust deed.

Rights and Obligations of Parties to a Trust Deed

1. Payment of principal and interest
2. Payment of taxes and insurance
3. Statement of how payments are to be made relating to the note
4. Charges to be made to borrower (if required to pay taxes and insurance without an impound account by lender) and  liens to be placed for non-payment
5. Requirements for hazard insurance coverage and application of insurance proceeds
6. Obligations to comply with the provisions of a lease (optional)
7. Statement of lender's right to take action if borrower defaults
8. Property inspection by lender before action is taken upon the default of borrower
9. Settlement agreement in case of eminent domain proceedings

10. Lender's right to give forbearance in certain cases, but no obligation in all cases
11. Description of liability for parties--both joint, several and co-signers, as well as all successors-- of interest.
12. Charges given for the loan
13. Provision for an acceleration clause if all terms are not met
14. Address of borrower and lender listed
15. Copy of document to borrower
16. Requirements of lender with transfer of ownership (due-on-sale, assumption)
17. Methods of curing default
18. Description of lender's right to foreclose upon default of borrower, and of default
19. Rents from property occupants, collected by lender or an appointed receiver, in case of default
20. Conditions for reconveyance after loan paid in full
21. Substitution of trustee allowed
22. Requirement for notification of default to be mailed to borrower at the property address (request for notice)
23. List of any special conditions of the loan
24. Possible fee by the lender for preparing a beneficiary's statement

Trust Deed as a Lien

A trust deed becomes a lien on the real property being conveyed when the buyer borrows money to buy the property. The escrow agent prepares the trust deed and it is then added to the loan document package supplied by the lender for the buyer's signature. The trust deed does not have to be recorded to be valid, but ordering recordation of the signed trust deed is normally part of the closing agent's responsibility.

Quitclaim Deed

Another type of deed that may be prepared by the closing agent is a quitclaim deed. In the past, this type of deed was commonly used to transfer real property interests between husband and wife. However, an inter-spousal grant deed is now used between spouses instead of a quitclaim deed.

A quitclaim deed is a deed of conveyance that operates as a release of whatever interest the grantor has in the property. The quitclaim deed contains similar language to a deed, with the important exception that rather than using the words *grant and release*, it contains language such as *remise, release and quitclaim*. Grantors therefore do not warrant title or possession. Grantors only pass on whatever interest they may have, if any. In effect, a grantor forever quits whatever claim he or she had, if in fact any existed.

Executing a quitclaim deed does not carry even an implied warranty as regards ownership, liens, encumbrances or the possibility that the grantor has not previously signed a deed to someone else. It does convey ownership of the property to another person.

A quitclaim deed is not commonly used to convey a fee, but is usually restricted to releasing or conveying minor interests in real estate for the purpose of clearing title defects or clouds on title. It may also be used to convey lesser interests such as life estates and to release such interests as a remainder or reversion.

Quitclaim deeds also are often used between close relatives, such as when one heir is buying out the other, or where a seller's finances are so troubled that it is inconsequential to the buyer whether he or she is getting any warranties or not.

Although a quitclaim deed may or may not vest any title in the grantee, it is not inferior to the other types of deeds in what it actually conveys. For example, if a grantor executes and delivers a grant deed to one person and subsequently executes and delivers a quitclaim deed to the same property to another person, the grantee under the quitclaim deed will prevail over the grantee under the grant deed, assuming the holder of the quitclaim is first to record the deed.

A title searcher will regard a quitclaim deed in the chain of title as a red flag, and most title companies will not guarantee titles derived out of a quitclaim, at least not without further clarification.

Bill of Sale

A bill of sale is a written agreement by which one person sells, assigns, or transfers to another his or her interest in personal property. A bill of sale sometimes is used by a seller of real estate to show the transfer of personal property, such as when the owner of a store sells the building and includes the store equipment and trade fixtures. The transfer of the personal property can be effected by mentioning in the deed, or more commonly, by a separate bill-of-sale document, which is prepared by the closing agent for signature by the seller.

Security Agreement

A security agreement is a document that creates a lien on personal property, including possessions intended to be attached to land as fixtures after the sale closes. Rather than recording the security agreement to give notice of the lien, however, the law provides for filing a financing statement to perfect the security interest. A closing agent usually will be required to prepare a security agreement in the sale of a business opportunity.

Financing Statement

A financing statement is a written notice (of credit given and ensuing terms in a security agreement) to be filed with the Secretary of State's Office. A closing agent will prepare a financing statement and order it to be recorded at the request of a seller who has given credit for the purchase of personal property. The purpose of recording the statement is to establish the creditor's interest in the personal property (separate from the real property being conveyed in the transaction) which is the security for the debt. The financing statement is the document that is recorded to show evidence of a security agreement.

Truth in Lending Documents

The main purpose of the Truth-in-Lending Law or Regulation Z, as it is commonly known, is to assure that borrowers in need of consumer credit are given accurate and meaningful information about the cost of the credit being extended. Most escrow agents are involved in these lender disclosures and will present them to the borrower as required by law.

Real Estate Settlement Procedures Act Disclosures

The Real Estate Settlement Procedures Act (RESPA) is a federal loan disclosure law applicable to first mortgage loans on residential property. It requires certain disclosures to borrowers and provides the consumer with information on loan settlement costs. A special information booklet and good faith estimate of costs must be given to a borrower when he or she applies for a loan. One day before the scheduled closing the borrower has the right under RESPA to inspect the *Uniform Settlement Statement* which gives an itemized account of all fees charged by the lender. Information containing these disclosures usually is provided by the closing agent.

Consideration/Cash Agreements

At the beginning of the printed escrow instructions there is a listing of the consideration included in the transaction. This listing describes the source and use of all funds in the transaction.

Any money required by the transaction is noted, with its source, whether it is a cash deposit or new financing. This amount, plus or minus any fees, adjustments or prorations, represents the true cash that passes through the escrow.

Any other consideration that is not to be given as cash is accounted for in the instructions. Items of value such as personal or other real property to be added to the transaction are listed, as well as the equities to be transferred if the transaction is a tax deferred exchange.

Other Information

Certain basic information must be available to answer questions that may be asked about the escrow instructions, title and transfer documents, new financing being obtained to complete the transfer or any liens being paid off through the transaction. After all necessary information has been gathered and noted in the take sheet, the closing agent is ready to utilize the data in preparing instructions.

Escrow Instructions

Instructions may be drawn when the escrow agent has gathered all information specific to the escrow and is ready to proceed with the task of completing the transaction according to the direction given by the principals.

Basic Information

The consideration in dollar amounts, including amount of good faith deposit, additional cash to be added for down payment, any deeds of trust to be recorded, and sales price, term of escrow, title insurance policy liability, legal description of property, street address of property, and vestingare listed at the beginning of the instructions.

Conditions

This section states that the closing and costs allocated to the parties are subject to payment of taxes, liens or other restrictions on financing.

Special Provisions

Preliminary title report approval, home warranty agreement, executed preliminary change of ownership requirement, disclosure of supplemental tax on property, condominium data if applicable, pest control agreement, authorization and instruction for collection and disbursement of funds, and a cancellation agreement are listed in this section.

Costs

Special and general allocation of costs to buyer and seller are mentioned specifically.

Possession

The time and date of property possession by the buyer is listed, even though it may not be essential to the transaction.

Prorations

Items to be prorated as of close of escrow are specified.

General Provisions

By signing the instructions, the buyer and seller agree to the general provisions of the instructions which disclose various elements of the transaction general to most escrows.

Signatures

Instructions are signed by all parties.

Local Differences

As we have seen in Chapter 6, there are differences in the closing practices. There are two main differences between the locales. The first is the timing of the signing of closing documents. The second is the type of instructions prepared for the principals to sign. In the north, the instructions are unilateral, where the buyer and seller sign different sets of instructions. Bilateral instructions where buyer and seller sign an identical set of instructions are used in the southern part of the state.

Third Party Instructions

When third parties are involved in the transaction, such as lenders or other lien holders, special instructions are required giving the escrow holder authority to deal with parties other than the principals. These might include documents, demands or the deposit of funds into escrow.

Parties other than the principals, typically, may execute a third-party instruction to claim or discard a financial interest in the transaction. All parties must accept the additional instruction and sign any amendments affecting a third party.

<u>Third Party Instructions</u>

- For fire insurance authorization
- For commission payment authorization
- For an interspousal transfer grant deed between spouses
- To lender regarding payoff or assumption of an existing loan
- For release of mechanic's and other liens
- For release of a judgment

General Instructions

As we have seen, processing varies in different areas, depending on local custom. In some places an estimated closing statement is issued as part of the instructions, showing, for example, the proceeds going to the seller and the estimated cash needed to close for the buyer. In other places the broker's net sheet serves the same purpose, except the closing statement is provided at the settlement.

The general instructions are usually the pre-printed part of any set of instructions. As important as the contract items of agreement between the buyer and seller, this part of the escrow contract describes the procedures that will be used to accomplish the task required of the escrow officer.

Because different escrow holders have varying ideas regarding the number and extent of protective and disclosure clauses in their general instructions, there are any number of provisions that may be included here. The general instructions also deal with practically every aspect of the escrow, explaining each item of the escrow process.

These instructions authorize the escrow holder to carry out the general procedures needed to complete the escrow.

Deposit of Funds

Escrow holder is authorized and directed to deposit any and all funds placed in this escrow with any state or national bank or savings bank in a trust account in the name of the escrow holder without any liability for interest to be withdrawn by escrow holder and disbursed in accordance with the instructions of the parties.

Disbursements

All disbursements of funds and/or delivery of other documents or instruments concerning this escrow will be mailed to parties entitled thereto by regular first-class mail, postage prepaid to their respective addresses shown on the escrow file.

Instructions Signed

Escrow holder's duty does not commence until mutual escrow instructions signed by all parties are received by escrow holder. Until such time either party may unilaterally revoke these instructions and upon written request delivered to  escrow holder, the party may withdraw any funds, instruments, documents or items previously handed to escrow holder by such party.

Prorations

All prorations and adjustments are to be made on the basis of a thirty (30) day month unless otherwise instructed in writing by all parties. For proration purposes, the buyer will have ownership of the real property which is the subject of this escrow for the entire day, regardless of the hour of recording. The "close of escrow" with reference to said prorations and adjustments of all purposes for this escrow shall be the day instruments of conveyance called for are recorded or filed with the county recorder.

Escrow holder is instructed to prorate taxes for the current fiscal year based on the most recent information furnished to you by title insurer herein. Prorations are made on the basis of a 360 day year. In view of the change of ownership of the subject property which will take place on the close of this escrow, it is to be expected that the taxing authorities will re-assess the property and issue a supplemental tax bill. Seller and buyer acknowledge their awareness of the foregoing and hereby release and relieve escrow holder of all liability in connection with same, and escrow holder shall not be further concerned with the above re-assessment in any manner.

Escrow holder is authorized to obtain a Statement of Fees from Homeowners' Association affecting subject property and to charge account of the seller to bring account current, if necessary, and to use said statement to determine amounts required for proration purposes. Seller has furnished or will furnish, prior to close of escrow, to buyer outside of this escrow a copy of CC&R's, By-Laws, Budget and Articles of Incorporation for said Association.

Escrow holder has no duty or responsibility regarding those documents. Escrow holder is instructed to charge to the account of the buyer any transfer fee as charged by the Homeowners' Association and to split any "move-in/move-out" fee 1/2 to seller and 1/2 to buyer.

In the event rents are to be prorated, escrow holder is instructed to prorate and charge seller and credit buyer with any deposits paid in advance on the basis of a statement furnished by seller. Seller represents that he or she will collect all rents which fall  due prior to the close of escrow. Escrow holder is to make all adjustments on the basis that all rents are current.

Title Company

Escrow holder is to immediately open an order with title company and request a preliminary title report concerning the subject property, regardless of the consummation of this escrow.

Charges

In addition to other costs and charges set forth in the escrow instructions, seller agrees to pay on demand, whether or not the escrow closes, any and all charges incurred by escrow holder on the seller's behalf, including but not limited to charges for owner's policy of title insurance, beneficiary statements and/or demands, offset statements, documentary transfer tax, preparation of, notarizing and recording of documents necessary on seller's behalf, seller's portion of sub-escrow fee, seller's escrow fee and other costs as charged.

Escrow holder is authorized to deduct from seller's net proceeds or buyer's net proceeds any amount which seller or buyer, as the case may be, may owe in any other matter or transaction. Escrow holder is authorized to charge and the parties agree to pay additional escrow fees for extraordinary services not within the range of customary escrow processing.

Documents

Escrow holder shall not be responsible in any way for the

sufficiency or correctness as to form, manner of execution or validity of any documents deposited in this escrow, nor as to the identity, authority or right of any person executing the same, either as to documents of record or those handled in this escrow.

Nor shall escrow holder be responsible in any way whatsoever for the failure of any party to comply with any of the provisions of any agreement, contract or other instrument filed or deposited in the escrow or referred to in the escrow instructions. Escrow holder duties shall be limited to the safekeeping of such money and documents received and for the disposition of the same in accordance with the written instructions.

> **Escrow holder shall not be required to take any action in connection with the collection, maturity or apparent outlaw of any obligations deposited in this escrow unless otherwise instructed in writing.**

Insurance

The closing agent must make arrangements for new fire and hazard coverage or the transfer of coverage from the seller to he buyer. New documents reflecting the change must be gathered or prepared for signature by all parties.

Where the assignment of any insurance policy from seller to buyer is concerned, seller guarantees, as to any insurance policy handed to escrow holder, that each policy is in force, has not been hypothecated and all necessary premiums have been paid. Escrow holder is authorized to

execute, on behalf of the parties, assignments of interest in any insurance policy (other than title insurance policies) called for in this escrow. Also to transmit for assignment any insurance policy to the insurance agent requesting that the insurer consent to such assignment and that it attach a loss payee clause or such other endorsement as may be required.

Such policy is to be forwarded to the lender and party entitled to it. Escrow holder shall not be responsible for verifying the acceptance of the request for assignment and the policy of insurance by the insurance company. The parties mutually agree that you will make no attempt to verify the receipt of the request for assignment by the insurance company. The parties are placed on notice that if the insurance company should fail to receive said assignment, the insuring company may deny coverage for any loss suffered by buyer. It is the obligation of the insured or a representative to verify the acceptance of the policy's assignment by the issuing company.

Personal Property Tax

Escrow holder is not responsible in any way for any personal property tax which may be assessed against any former or present owner of the subject property described in these escrow instructions, nor for the corporation or license tax of any corporation as a former or present owner.

Sub-Escrow

In the event it may be necessary, proper or convenient for the completion of this escrow, you are authorized to deposit or have deposited funds or documents or both, handed you under these escrow instructions, with any duly authorized sub-escrow agent. These may include, but are not limited to, any bank, trust company, title insurance company, title company or licensed escrow agent. The above described sub-escrow agent is to be subject to the escrow holder's order at or prior to close of that sub-escrow in the course of carrying out the close of this escrow. Any such deposit shall be considered as one in accordance with the meaning of these escrow instructions.

Subdivision

The parties to this escrow have satisfied themselves outside of escrow that the transaction covered is not in  violation of the Subdivision Map Act, any law regulating land division, zoning ordinances or building restrictions. Escrow holder is relieved of all responsibility and/or liability in connection with the above mentioned regulations and is not to be concerned with the enforcement of any laws, restrictions, ordinances or regulations.

Purchase Agreement

In the event any Offer to Purchase, Deposit Receipt or any other form of Purchase Agreement, amendment or supplement is deposited in this escrow, it is understood that such document shall be effective only as between the parties signing the document. Escrow holder is not to be concerned with the terms of such Purchase Agreement and is relieved of all responsibility and/or liability for the enforcement of such terms. The only duty is to comply with the instructions set forth in this escrow.

Escrow holder is not responsible for knowing or interpreting any provisions of any Purchase Agreement on which these instructions may be based. Escrow holder shall not rely on any knowledge or understanding of the Purchase Agreement in performing the duties required by this escrow. In connection with any loan transaction, escrow holder is authorized to deliver a copy of any such Purchase Agreement, along with any supplement or amendment to that document to the lender.

Disclosures

Escrow holder is not to be concerned with the giving of any disclosures required by federal or state law, including, but not limited to, RESPA (Real Estate Settlement Procedures Act), Regulation Z (Truth-In-Lending Disclosures), FIRPTA (Foreign Investment Real Property Tax Act), or other warnings, or any other warranties, expressed or implied.

Escrow holder shall not be responsible in any way and is released from any liability, obligation or responsibility with respect to withholding of funds in response to FIRPTA regulations. Escrow holder is not responsible in determining whether the transferor is a foreign person, or for obtaining a nonforeign affidavit or exemption from withholding under FIRPTA.

Copies Delivered

Escrow holder is authorized to deliver copies of all escrow instructions, supplements and amendments, estimated and final closing statements, preliminary title reports and notices of cancellation, if any, to the real estate broker, real estate agent, lender, lender's agent and/or attorney for the parties, upon their oral or written request. Escrow holder shall not incur any liability in doing so.

231

Physical Inspection

Escrow holder shall make no physical inspection of the real and/or personal property described in any instrument deposited in this escrow. Escrow holder shall make no representations and/or warranties concerning any such real and/or personal property and is not to be concerned with nor liable for the condition of such properties.

Recording, Delivery of Instruments or Funds

The parties to this escrow authorize the recordation of any instrument necessary or proper for the issuance of the policy of title insurance called for or to effect the closing of this escrow. Funds, instructions or instruments received in this escrow may be delivered to, or deposited with, any title insurance company or title company for the purpose of complying with the terms and conditions of this escrow. Escrow holder is not responsible for the sufficiency, correctness of form or authority of person signing of any documents drawn outside of escrow and deposited with escrow holder.

Pest Control Report

If a structural pest control report and/or notice of work completed are handed to escrow holder, a copy shall be mailed to buyer as soon as is practicable after receipt.

Forms

Escrow holder is to use the usual instrument forms such as notes, deeds or deeds of trust, or the usual forms of any title insurance company. Dates and terms are to be inserted on the usual instruments if they are incomplete in such particulars, provided the insertions comply with the instructions contained in these escrow instructions.

Performance

Escrow holder shall conduct no lien or title search of chattels or personal property in connection with the sale or transfer of same through this escrow.

Usury

Escrow holder shall not be responsible in any way nor concerned with any question of usury in any loan or encumbrance, whether new or of record, which may arise during the processing of this escrow.

Delivery of Documents

The parties agree to deliver to escrow holder all documents, instruments, escrow instructions and funds required to process and close this escrow in accordance with these instructions.

Title

Escrow holder is instructed to clear title to the subject real property according to the beneficiary demands and/or beneficiary statements delivered to escrow holder by the existing lienholders. Escrow holder is not responsible for the correctness of the above. Escrow holder is not required to submit any such beneficiary statement and/or beneficiary demand to the parties for approval prior to the close of escrow unless expressly instructed to do so, in writing, by the parties.

Terms of New Loan

Escrow holder is not to be responsible in any way nor to be concerned with the terms of any new loan or the content of any loan documents obtained by buyer or seller in connection with the escrow except to order such loan documents into the escrow file and to transmit the same to buyer for execution and transmit the executed loan documents to lender. The parties understand and agree that escrow holder is not involved nor concerned with the processing of any loan and cannot advise or give an opinion regarding the processing of any loan.

Statement of Information

Each principal agrees to immediately deliver to escrow holder a fully completed and executed "Statement of Information", to be delivered to the title company as required. Parties acknowledge that refusal to deliver the "Statement of Information" may be cause for delay in closing.

Tax Information

In connection with the Federal Tax Reform Act of 1986 and the California Revenue and Taxation Code, certain transactions are required to be reported to the Internal Revenue Service and the California State Franchise Tax Board. In those transactions required to be reported, seller will furnish a correct tax identification number to escrow holder for reporting purposes as required by law.

Seller understands that he or she may be subject to civil or criminal penalties for failure to do so.

Third Party Claims

The parties expressly indemnify and hold escrow holder harmless against third party claims for any fees, costs or expenses where escrow holder has acted in good faith, with reasonable care and prudence and/or in compliance with escrow instructions.

Liability for Disclosure

The parties agree that as far as the responsibilities and liabilities of the escrow holder are concerned, this transaction is an escrow, and does not create any other legal relationship except that of an escrow holder upon the terms and conditions expressly set forth in these instructions.

Escrow holder shall have no duty or responsibility to disclose any profit realized by any person, firm or corporation including, but not limited to, any real estate broker, real estate sales agent and/or a party. However, if escrow holder is instructed by any party to this escrow, in writing, to disclose any sale, resale, loan, exchange or other transaction involving any real or personal property described herein or any profit realized by any person, firm or corporation as set forth herein, escrow holder shall do so without incurring any liability to any party.

Escrow holder shall not be liable for any acts or omissions done in good faith nor for any claims, demands, losses or damages made, or claims suffered by any party to this escrow, excepting such as may arise through or be caused by willful neglect or gross misconduct on the part of escrow holder.

Change of Ownership Form

Buyer acknowledges that a Change of Ownership form is required by the county recorder to be completed and affixed to any documents submitted for recording which indicate a conveyance of title. The Change of Ownership form shall be furnished to buyer by escrow holder and buyer is aware that if buyer does not complete the form in full, sign and return to escrow holder prior to closing, a penalty will be assessed by the county recorder.

If the Change of Ownership form is not filed after the close of escrow within the time limits set forth by the county recorder, additional penalties will be assessed against the buyer. For information or assistance in completing the Change of Ownership form, buyer may contact the county assessor's office in the county in which the subject property is located.

Hold Open Fee

Notwithstanding any other provisions contained in escrow instructions, and in addition to such other fees and costs to which escrow holder may be entitled, the parties, jointly and severally, agree that in the event the escrow is not consummated within ninety (90) days of the date set for closing, escrow holder is instructed to withhold the escrow hold open fee of $25.00 per month from the funds on deposit with you regardless of the depositor.

Agency

The agency between the principals to this escrow and the escrow holder shall automatically terminate six (6) months following the date set for the close of escrow. It shall be subject to earlier termination if the parties to the escrow submit mutually executed cancellation instructions.

In the event the conditions of this escrow have not been complied with at the expiration provided, escrow holder is instructed to complete the termination at the earliest possible date, unless any of the parties have made written demand upon the escrow holder for the return of funds and/or instruments deposited by either of the parties.

If there are funds or instruments to be disbursed, escrow holder is instructed to stop proceedings, without liability for interest on funds held, until mutual cancellation instructions are received from the parties. The parties, jointly and severally, agree that in the event of cancellation or other termination of this escrow prior to closing to pay for any expenses which escrow holder has incurred while following these instructions.

The principals agree, if this escrow is mutually terminated prior to the closing date, to pay a reasonable escrow fee for services contracted by them and to deposit such funds into escrow prior to cancellation. Buyer and seller agree that any cancellation charges or fees for services shall be divided fairly between the parties in a manner the escrow holder considers equitable. Escrow holder's decision regarding the distribution of fees will be considered binding and conclusive upon the parties.

Upon receipt of mutual cancellation instructions or a final order or judgment of a court, the escrow holder is instructed to disburse any funds and instruments in accordance with such instructions, order or judgment. This escrow, without further notice, will then be considered terminated and canceled.

Cooperation of Parties

The parties shall cooperate with escrow holder in carrying out the instructions and completing the escrow. In the interest of following the instructions, the parties shall deposit into escrow any additional funds, instruments, documents or authorizations as requested. These additions shall be reasonably necessary to enable escrow holder to comply with demands made by third parties, to secure policies of title insurance, or otherwise carry out the terms of the instructions and close this escrow.

In the event conflicting demands are made upon the escrow holder or controversy arises between the parties or with any third person arising out of this escrow, the escrow holder shall have the absolute right to withhold and stop any further proceedings in the performance of this escrow until receiving written notification of the dispute's settlement.

All parties to this escrow promise to compensate the escrow holder for specific, unexpected costs connected with the escrow. These might be litigation costs, judgments, attorney's fees, expenses, obligations and liabilities of any kind which, in good faith, the escrow holder may incur in connection with carrying out this escrow.

As a safeguard, the escrow holder is given a lien on all rights, titles and interests of parties to this escrow as well as all escrow papers, other property and money deposited in case there is a need for escrow holder to be reimbursed. In the event of failure to pay fees or expenses due escrow holder or for costs and attorneys fees incurred in any litigation or interpleader, the parties agree to pay a reasonable fee for any attorney services which may be required to collect such fees or expenses, whether such attorney's fees are incurred prior to trial, at trial or on appeal.

In Writing

All notices, demands and instructions must be in writing. No notice, demand, instruction, amendment, supplement or modification of these instructions shall be of any effect in this escrow until delivered in writing to the escrow holder. All documents must be executed by all parties affected.

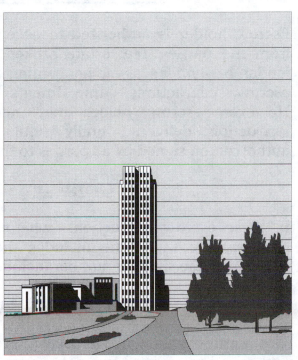

Any purported oral instruction, amendment, supplement, modification, notice or demand deposited with escrow holder by the parties shall be invalid.

Escrow holder is to be concerned only with the directives expressly set forth in the escrow instructions, supplements and amendments. Escrow holder is not to be concerned with nor liable for items designated as "memorandum items" in the escrow instructions.

Counterparts

These instructions may be executed in counterparts, each of which shall be considered an original regardless of the date of its execution and delivery. All such counterparts together shall constitute one and the same document. Together they make up the entire contract.

Dishonored Checks

If any check submitted to the escrow holder is dishonored upon presentment for payment for any reason, escrow holder is authorized to notify all parties to the escrow and/or their respective real estate broker or real estate sales agent.

Oral Instructions

Escrow holder is authorized to accept oral instructions from the parties' real estate broker, real estate agent, lender or lender's agent concerning the preparation of escrow instructions, amendments or supplements. However, escrow holder may not act upon any instruction delivered orally until receiving written authorization signed by all parties to this escrow.

Gender

In these escrow instructions, wherever the context so requires, the masculine includes the feminine and/or neuter and the singular number includes the plural.

Legal Limitations

The parties acknowledge that escrow holder is not authorized to practice law nor to give legal advice. Each of the parties is advised to seek legal or financial counsel and advice concerning the effect of these escrow instructions. Further, the parties acknowledge that no representations are made by escrow holder as to the legal sufficiency, legal consequences, financial effects or tax consequences of this transaction.

Authorization to Dispose of Escrow Paperwork

Escrow holder is authorized to destroy or otherwise dispose of any and all documents, papers, instructions, correspondence and records or other material in this escrow file at any time after five (5) years from the date of close of escrow or cancellation. Escrow holder shall have no liability for disposing of the above without further notice to the parties.

Signatures

The parties' signatures on all escrow instructions and instruments indicate their unconditional acceptance and approval. Escrow holder is entitled to rely on the signatures contained in these instructions.

Electronic Signatures

Federal legislation enacted in 2000, electronic contracts and electronic signatures are just as legal and enforceable as traditional paper contracts signed in ink. The law is known as The Electronic Signatures in Global and (Inter) National Commerce Act, (E-SIGN) and allows for certain transactions to be confirmed electronically.

However, for purposes of real estate, escrow, and banking, electronic signatures are not allowed for signatures required under the Uniform Commercial Code. It also includes Notice of Default, Acceleration, Repossession, Foreclosure, Eviction, Right to Cure (when individual's residence is used to secure a loan).

Parties to a transaction or contract are allowed to negotiate document integrity and electronic signing, but there are specific standards regarding promissory notes, pertaining to photocopies, faxes, and electronic transmissions of original documents, and does not include voice or audio transmissions. Documents that are notarized and recorded cannot be signed electronically.

San Clemente Escrow, Inc.

34932 Calle del Sol, Suite B, Capistrano Beach, CA 92624
(714) 361-1725 telephone-(714) 240-0233 fax

BUYER AND SELLER ESCROW INSTRUCTIONS
Escrow No: 1-4035-J
Joan Thompson: Escrow Officer
Date: January 17, 1997
Page: 1 of 5

THIS COMPANY IS LICENSED BY DEPT. OF CORPORATIONS

BROKER WILL HAND YOU FOR BUYER	$5,000.00
BUYER WILL HAND YOU PRIOR TO CLOSE OF ESCROW	$11,050.00
DEED OF TRUST TO RECORD	$304,950.00
TOTAL SALES PRICE	$321,000.00

Buyer to deliver to you any instruments and/or funds required from Buyer to enable you to comply with these instructions, all of which you are authorized to use and/or deliver on or before March 6, 1997, and when you are in a position to obtain a standard Policy of Title Insurance through CHICAGO TITLE, provided that said policy has a liability of at least the amount of the above total consideration, (new title policy to be delivered to lien holder), covering the following described property in the City of SAN CLEMENTE, County of ORANGE, State of CALIFORNIA:

SEE LEGAL DESCRIPTION ATTACHED HERETO AND MADE A PART HEREOF
AS EXHIBIT "A"
SELLER STATES PROPERTY ADDRESS IS:
310 AVENIDA CRISTOBAL, SAN CLEMENTE, CALIFORNIA 92672
INSURING TITLE VESTED IN:

ONOFRE AND RUBY ARCHULETA, HUSBAND AND WIFE AS COMMUNITY
PROPERTY

SUBJECT ONLY TO:
CURRENT installment(s) of the General and special county, and city (if any) Taxes, including any special district levies, payments which are included therein and collected therewith, for current fiscal year, not delinquent, including taxes for ensuing year, if any, a lien not yet due or payable; personal property taxes, if any; covenants, conditions, reservations (including exceptions of oil, gas, minerals, and hydrocarbons, without right of surface entry), restrictions, rights, rights of way and easements for public utilities, districts, water companies, alley and streets, and any gas and oil leases.

INITIAL HERE: **SELLER (   ) (   )   BUYER (   ) (   )**

San Clemente Escrow, Inc.

34932 Calle del Sol, Suite B, Capistrano Beach, CA 92624
(714) 361-1725 telephone-(714) 240-0233 fax

BUYER AND SELLER ESCROW INSTRUCTIONS
Escrow No: 1-4035-J
Joan Thompson: Escrow Officer
Date: January 17, 1997
Page: 2 of 5

THIS COMPANY IS LICENSED BY DEPT. OF CORPORATIONS

DEED OF TRUST to file, as obtained by the BUYER herein securing a Note in the amount of $304,950.00, in favor of Lender of BUYERS choice. Exact terms of loan to follow with loan documents and BUYERS execution of same shall indicate their full approval of all terms and conditions contained therein. Escrow Holder is authorized and instructed to comply with lenders instructions and requirements.

CLOSE OF ESCROW is subject to BUYER and PROPERTY qualifying for above financing with 6.5% initial adjustable rate with a maximum lifetime interest rate cap of 11% for 30 years, points not to exceed 1%. BUYER to provide verification of down payment funds within 48 hours of 1/17/97.

SELLER agrees to pay a maximum of $6,000.00 towards BUYERS non-recurring closing costs.

CLOSE OF ESCROW subject to Buyers approval of Preliminary Title Report within 7 days of receipt of same. In the event Escrow Holder is not in receipt of written disapproval within time period stated, Escrow Holder shall deem this contingency waived.

Seller to furnish Buyer with a One Year Home Protection Policy issued by SIERRA NATIONAL HOME WARRANTY CO., the cost of which is not to exceed $400.00 and is to be paid from Sellers Net Proceeds upon Close of Escrow.

BUYER shall hand you, prior to the close of escrow, completed, executed preliminary change of ownership to be attached to deed for recording per section 480.30 of revenue and taxation code and in the absence of said report or in the event the recorder deems said report to be incomplete, recorder shall impose $20.00 fee to BUYER.

INITIAL HERE: **SELLER (   )(   )BUYER (   )(   )**

San Clemente Escrow, Inc.

34932 Calle del Sol, Suite B, Capistrano Beach, CA 92624
(714) 361-1725 telephone-(714) 240-0233 fax

BUYER AND SELLER ESCROW INSTRUCTIONS
Escrow No: 1-4035-J
Joan Thompson: Escrow Officer
Date: January 17, 1997
Page: 3 of 5

THIS COMPANY IS LICENSED BY DEPT. OF CORPORATIONS

BUYER is made aware that the tax assessor has the right to impose a supplemental tax on subject property after the close of escrow, and in such event, said tax shall be the BUYER'S responsibility. BROKER, ESCROW HOLDER, and SELLER are relieved of any liability with regard to same. If the SELLER receives a supplemental tax bill prior to the close of escrow, escrow holder is to be notified, and same shall be paid accordingly.

CONDOMINIUM PLAN/P.U.D.: The subject of this transaction is a condominium/planned unit development (P.U.D.) designated as unit specified and specified parking space and an undivided interest in community areas, and _____.
The current monthly assessment charge by the homeowner's association or other governing body is _$43_ approx. As soon as practicable, Seller shall provide Buyer with copies of covenants conditions and restrictions, articles of incorporation, by-laws, current rules and regulations, most current financial statements, and any other documents as required by law. Seller shall disclose in writing any known pending special assessment, claims, or litigation to buyer. Buyer shall be allowed _7_ calendar days from receipt to review these documents. If such documents disclose conditions or information unsatisfactory to Buyer, Buyer may cancel this agreement. BUYER'S FAILURE TO NOTIFY SELLER IN WRITING SHALL CONCLUSIVELY BE CONSIDERED APPROVAL.

BUYER to pay Homeowners Association transfer fee at close of escrow.

A pest control report per item 20 of the Real Estate Purchase Contract and Receipt for Deposit is a requirement of this escrow. Seller to pay for report and any corrective work required for a Notice of Completion. Buyer to pay for work in Section 2, if any.

INITIAL HERE: BUYER(   )(   )   SELLER(   )(   )

San Clemente Escrow, Inc.

34932 Calle del Sol, Suite B, Capistrano Beach, CA 92624
(714) 361-1725 telephone-(714) 240-0233 fax

BUYER AND SELLER ESCROW INSTRUCTIONS
Escrow No: 1-4035-J
Joan Thompson: Escrow Officer
Date: January 17, 1997
Page: 4 of 5

THIS COMPANY IS LICENSED BY DEPT. OF CORPORATIONS

ESCROW HOLDER is specifically instructed by the undersigned Buyer and Seller to request that the new loan proceeds be deposited directly in the San Clemente Escrow, Inc. Trust Account for payoff of existing encumbrances and disbursement in accordance with these escrow instructions without the use of the title company subescrow. In the event the new Lender refuses to fund to San Clemente Escrow, Inc. and instead should direct funds to the title company in this transaction, Buyer and Seller herein instruct Escrow Holder to authorize recordation, regardless and agree to hold San Clemente Escrow, Inc. harmless and without liability in connection with funds on deposit with the title company.

CANCELLATION FEE: In the event of cancellation of this escrow, all parties are aware and agree that escrow holders is hereby authorized and instructed to charge a cancellation fee. Said Fee shall be determined upon the stage in the escrow and work done to date.

SELLER, BUYER or BORROWER shall each pay their own respective closing costs, including their own portion of escrow fees, in connection with this transaction, unless otherwise stated herein.

AS A MEMORANDUM ITEM ONLY WITH WHICH ESCROW HOLDER IS NOT TO BE CONCERNED, it is agreed between BUYER AND SELLER outside of escrow that: BUYERS do intend to occupy subject property.

Possession of subject property is to be granted to BUYER 72 hours after close of escrow.

****

In accordance with the manner specified under the "General Provisions" attached hereto, you are authorized and instructed to adjust or prorate the following to CLOSE OF ESCROW: **PROPERTY TAXES AND HOMEOWNERS DUES.**

INITIAL HERE: **BUYER( )( )**   **SELLER( )( )**

San Clemente Escrow, Inc.

34932 Calle del Sol, Suite B, Capistrano Beach, CA 92624
(714) 361-1725 telephone-(714) 240-0233 fax

BUYER AND SELLER ESCROW INSTRUCTIONS
Escrow No: 1-4035-J
Joan Thompson: Escrow Officer
Date: January 17, 1997
Page: 5 of 5

THIS COMPANY IS LICENSED BY DEPT. OF CORPORATIONS

THE FOREGOING TERMS, CONDITIONS AND INSTRUCTIONS, INCLUDING THE "GENERAL PROVISIONS" ATTACHED HERETO, (AS IF FULLY SET FORTH HEREIN), HAVE BEEN READ AND ARE UNDERSTOOD BY EACH OF THE UNDERSIGNED, WHO HEREBY AGREE TO, CONCUR WITH, APPROVE AND ACCEPT THE SAME IN THEIR ENTIRETY.

SELLER'S SIGNATURE: BUYER'S SIGNATURE:

_____   _____
KATE OLIVER   RUBY ARCHULETA

_____   _____
QUENTIN OLIVER   ONOFRE ARCHULETA

Post Test

The following self test repeats the one you took at the beginning of this chapter. Now take the exam again--since you have read all the material-- and check your knowledge of escrow closing procedures.

True/False

1. A "take sheet" is the framework for the escrow instructions.

2. Collecting the information needed to provide complete escrow instructions is the first step for an escrow agent.

3. The three documents that serve as the heart of a sale escrow are the grant deed, promissory note and bill of sale.

4. A promissory note is the security for a debt.

5. General instructions authorize the escrow holder to carry out general procedures needed to complete the escrow.

6. General instructions are special instructions given by a buyer or seller to the escrow holder.

7. Third party instructions may include a demand or claim from a person not involved in the escrow as a principal.

8. The escrow holder's obligation to the parties starts as soon as escrow instructions are written.

9. Prorations are made on the basis of a 25- day month.

10. If rents are to be prorated, escrow holder should prorate and charge seller and credit buyer with any deposits paid in advance to the seller by tenants.

chapter 8

RECORD KEEPING & PRORATIONS

Focus

- Introduction
- Closing statement
- Escrow checklist for selling broker
- Escrow checklist for listing broker
- Prorations

Pre-Test

The following is a self test to determine how much you know about record keeping and prorations before reading this chapter. Take it without studying, then read the material presented in the text. At the end of the chapter you will find a repeat of this exam. Test your knowledge by answering the questions again, then check your improvement. (The answers are found at the end of the book.) Good luck.

True/False

1. Items that are credits to the seller are debits to the buyer.

2. Taxes, rents and deposits are usually prorated.

3. The day of closing is included for proration purposes.

4. Prorations are based on a 30-day month.

5. Proration of taxes are based on 180 days or six months.

6. The first installment of property tax is due December 1.

7. Supplementary taxes are paid by the seller.

8. The buyer's new taxes are generally calculated on 1% of the purchase price plus part of a percentage for local or county taxes or special assessments.

9. Life insurance is required by most lenders.

10. Property taxes are due twice yearly.

Introduction

If you recall, Onofre and Ruby Archuleta are buying a house from Kate and Quentin Oliver for $400,000. The transaction is due to close and all parties expect to be informed of the costs incurred during the escrow, as well as receive an accounting of the process.

One of the closing agent's main jobs is to represent the obligations of each party in a personalized closing statement. The flow of consideration through escrow is outlined in the closing statement, as well as adjustments and disbursements reflecting the prior agreement of the parties.

Closing Statement

The closing statement is where the accounting for the escrow is set down for the buyer and seller. It is a reflection of the parties' agreements and matches their wishes exactly. Both the seller and buyer are credited

and debited for their agreed upon share of costs, ending statement for the transaction.

The debit-credit columns shown on the closing statement are marked *seller/lender* or *buyer/ borrower*, depending on whether it describes a sale or loan escrow. The information from this statement will be used at the closing to conform to the Real Estate Settlement Procedures Act (RESPA).

251

Seller's Statement

This represents the accounting the Olivers will receive upon the transaction's closing.

Credits

The total consideration in the transaction is $400,000.00 as specified in the escrow instructions. Credit the seller, debit the buyer.

The first installment of taxes for the tax year was paid by the seller. A credit in the amount of $77.34, representing 15 days of prepaid property tax, is given to the seller. Credit the seller, debit the buyer.

The seller has prepaid 15 days of monthly homeowners association dues at the rate of $50.00 per month, or 25.00. Credit the seller, debit the buyer.

Debits

The escrow holder was instructed to calculate rent from 12/16 to 12/31, or $400.00. Debit the seller, credit the buyer.

The payoff on the existing loan plus interest charges is a debit to the seller.

The commission paid to the real estate broker, $24,000, is a debit to the seller.

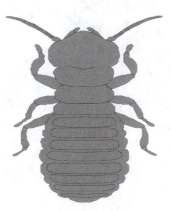

The seller has agreed to pay for the termite report in the amount of $200.00. Debit the seller.

It is the job of the title company to transfer the insured title to the buyer. Seller is debited for the following items:

• Title policy premium	$579.00
• Reconveyance fee	$60.00
• Documentary transfer tax	$440.00
• Recording fee (reconveyance)	$3.00
• Total	
	$1,082.00

Balance

This figure represents the proceeds the seller can expect to receive.

Total Debits to Seller

The end debits must balance with the corresponding credits.

Checklist of Seller's Costs and Credits

Seller's Costs

Selling Commission
Title Insurance
Escrow Fee
Legal Fees
Prepayment Penalty
State or Local Transfer Tax
Pest Control Inspection Fee
Pest Control Work
Recording Fee
FHA or VA points

Seller's Costs (continued)

Reconveyance Fees
Notary Fee
Prorated Taxes
Personal Property Tax
Interest if paid in arrears
Prorated Rents
Security Deposits on hand

Seller's Credits

Interest if paid in advance (from recordation to date of next loan payment)
Refund existing Trust Fund (Impound Account), if any
Prorated Taxes (if paid beyond recordation)

Buyer's Statement

This statement represents the accounting the Archuletas will receive upon the closing of the transaction.

Credits

The money deposited by the buyer to open the escrow is noted as a credit to the buyer.

The amount of the new loan, $240,000.00, is a credit to the buyer.

The rental credit of $400, noted as a debit to the seller, is a credit to the buyer (for seller rent back).

The total amount credited to the buyer includes the remainder of the down payment which is due at the closing.

Debits

Items that have been credited to the seller are noted as debits to the buyer, such as the amount of total consideration, tax prorations and association dues.

Charges made by the lender in connection with the new loan may be loan fees or advance collections for taxes or insurance. In this case one month's interest is charged to the buyer. In addition, a tax service charge, credit report, appraisal fee, impound account deposit for taxes, two months' insurance, document fee and mortgage insurance are all listed as debits to the buyer.

Fees related to title company charges are debited to the buyer (lender's title policy premium and recording fees for deed and trust deed).

The end debits must balance with the corresponding credits.

Checklist of Buyers Closing Costs

Non-Recurring Costs

Title Insurance (where payable by buyer)
Escrow Fee
Legal Fees
Loan Fee
Appraisal Fee
Tax Service
Credit Report
Notary Fee
Recording Fee
Pest Control Inspection
Document Preparation Fee
Review Fee

Non-Recurring Costs (continued)

Application Fee
Underwriting Fee
Courier Fee
Verification Fee
Warehousing Fee

Recurring Costs

Hazard Insurance
Trust Fund or Impound Account
Prorated Taxes (if paid beyond recordation)
Prorated Interest (if charged in arrears: to end of month/if charged in advance: to date of first payment?

Credits

Prorated Taxes
Prorated Rents
Security Deposits on hand

Escrow Checklist for Selling Broker

As we have seen, in some areas the real estate broker handles many of the details of collecting information for the escrow and making sure all contingencies are met. In varying degrees, then, the real estate agent is important to the closing process. The following is a list of functions that may be performed by the selling broker.

<u>Selling Broker may:</u>

- Obtain increase of deposit
- Open the escrow
- Order credit report on buyer (if required)
- Order pest control inspection
- Order other inspections (roof, etc., if required)
- Check on any contingencies to be eliminated
- Check occupancy permit
- Order loan commitment
- Assist buyer with loan application and submit to lender
- Arrange for hazard insurance
- Have closing instructions prepared and signed by buyer

Escrow Checklist for Listing Broker

Once again, in different areas, a real estate agent performs particular duties. The listing broker has a special list of jobs to perform in completing his or her commitment to the seller.

<u>Listing Broker may:</u>

- Notice of sale to multiple listing office
- Check on increase of deposit
- Examine preliminary title report and assist in eliminating clouds on the title, of any
- Check on any contingencies to be eliminated

Listing Broker may (continued)

- Request title company or escrow company to order pay-off demand, or statement of condition and assumption papers from lender
- Check with selling broker on buyer's loan
- If income property, obtain: rent schedule, rent due dates, Security deposits, copies of leases, names and phone numbers of tenants
- Have seller's instructions prepared and signed
- If seller carries a second loan, have escrow holder record a "Request for copy of Notice of Default and subscribe to a tax agency
- Obtain seller's future address and phone

Prorations

Items to be prorated by the closing agent such as taxes and insurance and rents may be calculated using proration tables, financial calculators or software created specifically for that purpose. The closing agent, however, must be aware of the principles used to determine the percentage or dollar figure shown on the proration tables as well as be able to determine simple prorations directly.

The proper time period in which to prorate items must first be established. The day of closing is not included for proration purposes. In completing the prorations for a transaction, time is converted to a day factor, either as an amount per day or as a percentage of the total time period for the transaction. Prorations are typically based on a 30-day month and a 360-day year.

> ## Time Periods for Prorations
>
> **Taxes:** based on 180 days or six months
>
> **Insurance:** usually based on a 360-day year
>
> **Rents:** based on a 30-day month

Taxes

Tax prorations are based on due dates for taxes. Real property tax becomes a lien on the property assessed on January 1st preceding the tax year for which the taxes are due. As you recall, the tax, or fiscal, year is from July 1 through the following June 30.

Regardless of the time other liens are created, real property taxes have priority over any other liens on the property. The payment of property tax is enforced by the sale of the subject property in a manner dictated by statute.

Taxes are due twice yearly. The first half is due on November 1 and becomes delinquent December 10. The second half is due February 1 and becomes delinquent April 10.

> ## Memory Aid for Tax Due Dates
> <u>N</u>o--Nov 1
> <u>D</u>arn--December 10
> <u>F</u>ooling--February 1
> <u>A</u>round--April 1

259

Each year, after April 10, a delinquent roll is prepared showing all property upon which taxes are due.

Also each year, before June 8, a delinquency list of real property taxes is published in local newspapers describing a date upon which the delinquent property will be "sold to the state."

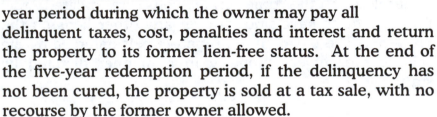

The property is not really "sold to the state," with the state taking possession or ownership. The taxpayer retains legal title to the property and enjoys possession during the five-year redemption period.

The term "sold to the state" refers to a bookkeeping transaction that starts a five-year period during which the owner may pay all delinquent taxes, cost, penalties and interest and return the property to its former lien-free status. At the end of the five-year redemption period, if the delinquency has not been cured, the property is sold at a tax sale, with no recourse by the former owner allowed.

Additional taxes may be levied at the time of a sale to reflect the sales price. These are called supplemental taxes and should be expected by the parties to an escrow. The buyer completes a Preliminary Change of Ownership form which informs the tax assessor of the possible change in value. At that time the tax assessor may levy a supplemental tax for that tax year based on the sales price, and send it to the buyer. This usually occurs outside of escrow and is not a matter for the closing agent.

A supplemental tax may also be assessed if an improvement to the real property is completed during the tax billing period (before November 1). After the improvement has been assessed, the tax collector will calculate the new taxes on a prorated basis, depending on the improvement's date of completion. The new tax generally is based on 1% of the market value or sales price, plus a part of a percentage for local or county taxes or special assessments. The tax is prorated based on the closing date of the transaction.

Taxes on a property may decrease if the value of the property has declined, and the supplemental tax will reflect the change.

Calculation of Prorated Taxes

The close of escrow is 10/25/02, and the seller has not paid the first installment of property taxes of $980.00, which is due 11/01/02. Both the buyer and the seller must pay a portion of the taxes. To calculate the amounts owed, prorate the tax according to the number of days in the tax year each party owned the property.

To Prorate Taxes:

1. First, calculate the cost of taxes per day for the six-month period in question.

   $980=taxes for 180 days (six months)
   $980 divided by 180=$5.44 daily

2. Count the number of days during the tax period in question when the seller owned the property.

   July 1 to September 30=90 days
   October 1 to October 24=24 days

3. Seller owned the property 114 days of current tax period

   114 x $5.44=$620.16 (amount owed by seller)

4. Subtract $620.16 from the total tax charged to the seller. The buyer owes the difference.

   $980.00 less $620.16=$359.84 (amount owed by buyer)

Insurance

Traditionally, the type of insurance required by lenders and expected by buyers was fire insurance. Today, there are several types of policies covering various types of damage, such as earthquake or flood destruction. In any case, the closing agent may prorate some of the policies and some might be done by the insurer. If calculations are required for insurance prorations, the following example will be helpful.

The buyer is taking over a three-year policy with a premium of $1,200, which the seller had prepaid. It was effective May 13, 1997, to be prorated as of the closing, October 25, 1999, using a 30-day month and a 360-day year:

1. Determine number of days to be prorated:

	Year	Month	Day	Total
10/25/99	1999	10	25	
5/13/97	-1997	-5	-13	
	2	5	12	
	x360	x30	x1	
	720	150	12	882

2. Then calculate the cost per day for the term of the policy by dividing $1,200 by 1,080 (the number of days in the three-year policy) to arrive at $1.11.

3. Finally, multiply the total number of days to be prorated, or 882, by $1.11 to arrive at $979.00, or the dollar amount of the premium that has been used.

4. Subtracting $979.00 from the cost of the policy, or $1,200, the seller would be credited $221, and the buyer debited the same amount.

Rents

Normally, a 30-day month is used to prorate rents. The closing agent must be aware that rents are collected in advance and should be prorated accordingly.

A triplex with the following rents is in escrow with the transaction to close on October 25, 1999.

> Apartment A = $780 paid through 11/1/99
> Apartment B = $780 paid through 11/1/99
> Apartment C = $780 paid through 11/1/99

Prorating Rents

1. The closing agent must first calculate the amount of daily interest by dividing the monthly rent of $780 by 30, or $26 a day.

2. The buyer will be taking title on the 25th day of October, and should be credited for 6 days of rent or the number of days between October 25 and November 1.

3. By multiplying 6 x $26 to get $156 per unit for the six days, the closing agent can multiply that amount by 3, to credit the buyer with $468.00.

Also, the seller must provide information about when the rents are collected, amounts of security deposits, cleaning deposits, and any other funds that are to be transferred at the closing. An accounting is done at the closing to reflect funds to be transferred to the buyer or remain with the seller.

Loan Assumptions/Loan Payoffs

The escrow holder must be very careful in calculating the amounts when loans are involved. Terms of a beneficiary statement in the case of a loan assumption, or the demand statement in the case of a loan payoff, must be observed carefully by the closing agent. There are certain items of which the closing agent must be especially aware.

Loan Assumption/Loan Payoff

A beneficiary statement is a statement of the unpaid balance of a loan and the condition of the indebtedness and is requested from the lender when a buyer is assuming an existing loan or purchasing the property subject to that loan.

A demand statement or demand for pay-off is requested from an existing lender when a buyer is obtaining a new loan.

Payment Date
Most loans are paid monthly. Even though this is usually the case, payments on some loans are due quarterly, semi-annually or annually.

Payment Status
The closing agent must be aware of whether or not all current loan payments are being made in a timely manner. In case the payments are not kept current, any statements of loan condition should not be ordered until the very last part of the escrow period.

<u>Loan Assumption/Loan Payoff (continued)</u>

Impounds

In the case where existing impounds must be credited to the correct party, the closing agent must receive instructions about the amount and to whom it is entitled.

If the buyer is obtaining a new loan with an impound account, the lender determines the amount of additional funds required from the buyer to establish the account and includes the amount in the loan documents.

How is the Loan Paid?
Are the payments interest only, partially amortized with a balloon payment or fully amortized?

Calculating Loan Payoff or Assumptions
In the typical loan payoff, the payment is being made in arrears. It also must be determined whether the lender requires payment to the date of closing or to the date the lender receives the payoff funds. Because of this requirement, the money required for closing could change. Interest between buyer and seller must be allocated carefully by the closing agent.

Miscellaneous Prorations

Closing agents should be aware that there may be items to prorate in addition to those normally required. Homeowners association assessments or other items that may have been prepaid by the seller or assumed by the buyer must be calculated and prorated to the close of escrow.

1004 E. Taft Avenue
Orange, CA 92865
(800) 767-7832

Escrow No. CRISTY2
Reference: 2566 Broadway
Laguna Beach, CA 91002

Closing Date: October 3, 2000
Page 1

Seller
CLOSING STATEMENT

SELLER:
Steve Silvers
Susan Sanders
257 Ocean Blvd.,
Corona Del Mar, CA 92665

	- - DEBITS - -	- - CREDITS - -
Consideration:		
Total Consideration		150,000.00
Existing & New Encumbrances:		
New Encumbrance	30,000.00	
Steve Silvers		
Adjustments:		
Credit for Ceiling Fan		200.00
Prorations:		
Beach Front Homeowners		84.00
at $ 90.00 per month		
From 10/03/00 to 11/01/00		
County Taxes	867.87	
at $ 1698.00 per 6 months		
From 07/01/00 to 10/03/00		
Payoff(s):		
Loan Payoff	95,742.10	
Re: Lucky Lender		
Interest @ 12.75%	1,170.55	
From 09/01/00 To 10/06/00		
Reconveyance Fee	100.00	
Statement / Forwarding Fee	100.00	
New Loan Charges:		
Origination fee	1,100.00	
Re: Steve Silvers		
Interest @ 10%		238.36
From 10/03/00 To 11/01/00		
Disbursements Paid:		
Pest Inspection	65.00	
pd to: Bug B Gone		
Dues paid by Seller October	90.00	
pd to: Beach Front Homeowners		
Commission	9,000.00	
Commission of $ 4,500.00		
pd to: Century 21 Surf and Sand		
Commission of $ 4,500.00		
pd to: Star Agency		
Home Warranty Plan	325.00	
pd to: We Fix It Warranty		
,Ref: 369852		
Credit card payment	800.00	
pd to: Bankroll Visa		
credit card payment	1,200.00	
pd to: Paymore Payment Center		
Title Charges:		
Owner's Title Policy	800.00	
Sub-title Fee	50.00	
County Document Transfer Tax	165.00	
Record Release/Reconveyance	25.00	
Escrow Fees:		
Seller's Portion of Escrow Fee	500.00	
Order Demand Statement	25.00	
Prepare Grant Deed	25.00	
Funds Held:		
Roof Repair Completion	350.00	
Check Herewith	$ 8,021.84	
Totals	$ 150,522.36	$ 150,522.36

SAVE FOR INCOME TAX PURPOSE

2566 Broadway
Laguna Beach, CA 91002

1004 E. Taft Avenue
Orange, CA 92865
(800) 767-7832

Escrow No. CRISTY2
Reference: 2566 Broadway
Laguna Beach, CA 91002

Closing Date: October 3, 2000

Buyer
CLOSING STATEMENT

BUYER:
Brandon Bowers
Brenda Bowers
2566 Broadway
Laguna Beach, CA 91002

	- - DEBITS - -	- - CREDITS - -
Consideration:		
Total Consideration	150,000.00	
Deposits:		
Deposit		
By: Brandon Bowers		2,500.000
Deposit		
By: Brandon Bowers		27,000.00
Existing & New Encumbrances:		
New Encumbrance		
Golden Coin Bank		95,000.00
New Encumbrance		
Steve Silvers		30,000.00
Adjustments:		
Credit for Ceiling Fan	200.00	
Credit from Selling Broker		2,000.00
Prorations:		
Beach Front Homeowners	84.00	
at $ 90.00 per month		
From 10/03/00 to 11/01/00		
County Taxes		867.87
at $ 1,698.00 per 6 months		
From 07/01/00 to 10/03/00		
New Loan Charges:		
Re: Golden Coin Bank		
Interest @ 8.5%	663.70	
From 10/02/00 To 11/01/00		
Discount Points	950.00	
Document Preparation	500.00	
Lender's Inspection Fee	100.00	
Impounds: Taxes	937.50	
6 months @ 156.25 per month		
Impounds: Fire Insurance	91.66	
2 months @ $45.83 per month		
Aggregate Account Adjustment	-325.00	
Re: Steve Silvers		
Interest @ 10%	238.36	
From 10/03/00 To 11/01/00		
Re: Fat Jack Lender		
*Yield Spread POC $ 1,200.00		
Disbursements Paid:		
Fire Insurance	550.00	
pd to: Red Hot Fire Insurance		
Transfer Fee	50.00	
pd to: Coast Villas Management		
Dues paid by Buyer November	90.00	
pd to: Beach Front Homeowners		
Title Charges:		
Lender's Title Policy	500.00	
Taxes: Paid by Title Company	1,698.00	
Sub-Title Fee	50.00	
Record Grant Deed	25.00	
Record Trust Deed	75.00	
Escrow Fees:		
Seller's Portion of Escrow Fee	500.00	
Prepare Grant Deed	25.00	
Loan Tie-in Fee	100.00	
Federal Express/Messenger Fees	35.00	
Check Herewith	$ 229.65	
Totals	$ 157,367.87	$ 157,367.87

SAVE FOR INCOME TAX PURPOSES

Post Test

The following self test repeats the one you took at the beginning of this chapter. Now take the exam again--since you have read all the material-- and check your knowledge of escrow closing procedures.

True/False

1. Items that are credits to the seller are debits to the buyer.

2. Taxes, rents and deposits are usually prorated.

3. The day of closing is included for proration purposes.

4. Prorations are based on a 30-day month.

5. Proration of taxes are based on 180 days or six months.

6. The first installment of property tax is due December 1.

7. Supplementary taxes are paid by the seller.

8. The buyer's new taxes are generally calculated on 1% of the purchase price plus part of a percentage for local or county taxes or special assessments.

9. Life insurance is required by most lenders.

10. Property taxes are due twice yearly.

chapter **9**

PROCESSING & CLOSING

Focus

- **Introduction**
- **Escrow instructions**
- **Requirements for closing**
- **The closing statement**
- **Transfer documents**
- **Financing documents**
- **Other documents needed for closing**
- **Document conveyance**
- **Final closing review**
- **Closing/recording**

Pre-Test

The following is a self test to determine how much you know about processing and closing an escrow before reading this chapter. Take it without studying, then read the material presented in the text. At the end of the chapter you will find a repeat of this exam. Test your knowledge by answering the questions again, then check your improvement. (The answers are found at the end of the book.) Good luck.

True/False

1. Buyers and sellers in Northern California do not sign separate escrow instructions.

2. Unilateral instructions are used in Northern California.

3. Bilateral instructions are used in Southern California.

4. Disclosure clauses limit the closing agent's liability regarding the complication of taxes and conformity to codes and other legal requirements.

5. Both federal and state tax laws are affected by the Foreign Investment in Real Estate Property Tax Act (FIRPTA).

6. Smoke detectors must be installed in all sold residential properties.

7. In most cases, the document of transfer will be a grant deed.

8. Loan documents are usually prepared by the title company.

9. A demand is a statement of loan default.

10. A grant deed does not *have* to be notarized to be recorded.

Introduction

The major commitment of an escrow holder is to complete all the terms of the agreement between the principals. Both in the manner desired and in the time period specified, the escrow holder must perform the appointed tasks. Upon satisfaction of all requirements of the escrow, including loan approval and removal of contingencies, then, and only then, can the escrow close.

One of the major tasks, as the closing nears, is to make sure all requirements of the escrow have been met. As we have seen, the escrow holder has the original take sheet to use as a guide to assure a smooth closing. Each part of the transaction must be evaluated and double checked for accuracy. The following is a list of items which have been ongoing throughout the processing of the escrow. This list can be used as a guide for review just prior to closing.

Items to be Reviewed

- Legal description of property as well as street address if applicable

- Current ownership information

- Any particular conditions or contingencies of the sale, such as the escrow being subject to the sale of the buyer's current home, or subject to loan approval

- Deeds of trust to be created, along with terms, conditions and responsibilities imposed by lender

- Loans to be assumed/impounds involved

- If the loan is current

- If the assumption is subject to lender approval

- Hazard and other insurance provisions

- Charges to buyer and seller

- Commission instructions

- Separate loan escrow instructions required for loans other than purchase money

- Legal name of buyer and method of taking title

- Personal property included in the sale (only personal property for identification purposes)

- Pest control inspection

- Prorations

- Other requirements particular to the transaction

Joint Escrow Instructions

Currently, the approach to conducting escrow is to use the Purchase Agreement as escrow instructions. The California Association of Realtors (CAR) updates their forms regularly, so it is critical to stay current with all documentation. The Residential Purchase Agreement and Joint Escrow Instructions initiates both the sale and escrow process, and allows for conformity in escrow practices throughout the state.

The purchase agreement combines the original contract between buyer and seller with the joint escrow instructions into one form. This should reflect the mutual and agreed upon desires of the the parties when it becomes the actual escrow instructions. Any mutual changes are made usuing an addendum to the original contract rather than amendment to escrow instructions.

An escrow is opened when a real estate agent brings the signed purchase agreement to the escrow holder, who makes a copy and accepts it by signing off in the required box in the document. The escrow holder should be concerned with whether or not the contract is complete, fully signed and initialed before accepting it. The contract must be valid before becoming instructions for the escrow.

In addition to the purchase agreement as escrow instructions, an escrow holder will submit acceptance or additional escrow instructions ofr buyer and seller signature. These instructions will include any other terms that need to be agreed upon by buyer and seller to complete the escrow.

Local Variations

As we have seen, processing is done differently in the northern and southern parts of California. In Northern California, an estimated closing statement is issued as part of the instructions, showing, for example, the proceeds going to the seller and the estimated cash needed to close for the buyer. In Southern California, the broker's net sheet serves the same purpose, except the closing statement is provided at the settlement.

Northern California

Buyers and sellers in Northern California each sign separate instructions at the end of the escrow period. These unilateral instructions represent the end of the transfer process and describe the agreement between the parties to the escrow. The closing agent, however, has been carrying out specific duties, as ordered by the principals, since the opening of the escrow, even though no instructions have been signed. The instructions also apportion closing costs to the appropriate parties. After signing the instructions, all that remains to be completed is the provision of funds from the buyer and the lender.

The contents of the buyer's and seller's instructions differ in requirements for closing. The buyer's instructions call for consideration to be given by the buyer when all documents of title transfer have been signed and the escrow is in a position to close. The seller's instructions provide for the necessary documents of transfer in exchange for consideration, either money or money and debt obligation by the buyer.

A complication that may arise out of having separate instructions is a breakdown of communication between the buyer and seller.

The buyer or seller may have changed some part of the transaction without getting the approval of the other party, and at the closing everyone is surprised. The buyer might decide to change financing arrangements, or one party could change his or her mind about the time of closing or possession. Any number of items could require amendments for all parties to sign before the closing can occur. In northern California, the real estate broker produces the amendments to the purchase contract and gives copies to the closer.

Basically, when buyer and seller sign unilateral escrow instructions they are approving the previously ordered actions of the escrow holder. They are acknowledging that demands have been satisfied, title reports completed, the amount of pest control work determined and any new loans approved. The unilateral instructions act principally as a closing statement. Closing costs for buyer and seller are disclosed separately in each of their instructions.

Southern California

In the bilateral escrow instructions of the southern part of California, the shared promises of buyer and seller are joined into one document. That instruction contains conditions of the buyer's purchase as well as general (boilerplate) instructions for both parties about requirements of the escrow. The seller agrees to the necessary steps to place title in the name of the buyer.

When bilateral instructions are used, amendments are common as a transaction progresses.
Because escrow instructions are a binding contract between the buyer and seller, any changes in the original instructions require the signature of both buyer and seller on an amendment stating the desired changes. No changes may be made without the agreement of all parties to the escrow.

Requirements for Closing

Certain protective or disclosure clauses may be included in escrow instructions which go beyond the personal, original agreements of the parties. These clauses limit the closing agent's responsibilities and liabilities regarding the complication of taxes and conformity to codes and other legal requirements.

Supplemental Tax Roll: All parties must be made aware that tax bills sent after the closing may increase or decrease the tax level imposed on the property being transferred.

Preliminary Change of Ownership Report: The buyer is required to complete this change of ownership form before closing. The purpose is to inform the county tax assessor of the change in ownership so new taxes can be calculated from the date of closing and the new owner billed appropriately.

FIRPTA: Both federal and state tax laws are affected by the Foreign Investment in Real Property Tax Act (FIRPTA). In both cases the buyer is responsible for making sure either the proper disclosures have been made and/or the proper funds have been set aside. This is the responsibility of the broker, originally, and ultimately, the closing agent. FIRPTA requires that every buyer of real property must deduct and withhold from the seller's proceeds ten percent of the gross sales price unless an exemption applies. Withheld funds must be reported and paid to the IRS within 20 days after the close of escrow.

<u>Transaction is Exempt from FIRPTA Withholding if:</u>

1. Seller's affidavit that he or she is not a "foreign person"

2. "Qualifying statement" from IRS stating no withholding is required

3. The purchase price is not over $300,000 and the buyer intends to live in the property

---

Form 1099-S: The Tax Reform Law of 1986 requires that all real estate transactions be reported to the IRS on the special Form 1099-S. The closing agent must complete this form and return it to the IRS.

Health and Safety Code Provisions

Retrofit Requirements: Smoke detectors must be installed in all sold residential properties and a disclosure must be given to the buyer as a result of state law.

The Closing Statement

An escrow has been completed when all documents have been signed, all contingencies have been met, all requirements fulfilled, all money (and other consideration) has been collected and deposited with the closing agent. The closing agent can now request recordation of documents and distribute the proceeds to the proper parties. A closing statement is then prepared by the closing agent for the buyer and seller, explaining the disposition of funds, and credits and debits made to their account.

When all is in order, the closing agent must determine the charges and account for the following items:

Sales price
Was the final sales price the same as it was originally?

Deposits
Have all moneys been disbursed or used according to instructions from all parties?

Trust deeds
Have all trust deeds of record been verified as to balance, interest rate and terms?

Payoff of existing debt
Did the seller approve a payoff of existing debt against the property, including any pre-payment penalty?

Impound account
How are existing impound accounts to be transferred to buyer?

New loan
Are all terms of the new loan agreeable to buyer (amount, interest rate, charges)?

Prorations
Have prorations been made according to instruction regarding interest on any existing debt, homeowners' association fees, taxes, insurance, rents?

Association transfer fee
Were instructions given regarding payment of association transfer fee (who pays it)?

Supplemental tax provisions
How is the supplemental tax bill to be paid?

Commission
Has the seller approved payment of commission to real estate broker?

Fees
Have buyer and seller agreed, in the instructions, to fees incurred during the escrow?

Incidental charges
Have instructions been given by the buyer and seller regarding supplementary charges such as judgments, tax liens, credit card payoffs, private note payments, or purchase of personal property?

Outside of escrow
Are there any special agreements between buyer and seller about money being disbursed outside of escrow?

Remaining balance
There may be a balance due to the seller or a refund to the buyer. If the buyer has not deposited enough money, the escrow is short and may not close.

Transfer Documents

A contract is formed between the parties as soon as the instructions are complete and signed by the principals. At the same time the escrow instructions are being prepared, the escrow holder is preparing documents needed for the transfer of ownership from the seller to the buyer.

In most cases, the document of transfer will be a grant deed. As you recall, a grant deed is a statement granting title, prepared according to written instruction from the parties. It must be signed and notarized by the seller and returned to the escrow holder with the signed escrow instructions.

An important job of the escrow holder at this point, when preparing to close, is to verify that the grant deed and the instructions conform exactly and to make sure the grant deed is completed as required by the county recorder.

The assessor's parcel number (AP number) must be identified correctly on the grant deed in order for the county recorder to accept the document for recording.

The documentary transfer tax must be computed by the escrow holder and the information added to the grant deed in the space provided. As you recall, the transfer tax is calculated based on $1.10 per thousand, or .55 per $500, of the purchase price or any fraction thereof. It is computed on the consideration or purchase price, or on the consideration or purchase price less remaining encumbrances if the buyer is assuming the existing loan.

The grant deed must be prepared exactly to the specifications of the county recorder or it will be rejected and sent back to the escrow holder. Some common mistakes made by escrow holders, requiring a new deed to be drawn, signed by the seller, notarized and submitted for recording, are:

Common Mistakes in Grant Deeds

- Notary seal unclear or incomplete
- Notarization incorrect or notary commissions expired
- Signatures not clear, missing or questionable
- Legal description of property not clearly visible in photocopy attached to deed
- Property in question in another county

Other documents of transfer might be a patent deed if the transfer is between the government and a private individual, a gift deed or a tax deed.

Financing Documents

When a property is sold, usually some form of financing is involved. Commonly the buyer applies for a new loan, and that, along with the buyer's down payment, constitutes the financing.

Other types of financing may be involved in a sale as well. The seller could carry back a note secured by a deed of trust, seller financing, outside secondary financing could be created, an All Inclusive Trust Deed or Contract of Sale could be used to secure the financing.

Types of Financing

- Note and Trust Deed
- Seller Financing
- Outside Secondary Financing
- All Inclusive Trust Deed
- Contract of Sale

Whatever the case, the escrow holder must be certain that all the documents are in order regarding the financing of the sale before the transaction can close.

The most common document used in a sale is a promissory note. The promissory note is the evidence of the debt created by a loan. It indicates the exact terms of the loan, including any special clauses agreed upon by the borrower and the lender. The note is included for the borrowers signature in the loan documents.

Loan documents are usually prepared by the lender and ordered in a timely manner by the escrow holder when the escrow is ready to close. Commonly, the borrower (buyer) brings in the remainder of the down payment and signs the loan documents, including the note and trust deed in the presence of the escrow holder.

The trust deed is the security for the loan and is also included in the loan documents. This document creates a lien on the buyer's new property once it is recorded. The trust deed includes the name of the borrower, the trustee, the beneficiary (lender), the amount owed, along with the legal description of the property. It does not have to be recorded to be valid, but should be recorded to preserve the lender's priority in case of default. In almost all cases, recording is a requirement of the lender.

Upon the close of the escrow the escrow holder sends the trust deed, along with the grant deed and any other documents requiring filing, to the county recorder's office for recording.

Other Documents Needed for Closing

Escrow instructions are reviewed by the escrow holder to determine what documents other than a grant deed and financing instruments are needed for the closing.

The preliminary title report, which most likely was ordered at the start of the escrow, is reviewed by the escrow holder for liens or other complications or disagreement with the escrow instructions. If any surprises show up, such as a lien for delinquent taxes or a trust deed not previously mentioned by the seller, the escrow holder must contact the principals for direction in the matter. Any changes must be approved, in writing, by all parties.

If any lienholders are to be paid off at the close, a demand must be ordered by the escrow holder. A demand is simply a statement of condition of a loan, including the amount owed along with a request for payment in full.

Document Conveyance

Certain documents require review and processing by the title company issuing the policy of title insurance as well as the tax assessor.

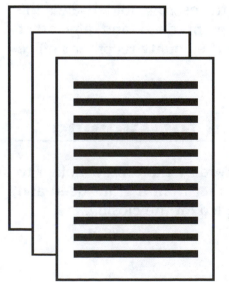

Prior to the close, the deed, properly notarized, is sent to the title insurance company whose title officer examines its acceptability for recording. Correct name and vesting for the buyer are verified, as well as the uninterrupted chain of title..

In Northern California, this requires little more than sending the documents to another department within the title company conducting the escrow.

After the notarized trust deed has been signed by the buyer it is sent to the title company for examination and held for further instruction from the escrow holder.

Certain confidential information about the buyer and seller is required by the title company to assure certain identity of the parties. Also, the general index at the title company is checked for judgments against either party that might affect the closing.

A preliminary change of ownership report is required by the tax assessor as a result of the sale. It must be prepared at the closing and sent to the assessor.

Final Closing Review

Most escrow holders will use a check list to make sure all parties have complied with the terms of the instructions. Some will use a checksheet as the escrow progresses, making note as each item is completed. Some of the more important items to be reviewed are emphasized below.

Instructions

Have escrow instructions been signed by all parties and returned to escrow holder? Have all parties with a vested interest in the transaction been included in the instructions?

Supplemental Instructions

Have there been amendments or modifications in the original instructions? Have all changes been reflected in writing and signed by all parties?

Disbursements

Has instruction been given to escrow holder regarding real estate broker commissions, existing loan payoff, loan escrow approval, title fees, pest control work, withholding of funds for work to be performed after the close of escrow, bills to be presented and any other disbursements required by the escrow?

Legal Description

A mistake in the legal description could cause the wrong property to be transferred and incur liability by the parties responsible for the error.

Fire Insurance

Escrow holder must check to make sure the coverage is sufficient and the insurance company approved by the lender.

Correct Names on Documents

The name of the buyer on the preliminary title report must agree with the name of the person taking title to the property. Has the buyer's name and vesting been correctly copied to the appropriate documents?

Sufficient Funds

The escrow file cannot be closed unless there are sufficient funds from the seller and buyer.

Checks Cleared

The buyer or seller should be notified prior to the closing that only cashier's or certified checks may be used to close the escrow. If, in fact, personal checks are used, time must be allowed for them to clear prior to closing.

Taxes

Have all laws relating to tax collection been followed by the escrow holder? Have funds been withheld or exemption filed to comply with the Foreign Investment in Real Property Tax Act (FIRPTA)? If a seller is not a citizen, escrow holder must hold a percentage of the sale proceeds for the IRS in single family residential sales of more than $300,000 and in transactions other than residential of more than $50,000, unless parties qualify for exemption.

Has Form 1099-S been filed by the escrow holder? The IRS requires every seller's name showing the taxidentification number and the amount of consideration passing in the transaction.

Pest Control

Has all required work been completed? If not, has escrow been instructed to withhold funds for work to be completed after the close of escrow?

Closing/Recording

Upon completion of all steps required in the escrow instructions, and after final escrow costs and prorations are computed as of the date of closing, the escrow holder arranges for the buyer to bring in a cashier's check for the amount needed to close the escrow. That would usually include the remainder of the down payment and closing costs.

At that point, depending on the locale of the escrow, the buyer might sign escrow instructions along with loan

289

documents. If escrow instructions have already been signed and returned to escrow, only the promissory note and trust deed still need to be signed by the buyer and notarized.

If the seller has not signed escrow instructions, or the grant deed, he or she must do so before the transaction is complete.

If all is ready, the grant deed, trust deed or deeds and any other documents that need to be recorded are sent to the title company for final examination and recording upon closing.

Upon notification from the escrow holder, funds are sent, by wire, to the title company from the lender with the requirement that the title company insures that the title is clear (all liens have been paid). The title company

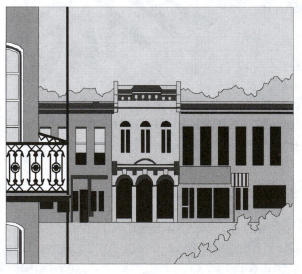

must have sufficient funds from the lender to pay the loan of record, tax liens, clear up any problems that show up on the preliminary title report and any other necessary payoffs before title insurance is issued.

When the title company has received all the necessary documents and has received the money from the lender, the escrow may close.

Before releasing any funds or recording any documents, the title company pays off all loans, taxes and any recorded liens against the property. The title company is only concerned, however, with paying off matters affecting the title. All other charges relating to the transaction are prorated and/or paid through the sale escrow.

Requirements for Closing

- All contingencies and requirements of escrow met

- Escrow instructions signed by all parties

- Grant deed signed by seller, notarized

- Escrow holder orders loan documents

- Buyer brings in closing funds

- Loan documents signed by borrower and notarized

- Escrow holder sends original signed promissory note and copy of signed trust deed back to lender

- Escrow holder funds to be sent from the lender to the title company

- Title company records original deed, trust deed or deeds in order of priority, as required by the transaction

- Title company pays off all liens and other amounts due to clear the title after a final review of documents

- Any surplus funds are sent to escrow holder for disbursement

---

After the title company records all documents and pays all existing loans and encumbrances of record, the balance of funds, if there are any, are sent to the escrow holder by the title company for disbursement and proration to the parties according to escrow instructions.

The escrow holder makes all payments, then, to the buyer, seller, real estate agents, termite company, insurance company, construction company and pays another demands on the escrow that may have accumulated.

The escrow holder prepares the closing statements for the buyer and seller, all deposits and other prorations are either debited or credited to the buyer or seller and the seller gets a check for the amount due after selling expenses.

Post Test

The following self test repeats the one you took at the beginning of this chapter. Now take the exam again -- since you have read all the material -- and check your knowledge of escrow closing procedures.

True/False

1. Buyers and sellers in Northern California do not sign separate escrow instructions.

2. Unilateral instructions are used in Northern California.

3. Bilateral instructions are used in Southern California.

4. Disclosure clauses limit the closing agent's liability regarding the complication of taxes and conformity to codes and other legal requirements.

5. Both federal and state tax laws are affected by the Foreign Investment in Real Estate Property Tax Act (FIRPTA).

6. Smoke detectors must be installed in all sold residential properties.

7. In most cases, the document of transfer will be a grant deed.

8. Loan documents are usually prepared by the title company.

9. A demand is a statement of loan default.

10. A grant deed does not *have* to be notarized to be recorded.

chapter **10**

CONTINGENCIES

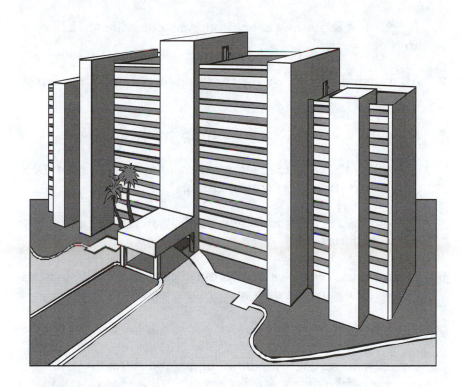

Focus

- **Introduction**
- **Contingencies**
- **Cancellations**
- **Variations on the sale escrow**

Pre-Test

The following is a self test to determine how much you know about contingencies and variations in escrow before reading this chapter. Take it without studying, then read the material presented in the text. At the end of the chapter you will find a repeat of this exam. Test your knowledge by answering the questions again, then check your improvement. (The answers are found at the end of the book.) Good luck.

True/False

1. A contract is binding even though all contingencies have not been met.

2. All principals to an escrow must agree to change contingencies.

3. A deposit receipt is an executory instrument.

4. Time is of the essence means that all parties can take their time in meeting any contingencies.

5. Escrow instructions may be signed by one or all parties to the transaction.

6. Buyers must receive and approve a copy of CC&R's within a certain number of days after receiving them.

7. The sale of the buyer's property may not be a contingency.

8. If parties to an escrow cannot agree about the disposition of funds when an escrow is cancelled, the escrow holder must release them to the seller.

9. Either party may initiate an action for funds, if the escrow is cancelled, through the courts or an arbitrator.

10. A wrap around trust deed is also known as an All Inclusive Trust Deed. (AITD)

Introduction

Escrows are opened, in the majority of cases, with the hopes and expectation that the agreement of the parties will prevail and the transaction will close. That, however, is not always the case. An escrow can fail to close, or "fall out", for many reasons. As a matter of fact, it's a miracle so many escrows manage to close considering all the contingencies that must be removed before the contract can be completed.

Along with contingencies, an escrow holder must deal with special types of transactions as well. While most escrows are typical, the escrow holder must be aware of all unusual factors and be able to provide instructions for escrows that vary from those commonly opened by buyers and sellers. We shall see here what an escrow holder can expect when special circumstances prevail. Instructions must reflect any uncommon or unusual meeting of the minds between the parties, as well as the familiar agreements.

Contingencies

A contingency requires the completion of a certain act or the happening of a certain event before a contract is binding. The parties themselves, by imposing contingencies, may cause obstacles to the closing process. In some cases, the contingencies are so abundant that it seems there can never be a meeting of the minds close enough for the transaction to be completed.

As you know, once escrow instructions have been signed by all parties, neither party may unilaterally change the content of the contract. All parties to the escrow may instruct the escrow holder to change the instructions, by mutual agreement.

At the opening of the escrow, the parties already have agreed, in the original deposit receipt, that certain items will be resolved during the process of the escrow. If one party decides that certain contingencies are no longer valid, or wants to add contingencies to the agreement, both must agree.

The problem is, people dislike rethinking decisions. Given another chance to decide, one party may balk at any change. Now we have a situation where someone must renegotiate between the parties or the escrow is at a stalemate. That person is *not* the escrow holder.

The escrow agent is considered a neutral party and is only required to provide written instructions reflecting the mutual thinking of the parties to the escrow. Joining the parties in their controversies or settling them is not part of the job. Keeping the escrow moving along and following the written instructions *is* the job, however.

No matter how carefully everyone tries to escape the possibility of new contingencies being created, it happens more times than not. One of the benefits to the deposit receipt commonly used is that the document includes just about every item buyers and sellers need to agree on at the start of the transaction. Even so, parties to any escrow must confirm or deny their acceptance of contingency removals, according to their prior agreement.

The unilateral instructions used in northern California also offer a benefit: Between the time escrow instructions are drawn and the end of the escrow process, changes have been arranged by the broker as amendments to the original deposit receipt. The escrow holder is presented with the finished agreement in writing.

In the southern part of the state, however, many times amendment after amendment to the escrow instruction is drawn to keep up with the sometimes demanding progression of the escrow. At the end, sometimes the demand overwhelms the ability of the parties to come to a decision and the escrow falls-out.

In reality, then, the deposit receipt is nothing more than an executory contract, with the parties waiting in suspense for the outcome of each contingency removal during the escrow period.

As is stated in the deposit receipt, time is of the essence, especially regarding contingencies. This means each contingency must be met in a timely manner exactly as described in the contract. If the contingency is not accepted or rejected in the manner specified, within the stated restriction of time, the contract is voidable.

There are certain parts of the deposit receipt that contain matters which must be resolved during the escrow and upon which the transaction depends. Escrow instructions will reflect these items also. If all contingencies are not met in a timely manner, the escrow is voidable by the injured party. In other words, the party waiting for satisfaction from the contingency being met has the right to cancel the escrow if the time period is not observed. Once again, the escrow holder must receive signed cancellation orders from all parties for the escrow to be terminated.

Financing

Financing must be obtained, obviously, before the buyer can complete the sale. Terms and conditions of financing are described in the deposit receipt as well as a time period for the buyer and property to qualify for any loans.The escrow also is contingent on agreements about existing and/or seller financing being executed.

Escrow Instructions

Escrow instructions must be signed within the time frame specified in the original deposit receipt.

Condominium

Buyer must receive and approve a copy of CC&R's as well as any pertinent information on the condition of the homeowners association within a certain number of days after receiving them.

Buyer's Investigation of Property Condition

Buyer has the right to inspect and approve of the property within a specified time frame. Seller must be given copies of all reports from inspections.

The buyer is advised to investigate the condition and suitability of all aspects of the property, as well as all matters affecting its value, including the following items:

- Built-in appliances, structural, foundation, roof, plumbing, heating, air conditioning, electrical, mechanical, security, pool/spa systems and components and any personal property included in the sale

- Square footage, room dimensions, lot size and age of improvements to the property

- Property lines and boundaries

- Sewer, septic and well systems and components (Property may not be connected to sewer, and applicable fees may not have been paid. Septic tank may need to be pumped and leach field may need to be inspected.)

- Limitations, restrictions and requirements regarding property use, future development, zoning, building, size, government permits and inspections

- Water and utility availability and use restrictions

- Potential environmental hazards including asbestos, formaldehyde, radon gas, lead-based paint or other lead contamination, fuel or chemical storage tanks, contaminated soil or water

- Geologic/seismic conditions, soil and terrain stability, suitability and drainage

- Neighborhood or property conditions including schools; proximity and adequacy of law enforcement;

proximity to commercial, industrial or agricultural activities; crime statistics; fire protection; other government services; existing and proposed transportation; construction and development; airport noise, noise or odor from any source; other nuisances, hazards or circumstances; and any conditions or influences of significance to certain cultures and/or religions.

Transfer Disclosure Statement

Buyer must approve the TDS (Transfer Disclosure Statement) which has been completed by the seller within three days after delivery. All parties, including the seller, buyer, seller's agent and buyer's agent, must sign the disclosure. Buyer may terminate the agreement if the TDS is not received in a timely manner.

Property Disclosures

When applicable to the property and required by law, the seller shall provide to the buyer, at the seller's expense, the following disclosures and information. The buyer shall then, within the time specified, investigate the disclosures and provide notice of disapproval (Southern California) or written notice of approval (Northern California).

- Geologic/Seismic Hazard Zones Disclosure

- Special Flood Hazard Areas Disclosure

- State Fire Responsibility Areas Disclosure

- Mello-Roos Disclosure

- Earthquake Safety Disclosure

- Smoke Detector Disclosure

- Environmental Hazards Booklet

- Lead Based Paint Disclosure

Governmental Compliance

Seller shall disclose to buyer any improvements, additions, alterations or repairs made without the required permits, final inspections or government approval (local or state). Buyer shall, within the time specified, either disapprove or approve in writing, depending on the custom and requirement of the escrow.

Pest Control

Buyer has the right to disapprove or approve the pest control report within a stated number of days after receiving it.

Sale of Buyer's Property

The escrow may be canceled if the contingency regarding the sale of the buyer's property is not removed in a timely and correct manner. Depending on the agreement between the buyer and seller, several variations on this contingency may be included in the instructions. Seller can continue to market the property or not, by agreement with the buyer. If a new buyer is found, buyer in this escrow has an agreed- upon time period to remove this contingency or the escrow is terminated.

Buyer can continue to market his or her property for a specified time period. If that time period comes and goes, the escrow may be terminated if buyer does not remove the contingency for the sale of his or her property.

Cancellation of Prior Sale/Back-up Offer

The escrow may be contingent on the cancellation of one entered into by the seller, prior to the current buyer's offer. This escrow is contingent on the successful cancellation of the earlier escrow.

Court Confirmation

Court confirmation may be required in a probate, conservatorship, guardianship, receivership, bankruptcy or other proceeding. Buyer understands that the property may continue to be marketed by a broker or others, and that others may represent different competitive bidders

prior to and at the court confirmation. If court confirmation is not obtained by the date shown in the instructions, buyer may cancel this agreement by giving written notice of cancellation to seller.

Cancellations

As we have seen, an escrow may be canceled with the mutual consent of all parties. The dissolution of the escrow must be concerned with the mutuality of everyone involved as well as the rights of third parties who are affected by the termination of the escrow.

Often, the parties cannot come to a mutual agreement about cancellation and the disposal of funds on deposit with the escrow holder or fees to be paid to the escrow holder. There are three options for funds being held by the escrow holder:

1. The funds may remain on deposit for three years, after which time they escheat to the state if there are no valid claims.

2. A court may determine the rightful owner of funds on deposit with the escrow holder. Either party may initiate an action for the funds through the court system or an arbitrator.

3. The parties can come to an agreement about the funds and direct escrow to disburse them accordingly.

Variations On the Sale Escrow

As you know, an escrow holder is obligated to produce and follow a set of escrow instructions that exactly mirrors the agreement of the parties in the deposit receipt.

The majority of sale escrows will be either a cash sale, with the buyer to qualify for a new loan sale, or seller financed.

Occasionally, however, certain situations arise where buyer and seller have agreed to a variation on commonly used financing to achieve the desired result.

All Inclusive Deed of Trust

Also known as an all-inclusive trust deed (AITD), or a wrap-around trust deed, this type of loan wraps an existing trust deed with a new trust deed, and the borrower makes one payment for both. In other words, the new trust deed (the AITD) includes the present encumbrances, such as first, second, third or more trust deeds, plus the amount to be financed by the seller.

The AITD is subordinate to existing encumbrances because the AITD is created at a later date. This means any existing encumbrances have priority over the AITD, even though they are included, or wrapped, by the new all-inclusive trust deed. At the close of escrow the buyer receives title to the property.

Typically an AITD is used in a transaction between buyer and seller to make the financing attractive to the buyer and beneficial to the seller as well. Instead of the buyer assuming an existing loan and the seller carrying back a second trust deed, the AITD can accomplish the same purpose with greater benefit to both parties in some instances.

AITD's are popular when interest rates are high and the underlying loans are not adjustable or have a low interest rate. When interest rates are low and a buyer can obtain a loan from an institution, it does not make sense to wrap an underlying loan, therefore paying a higher rate of interest to the seller than if an outside loan were obtained.

Benefits of an All Inclusive Trust Deed

Seller:
- Usually gets full-price offer
- Higher interest rate on amount carried

Buyer:
- Low down payment
- No qualifying for a loan or payment of loan fees

The AITD does not disturb the existing loan. The seller, as the new lender, keeps making the payments while giving a new increased loan at a higher rate of interest to the borrower. The amount of the AITD includes the unpaid principal balance of the existing (underlying) loan, plus the amount of the new loan being made by the seller. The borrower makes payment on the new larger loan to the seller, who in turn makes payment to the holder of the existing underlying loan. The new loan "wraps around" the existing loan.

A seller usually will carry back a wrap-around trust deed at a higher rate of interest than the underlying trust deed, thereby increasing the yield. The seller continues to pay off the original trust deed from the payments on the wrap-around, while keeping the difference. This type of financing works best when the underlying interest rate is low, and the seller can then charge a higher rate on the wrapped loan.

A wrap-around loan isn't for everyone. If a seller needs to cash out, it won't work. Also, most loans contain a due-on-sale clause, and cannot be wrapped without the lender's knowledge and approval. Depending on the buyer's and seller's motivation, sometimes an AITD will be created, with full knowledge of the risk. This is how the term "creative financing" came into being.

Generally, these payments are collected by a professional collection company and sent on to the appropriate parties. This assures the maker (borrower) of the AITD that all underlying payments are being forwarded and are kept current by a neutral party.

In some instances, a "rider" containing additional agreements between a buyer and seller will be attached to an all inclusive deed of trust.

Additions to an AITD

The AITD may be placed on contract collection with a professional collection company authorized to do business. Money is collected and disbursed for current installments, payments of taxes and insurance if necessary. Any amount then remaining is disbursed to the holder of the note secured by the AITD.

If the trustor (borrower) defaults, beneficiary obligations (lender) will be suspended until the default is cured. If the trustor is delinquent in making any payments due under the note, and the beneficiary incurs any penalties or other expenses on account of the underlying obligations during the period of trustor delinquency, the amount of any penalties and expenses will be added to the amount of the note and will be payable by the trustor with the next payment due under the note.

In the event of foreclosure of the all inclusive deed of trust, the beneficiary agrees that he or she will, at the trustee's sale, bid an amount representing that due under the AITD, less the total balance due on the underlying notes, plus any advances or other disbursements which the beneficiary is allowed by law to include in the bid.

When the note secured by the AITD becomes due or the trustor requests a demand for payoff of the note, the main amount payable to the beneficiary will be reduced by the unpaid balances of the underlying obligations.

If any installment payment under the note secured by the AITD is not paid within 15 days after the due date, a late charge may be incurred by the trustor and be due and payable upon the beneficiary's demand.

Adequate funds for the payment of taxes and fire insurance will be deposited and held by the collection account holder. Monthly, an amount equal to one-twelfth of the annual tax amount and one-twelfth the amount of the annual fire insurance billing will be deposited by the trustor. Taxes and insurance reserves have been provided by the trustor to the beneficiary for the initial reserve fund.

If the trustor makes any additional payments or added increments beyond the required monthly amount, the beneficiary, upon a request by the trustor in writing, will forward any extra funds to the holders of the underlying notes for application to the unpaid principal balances.

Wrap-Around Loans (AITD's)

- Secured by a trust deed that "wraps," or includes existing financing plus the amount to be financed by the seller

---

Contract of Sale

The contract of sale is the financing instrument with many names. It may be called an installment sales contract, a contract of sale, an agreement of sale, a conditional sales contract or a land contract.

In this type of agreement, the seller retains legal ownership of the property until the buyer has made the last payment, much like buying a car. This is a contract between a buyer and seller, and can be used during times when usual financing is difficult.

The buyer, or vendee, holds what is known as equitable title. The vendee may enjoy possession and use of the property even though legal title is held by the seller, or vendor. Like the holder of an AITD, the vendor pays off the original financing while receiving payments from the vendee on the contract of sale. Indeed, a contract of sale and an AITD are very similar. The most important distinction is that with the AITD--title passes to the buyer; under a contract of sale--title stays with the seller until the contract is paid off.

Difference Between AITD and Contract of Sale

- AITD: buyer gets title to property

- Contract of Sale: seller keeps title until loan is paid off

---

Contracts of sale are not commonly used except in special circumstances and under the guidance of an attorney, who will draw the document. They were heavily used in the 80s, but fell out of favor because of the risk involved and the difficulty of foreclosure in many cases.

Deed in Lieu of Foreclosure

Normally, when a trustor (borrower) defaults on a loan, the property in question is sold at a trustee's sale or title is conveyed to the beneficiary as a result of the foreclosure. The borrower has a ding on his or her credit as a result of the default and subsequent foreclosure and the lender must pick up any costs accrued by the sale.

Occasionally, however, the lender is willing to forgo the trustee's sale and allow the borrower to deed the property back to them voluntarily. This is most likely to happen if the lender is the former owner. The unpaid debt is then canceled, removing the lien against the property and in the process, saves the borrower's credit. If the beneficiary is an institutional lender, the property would be accepted and become one more unloved and difficult REO (Real Estate Owned) property needing a new owner. This is known as a "deed in lieu of foreclosure."

The escrow holder considers the "deed in lieu" as the principal instrument of conveyance in a transaction where this is the agreement between the parties. The consideration in this sale escrow is the satisfaction of the debt to the lender in return for a deed from the borrower, who executes a grant deed in favor of the beneficiary.

In order to guarantee the insurability of the deed, a disclaimer is added to the deed or a separate affidavit is prepared for the trustor to sign.

The note holder should always get a policy of title insurance with a deed in lieu of foreclosure so that any liens or judgments against the former owner (party in default) will not attach to the note holder.

"Subject to" Sale

A buyer may also purchase a property "subject to" the existing loan. The original borrower remains responsible for the loan, even though the buyer takes title and makes the payments. In this case, also, the property remains the security for the loan. In the case of default, it is sold and the proceeds go to the lender, with no recourse to the original buyer other than the foreclosure going against the buyer's credit.

However, a deficiency judgment is allowed if the loan was not a purchase money loan, or one made specifically upon purchase of the property. If the loan was a hard money loan, or a loan made to get cash, the original borrower could be held personally liable until the loan is paid off.

> *Roberto bought his home 20 years ago, and refinanced it after 10 years for money to add on a room. His first deed of trust was a purchase money loan in the amount of $10,000, and the second loan was a hard money loan, secured by the property.*
>
> *Roberto sold the property to Vicki, who bought the property "subject to" his two loans. When she defaulted on the loans and the property went into foreclosure, Roberto was responsible for the second loan, even though he no longer owned the property.*
>
> *What Roberto should have done, in this case, was to ask the lender, upon sale of the property, for a substitution of liability and agreement to pay (novation), relieving himself of any liability.*

Many times a property will be sold "subject to" existing loans because there is a due-on-sale clause in the present note. It may be the buyer's desire to take over the loan without triggering the due-on-sale clause.

When an escrow holder deals with an existing institutional lender, there is rarely any contact with the lender. Escrow instructions are written to include the appropriate exculpatory language relative to the transfer without compliance with normal lender requirements such as the buyer qualifying for the loan or paying loan fees.

> *"Escrow holder is authorized and instructed not to order a beneficiary statement on existing trust deed of record and both buyer and seller herein release San Clemente Escrow, as escrow holder, from any liability in any manner or way in connection herewith. Seller shall furnish escrow holder with an offset statement and a copy of promissory note setting forth the exact unpaid balance, terms and conditions of said loan for buyer's approval prior to close of escrow. Seller herein shall keep all payments current during the escrow period. In the event offset statement reflects the balance to be more or less than the amount stated herein, escrow holder is instructed to adjust any differences in buyer's cash downpayment.*
>
> *Buyer herein acknowledges that the within loan of record does contain a "due on sale" clause in the note which may cause an acceleration of maturity upon transfer of title. Regardless of this matter, escrow holder is authorized and instructed to close this escrow at the earliest possible date. All parties hold San Clemente Escrow, as escrow holder, from any liability in any manner or way in connection herewith."*

Loan Assumption Sale

When a property is sold, a buyer may assume the existing oan. Usually with the approval of the lender, the

315

buyer takes over primary liability for the loan, with the original borrower secondarily liable if there is a default.

What this means is that even though the original borrower is secondarily responsible, according to the loan assumption agreement, no actual repayment of the loan may be required of that person. If the new owner defaults, the property is foreclosed, and no deficiency judgment is allowed beyond the amount received at the trustee's sale, even though the original borrower's credit is affected by the foreclosure.

An assumption is much like an escrow where the buyer is getting a new loan, as far as the escrow holder is concerned. The escrow is contingent on the buyer qualifying with the existing lender. The buyer completes a loan package and escrow submits it to the lender with a request for a beneficiary statement. When the lender approves, they send the escrow holder a set of assumption documents for the buyer to sign and a beneficiary statement for escrow to follow for closing.

Post Test

The following self test repeats the one you took at the beginning of this chapter. Now take the exam again--since you have read all the material-- and check your knowledge of escrow closing procedures.

True/False

1. A contract is binding even though all contingencies have not been met.

2. All principals to an escrow must agree to change contingencies.

3. A deposit receipt is an executory instrument.

4. Time is of the essence means that all parties can take their time in meeting any contingencies.

5. Escrow instructions may be signed by one or all parties to the transaction.

6. Buyers must receive and approve a copy of CC&R's within a certain number of days after receiving them.

7. The sale of the buyer's property may not be a contingency.

8. If parties to an escrow cannot agree about the disposition of funds when an escrow is cancelled, the escrow holder must release them to the seller.

9. Either party may initiate an action for funds, if the escrow is cancelled, through the courts or an arbitrator.

10. A wrap around trust deed is also known as an All Inclusive Trust Deed. (AITD)

chapter **11**

TITLE INSURANCE

Focus

- **Introduction**
- **What is title insurance?**
- **History of title insurance**
- **Types of policies**
- **Policy of title insurance**

Pre-Test

The following is a self test to determine how much you know about title insurance before reading this chapter. Take it without studying, then read the material presented in the text. At the end of the chapter you will find a repeat of this exam. Test your knowledge by answering the questions again, then check your improvement. (The answers are found at the end of the book.) Good luck.

True/False

1. Title insurance is a contract to protect against losses arising through defects in title to real estate.

2. The foundation of real property ownership is title.

3. Title officers today are called conveyancers.

4. Standard coverage insures against matters not of record.

5. A CLTA policy of title insurance is designed primarily for the lender.

6. An extended policy of title insurance protects only against matters of record.

7. A basic policy of title insurance may be expanded or modified by special endorsements.

8. Title insurance covers defects known by the parties prior to the transfer, even though not disclosed.

9. The preliminary title report contains all encumbrances against the property in question.

10. If an untrue statement about the quality of the title to a property is made, the insurance is not valid.

Introduction

The business of title insurance has grown out of increased real estate activity together with the need to process the sale of real property quickly, safely and effectively. Early guarantees of the accuracy of title started with abstractors who established a chain of title by checking land records from the old Spanish and Mexican land grants, along with any records that had been kept from land sales to early settlers.

With the growth of the real estate industry, consumers began making demands for a guarantee of the accuracy of these early searches. Buyers and sellers wanted the title searchers to take responsibility for their comprehensive conclusions about all matters of record. Meeting this demand evolved into the title industry we know today.

What Is Title Insurance?

Title insurance is a contract to protect against losses arising through defects in title to real estate. In other words, the insurer guarantees the title to be free of liens or other encumbrances that would cause title to be unclear or clouded for the new owner. Title insurance is the application of insurance principles to hazards inherent in real estate titles.

Title, as you know, is the foundation of property ownership. It means that the owner has a legal right to possess that property and to use it within the restrictions imposed by authorities or limitations on its use.

No other property has a useful life that compares with the life of land. Owners die, new ones succeed, but land goes on forever. Owners of goods may change their locations at will, but land is immovable. Being both permanent and immovable, it lends itself to the absorption of innumerable rights. Over the ages, this so impressed lawyers and jurists that they formed a separate body of laws for land. These laws, creating many types of rights in land, are so numerous and so complex it is impossible for there to be a mathematical certainty of ownership.

The basic function of a title insurance company is to take positive steps that will minimize the risk that a policy holder will suffer any loss or be subject to any adverse claim, as well as to safeguard his or her ownership of or claim in the property.

The primary purpose of title insurance is to eliminate risks and prevent losses caused by defects in title arising out of events that have happened in the past.

A title defect is anything in the entire history of ownership of a piece of real estate which may encumber the owner's right to the "peaceful enjoyment" of the property or which may cause the owner to lose any portion of the property.

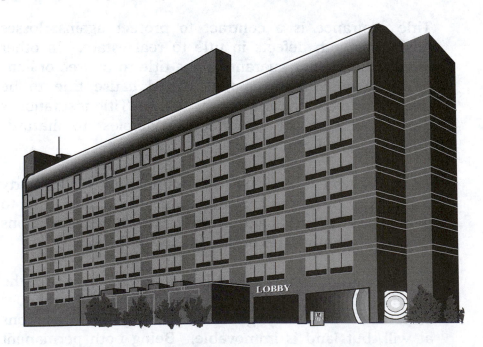

There are many title risks that cannot be revealed by even the most thorough search. Some examples of these risks:

Title Risks

- Mistakes in interpretation of wills or other legal documents
- Impersonation of the real owner
- Forged deeds or reconveyances
- Instruments executed under a fabricated or an expired power of attorney
- Deed delivered after the death of the grantor or grantee or without the consent of the grantor
- Undisclosed or missing heirs
- Wills not probated
- Deeds signed by persons of unsound mind, by minors, or by persons supposedly single but actually married
- Birth or adoption of children after the date of a will
- Mistakes in recording of legal documents
- Want of jurisdiction over persons in judicial proceedings affecting the title
- Errors in indexing of public records
- Falsification of records
- Confusion arising from similarity of names
- Title passing through a foreclosure sale where compliance of the requirements of the applicable foreclosure statutes have not been strictly met

Title insurance, however, is not always used in property transfers. It is not required by law and is usually a matter of agreement between the buyer and seller. A lender's policy usually is required by a lender as a requisite for obtaining new financing.

An abstract of title is one way to research the title to a property and is good as far as it goes. But an abstract is simply a condensed version of the recorded documents affecting title to the property. The limitations on the liability of an abstracter who issues an abstract are the same as those of an attorney who issues an opinion of title.

Sometimes an abstract of title is considered sufficient by the buyer or an attorney will offer an opinion or certificate of title which a purchaser might accept as sufficient protection. There are, however, many title defects which even the most careful title examination will not uncover. Then, chance of recovery in the event of a title loss in this case depends entirely upon the solvency of the attorney examining the title.

The attorney's liability is limited to errors and oversights that would not be made by a diligent attorney. The attorney is not liable for loss caused by hidden defects.

Every attorney knows that there are hazards in real estate title which cannot possibly be discovered with even a diligent search of the public records. For instance, the attorney cannot be sure:

- That the marital rights of all previous owners have been properly relinquished
- That all mortgages, judgments and other liens affecting the property have been properly indexed in the record room
- That all signatures on all recorded documents are genuine
- That no unknown heir of a former owner can appear to assert his or her claim

These are but a few of the matters that can defeat real estate titles. Among others are such circumstances as fraud, duress, insanity or false impersonations.

An attorney is not liable if the buyer should suffer loss because of any of the "hidden defects" in a real estate title. Liability extends only to losses caused by oversights or carelessness in the attorney's work. Then, too, liability is limited by the attorney's ability to pay, as well as by his or her life span.

Title insurance is usually required by a lender before funding a new loan. While the title insurance coverage afforded the lender and owner is somewhat the same, it is also substantially different in important areas. Because of the diminishing debt of the mortgage and the increasing equity of the owner as payments are made, it is apparent that there could be a complete title failure with the lender suffering no loss because of title insurance coverage and the owner suffering substantial loss because he or she had no title insurance.

Many buyers think that the purchase contract they signed makes the sale subject to their getting clear title. While that generally is true, there are cases where the seller cannot be absolutely certain the title is good. The seller knows about the title during his or her property ownership, but what about previous owners? Even a perfect looking title can be seriously unsound because of hidden defects. If anything would happen to defeat the title after escrow has closed

and the buyer is the new owner, the chance of recovery of damages would depend upon finding and suing the seller, winning the suit and, finally, on whether or not the seller was able to pay the judgment. In any event, the attorney's fees and expenses would be the buyer's loss.

Title insurance services are designed to give home owners, lenders and others with interests in real estate the maximum degree of protection from adverse title claims or risks. The financial assurance offered by a title insurance policy--both in satisfying any valid claims against the title as insured and in defraying the expenses of defending against any attacks on the insured title--is, of course, a key aspect of this title protection.

The risk elimination aspects of the title search and examination, performed as a prerequisite to the issuance of a title insurance policy, are equally important, however, since they ensure that all parties have a clear understanding of their interests *before* the transaction is consummated. The parties are enabled, then, to resolve potential title claims before they result in losses.

History of Title Insurance

The need for title insurance arose historically from the fact that traditional methods of conveying real property did not provide adequate safety to the parties involved. Until a century ago, transferring title to real property was handled primarily by conveyancers, who were responsible for all aspects of the transaction. The conveyancer conducted a title search to determine the ownership rights of the seller and any other rights, interest, liens or encumbrances that might exist with respect to the property, and, based on that search, provided a signed abstract (or description) of the status of the title.

Although the conveyancer generally was not a lawyer, he or she was recognized as an authority on real estate law. The origin of title insurance is directly traceable to the limited protection that the work of such a conveyancer provided the buyer of real property.

In 1868, the famous lawsuit of <u>Watson</u> v. <u>Muirhead</u> was filed in Pennsylvania. In that case, Muirhead, a conveyancer, had searched and abstracted a title for Watson, the buyer of a parcel of real estate. In good faith and after consulting an attorney, Muirhead chose to ignore certain recorded judgments and to report the title was good and unencumbered.

On the basis of Muirhead's abstract, Watson went ahead with the purchase, but subsequently was presented with, and required to satisfy, the liens that Muirhead had concluded were not impairments of title. Watson sued Muirhead to recover his losses, but the Pennsylvania

Supreme Court ruled that there was no negligence on the conveyancer's part and dismissed the case. Watson, an innocent buyer who had suffered financial damages because of the encumbrances on his title, had no recourse.

The decision in <u>Watson</u> v. <u>Muirhead</u> showed clearly that the existing conveyancing system could not provide total assurance to purchasers of real property that they would be safe and secure in their ownership. As a result of that decision the Pennsylvania legislature shortly thereafter passed an act "to provide for the incorporation and regulation of title insurance companies." On March 28, 1876, the first land title insurance company, The Real Estate Title Insurance Company, was founded in Philadelphia. During the next few years title insurance companies were organized in other cities throughout  the country, including New York, Chicago, Minneapolis, San Francisco and Los Angeles.

The nature and complexity of real estate titles and transfers have increased immeasurably since that time (as a result, in part, of the greater amount of interest and rights that are now recognized in real property). Services provided by title insurance companies also have expanded and adapted to the changing needs of our society. However, the same goals are still sought by title insurance companies today.

Types of Policies

Title requirements vary between transactions, depending on the complexity of the sale, therefore requiring the escrow holder to have a complete understanding of title insurance and the specific coverage that is available with each kind of policy.

<u>In matching the title insurance coverage to the transaction, the elements to be considered are:</u>

- Type of coverage--standard coverage, extended coverage, coverage modified by special endorsements

- Type of estate--fee, leasehold, equitable interest

- Parties insured--owner, lender, lessee, vendee, vendor

Standard Coverage

A Standard Coverage or CLTA (California Land Title Association) policy of title insurance is designed especially for the home buyer. It may be used, however, to insure a lender as well.

The title company insures the buyer, as of the date of the policy, against loss or damage not exceeding the amount of insurance stated in the policy, and any costs, attorneys' fees, and expenses which the title company may be obligated to pay in satisfying the buyer in case of a loss.

The Standard Coverage Policy is limited because it will insure against only those matters which are disclosed in public records and will not cover any defects which are concealed from the title company. Off-record items such as an encroachment, an unrecorded easement, a discrepancy in boundary lines or an interest of parties in possession of the property, which are discovered only by a survey or inspection of the property, are not covered by a CLTA Standard Policy.

The CLTA policy, when issued to insure a lender, provides coverage against a loss suffered because of an invalid trust deed, if the trust deed proved to be in a lessor position than shown or if an assignment in the policy was shown to be invalid.

A CLTA policy may be issued as follows:

- As an owner's policy
- As a lender's policy (either private or institutional)
- As a joint protection policy for both the owner and lender (commonly used when the seller acts as the lender and carries back a trust deed)

If an insured wants coverage against items not included in the standard policy, endorsements may be added to the Standard Coverage policy. Most title companies add an inflation endorsement, at no charge, which requires them, in case of a claim against the title, to cover the appreciated or inflated value of the property rather than the original sales price. Another endorsement usually available is the homeowner's endorsement. This coverage is issued only on owner occupied dwellings with four or less units. It insures against limited off record risks involving certain matters related to access, encroachments, restrictions, zoning, taxes and mechanics' liens.

While a standard title policy offers only limited coverage of off-record matters, an extended policy offers comprehensive protection for a much broader coverage. A standard policy is usually purchased by buyers of single family residences and is normally adequate. In some cases, however, it may not be enough. Some common extensions of standard coverage might be:

- Expanded encroachment coverage
- Expanded access to a public street coverage
- Unrecorded taxes or assessments--limited coverage
- Unrecorded mechanics' liens
- Violation of covenants, conditions and restrictions
- Violation of zoning ordinances
- Damage from a holder of mineral rights searching for or removing minerals from the insured property
- An inflation endorsement which can increase policy coverage up to 150% of the original policy amount

---

Standard Coverage Policy (CLTA)

Risks normally insured against:
- Most matters revealed by public records
- Some off-record risks, such as forgery or incompetence

Risks not normally insured against:
- Matters not disclosed by public records
- Environmental laws, zoning, and laws regarding the use of the property
-
- Defects known to the insured before the property was purchased and not revealed to the title company before the sale

---

Extended Coverage

While a standard title policy offers only limited coverage of off-record matters, an extended policy offers comprehensive protection for much broader coverage.

Extended Coverage Policy (ALTA)

- Matters disclosed by a physical inspection of the property
- Off-record matters disclosed by asking the occupants of the premises
- Matters disclosed by a current survey
- Violations of recorded covenants, conditions and restrictions
- Encroachments of improvements onto existing easements
- Any unrecorded easement rights disclosed by inspection
- The right of other parties, possessory or otherwise
- Unrecorded leases of tenants occupying the land
- Unrecorded assessments and inspection of tax office records
- Unrecorded claims resulting from work performed or materials supplied for improvement of the property

---

In the 1920s the American Title Association, now called the American Land Title Association (ALTA), and lenders from the East formed a partnership which resulted in the ALTA lender's policy of title insurance being offered. The extended coverage, provided at a higher price than standard coverage, protects against many risks which are not a matter of record. A lender's title requirements include any problems that affect the value of the loan security. Today, in almost all transactions where there is a new institutional lender, an ALTA extended coverage policy is required. Some of the risks covered by an ALTA extended coverage lender's policy are listed below.

Extended coverage surveys may reveal information not shown on record, An ordinary survey confirms matters of record and shows where improvements are with regard to lot lines.

An Extended Coverage Survey May Show:

- Shortages or overages in lot dimensions
- Natural watercourses crossing the property
- Unrecorded easements above or below the surface of the property
- Encroachments of existing improvements from adjoining property onto the property to be insured
- Anything existing on the surface or subsurface of the land from which a title claim may arise from other than the owner
- Claims to the title that are not a matter of record by asking the current owner about the occupancy of the land or whether there has been any work done recently on the property

---

Special Endorsements

A basic policy of title insurance may be expanded or modified by special endorsements. Adjustments of coverage requirements are usually made because the parties require special coverage, of the amount of consideration, the type of property being insured, the complexity of the transaction or any title exceptions or encumbrances affecting the property.

Guarantees

Specific limited-use coverages for special situations are called guarantees in the title insurance industry. They may include:

- Subdivision guarantee--When only a *preliminary* subdivision report has been filed with the Real Estate Commissioner on the property in question, this special coverage guarantees a final report will be filed.

- Chain of title guarantee--A chain of title is researched in every transaction and a preliminary title report is produced prior to issuing the policy of title insurance. Occasionally, a chain of title guarantee is required, however. As you know, the preliminary title report contains the legal description of the property to be insured, title vesting and all encumbrances against the property. The encumbrances show what exceptions will be in the title insurance policy desired and will allow the insured to choose what exceptions he or she can live with and which ones will have to be removed before the close of escrow.

No Liability

Title insurance does not cover any defect that was known by the parties prior to the transfer. So, if anyone, such as the real estate broker, escrow agent or seller, lies or knows of an untrue statement that would affect the quality of the title, the insurance is not valid. The title company must prove that the defect was known and mis-stated and is then not liable.

Policy of Title Insurance

LAWYERS TITLE COMPANY
Policy No._____

Subject to the Exclusions from Coverage, the exceptions contained in schedule B and the conditions and stipulations hereof, Lawyers Title Company, a California Corporation, herein called the Company, insures the insured, as of Date of Policy shown in Schedule A, against loss or damage, not exceeding the amount of insurance stated in Schedule A, and costs, attorneys' fee and expenses which the Company may become obligated to pay hereunder, sustained or incurred by said insured by reason of:

1. Title to the estate or interest described in Schedule A being vested other than as stated therein;

2. Any defect in or lien or encumbrance on such title;

3. Unmarketability of such title;

4. Any lack of the ordinary right of any abutting owner for access to at least one physically open street or highway if the land, in fact, abuts upon one or more such street or highway; and in addition, as to an insured lender only:

5. Invalidity of the lien of the insured mortgage upon said estate or interest except to the extent that such invalidity, or claim thereof, arises out of the transaction evidenced by the insured mortgage and is based upon

a. usury, or

b. any consumer credit protection or truth in lending law;

6. Priority of any lien or encumbrance over the lien of the insured mortgage, said mortgage being shown in Schedule B in the order of its priority; or

7. Invalidity of any assignment of the insured mortgage, provided such assignment is shown in Schedule B

IN WITNESS WHEREOF, LAWYERS TITLE COMPANY has caused its corporate name and seal to be hereunto affixed by its duly authorizes officers as of the date shown in Schedule A.

Lawyers Commonwealth Title Company

By:_____
President

Attest:_____

SCOTT SUGAR
UNITED AMERICAN MORTGAGE
2030 MAIN STREET, #120
IRVINE, CALIF. 92714

Dated as of March 6, 1996, at 7:30 AM

In response to the above referenced application for a policy of title insurance ,

CHICAGO TITLE COMPANY

hereby reports that is prepared to issue, or cause to be issued, as of the date hereof, a Policy or Policies of Title Insurance describing the land and the estate or interest therein hereinafter set forth, insuring against loss which may be sustained by reason of any defect, lien or encumbrance not shown or referred to as an Exception in Schedule B or not excluded from coverage pursuant to the printed Schedules, Conditions and Stipulations of said Policy forms.

The printed Exceptions and Exclusions from the coverage of said Policy or Policies are set forth in Exhibit A attached list. Copies of the Policy forms should be read. They are available from the office which issued the report.

Please read the exceptions shown or referred to in Schedule B and the exceptions and exclusions set forth in Exhibit A of this report carefully. The exceptions and exclusions are meant to provide you with notice of matters which are not covered under the terms of the title insurance policy and should be carefully considered.

It is important to note that this preliminary report is not a written representation as to the condition of title and may not list all liens, defects, and encumbrances affecting title to the land.

THIS REPORT (AND ANY SUPPLEMENTS OR AMENDMENTS HERETO) IS ISSUED SOLELY FOR THE PURPOSE OF FACILITATING THE ISSUANCE OF A POLICY OF TITLE INSURANCE AND NO LIABILITY IS ASSUMED HEREBY. IF IT IS DESIRED .THAT LIABILITY BE ASSUMED PRIOR TO THE ISSUANCE OF A POLICY OF TITLE INSURANCE, A BINDER OR COMMITMENT SHOULD BE REQUESTED.

This form of policy of title insurance contemplated by this report is:
A.L.T.A. RESIDENTIAL TITLE INSURANCE POLICY
AMERICAN LAND TITLE ASSOCIATION LOAN EXTENDED COVERAGE POLICY

_____

Title Officer

SAN CLEMENTE ESCROW
34932 CALLE DEL SOL, #B
CAPISTRANO BEACH, CALIF. 92624

Dated as of March 6, l996, at 7:30 AM

In response to the above referenced application for a policy of title insurance,

CHICAGO TITLE COMPANY

hereby reports that it is prepared to issue, or cause to be issued, as of the date hereof, a Policy or Policies of Title Insurance describing the land and the estate or interest therein hereinafter set forth, insuring against loss which may be sustained by reason of any defect, lien or encumbrance not shown or referred to as an Exception in Schedule B or not excluded from coverage pursuant to the printed Schedules, Conditions and Stipulations of said Policy forms.

The printed Exceptions and Exclusions from the coverage of said Policy or Policies are set forth in Exhibit A attached list. Copies of the Policy forms should be read. They are available from the office which issued the report.

Please read the exceptions sworn or referred to in Schedule B and the exceptions and exclusions set forth in Exhibit A of this report carefully. The exceptions and exclusions are meant to provide you with notice of matters which are not covered under the terms of the title insurance policy and should be carefully considered.

It is important to note that this preliminary report is not a written representation as to the condition of title and may not list all liens, defects, and encumbrances affecting title to the land.

THIS REPORT (AND ANY SUPPLEMENTS OR AMENDMENTS HERETO) IS ISSUED SOLELY FOR THE PURPOSE OF FACILITATING THE ISSUANCE OF A POLICY OF TITLE INSURANCE AND NO LIABILITY IS ASSUMED HEREBY. IF IT IS DESIRED .THAT LIABILITY BE ASSUMED PRIOR TO THE ISSUANCE OF A POLICY OF TITLE INSURANCE, A BINDER OR COMMITMENT SHOULD BE REQUESTED.

The form of policy of title insurance contemplated by this report is:
A.L.T.A RESIDENTIAL TITLE INSURANCE POLICY
AMERICAN LAND TITLE ASSOCIATION LOAN EXTENDED COVERAGE POLICY

Title Officer

SCHEDULE A

Title Order No:6805790

The estate or interest in the land hereinafter described or referred to covered by this report is:

A FEE AS TO PARCEL 1
AN EASEMENT MORE FULLY DESCRIBED BELOW AS TO PARCEL 2

2. Title to said estate or interest at the date hereof is vested in:

LARRY WILD AND NOBUKO WILD, HUSBAND AND WIFE, AS JOINT TENANTS

3. The land referred to in this report is situated in the State of California, County of ORANGE and is described as follows :

PARCEL 1:

LOT 6 OF TRACT NO. 13914, IN THE CITY OF SAN CLEMENTE, COUNTY OF ORANGE, STATE OF CALIFORNIA, AS SHOWN ON A MAP FILED IN BOOK 638, PAGES 45 THROUGH 50, INCLUSIVE OF MISCELLANEOUS MAPS, RECORDS OF ORANGE COUNTY, CALIFORNIA.

EXCEPTING THEREFROM ONTO THE GRANTOR, WITH THE RIGHT TO ASSIGN, TRANSFER OR LEASE TO ANY THIRD PARTY, ALL OIL, GAS AND CASINGHEAD GAS AND OTHER HYDROCARBONS LYING BELOW THE SURFACE OF THE LAND CONVEYED HEREBY, WITHOUT ANY SURFACE ENTRY RIGHTS, AS RESERVED IN THE DEED RECORDED NOVEMBER 1, 1990, AS INSTRUMENT NO. 90-581069, OFFICIAL RECORDS.

PARCEL 2:

A NON-EXCLUSIVE EASEMENT FOR INGRESS AND EGRESS PURPOSES OVER LOTS L, M AND N (THE PRIVATE STREETS) OF TRACT NO. 14682 AS SHOWN ON A MAP IN BOOK 539, PAGES 45 THROUGH 50, INCLUSIVE OF MISCELLANEOUS MAPS, RECORDS OF ORANGE COUNTY, CALIFORNIA.

SCHEDULE B

Title Order No. 6805790

At the date hereof exceptions to coverage in addition to the printed Exceptions and Exclusions in the policy form designated on the face page of this Report would be as follows:

A. 1. PROPERTY TAXES, INCLUDING ANY ASSESSMENTS COLLECTED WITH TAXES, TO BE LEVIED FOR THE FISCAL YEAR 1996-1997 THAT ARE A LIEN NOT YET DUE.

B. 2. PROPERTY TAXES, INCLUDING ANY PERSONAL PROPERTY TAXES AND ANY ASSESSMENTS COLLECTED WITH TAXES, FOR THE FISCAL YEAR 1995-1996

FIRST INSTALLMENT;	$1,749.93 (PAID)
2ND INSTALLMENT;	$1,749.93
PENALTY AND COST;	$184.99 (DUE AFTER APRIL 10)
HOMEOWNERS EXEMPTION;	$7,000.00
CODE AREA	10002
ASSESSMENT NO:	680-561-14

C 3. AN ASSESSMENT BY THE IMPROVEMENT DISTRICT SHOWN BELOW

ASSESSMENT (OR BOND) NO;	829-73
SERIES;	35-1
DISTRICT;	CITY OF SAN CLEMENTE-10
FOR;	30 AMD 85-1
BOND ISSUED;	FEBRUARY 21, 1989
ORIGINAL AMOUNT;	$ NOT SET OUT

SAID ASSESSMENT IS COLLECTED WITH THE COUNTY/CITY PROPERTY TAXES.

D A REPORT ON SAID TAXES AND ASSESSMENTS HAS BEEN ORDERED. WE WILL SEND A TAX SUPPLEMENT WHEN IT IS RECEIVED.

E 4. AN ASSESSMENT BY THE IMPROVEMENT DISTRICT SHOWN BELOW

ASSESSMENT (OR BOND)	NO: 6628
SERIES	95
DISTRICT	CITY OF SAN CLEMENTE-10
FOR	STREET IMPROVEMENTS
BOND ISSUED	JULY 14, 1995
ORIGINAL AMOUNT:	$ NOT SET OUT

SAID ASSESSMENT IS COLLECTED WITH THE COUNTY/CITY PROPERTY TAXES.

SCHEDULE B (CONTINUED)

Title Order No. 6805790

F. A REPORT ON SAID TAXES AND ASSESSMENTS HAS BEEN ORDERED.
WE WILL SEND A TAX SUPPLEMENT WHEN IT IS RECEIVED.

G. 5. THE LIEN OF SUPPLEMENTAL OR ESCAPED ASSESSMENTS OF PROPERTY
TAXES, IF ANY, MADE PURSUANT TO THE PROVISIONS OF PART 0.5,
CHAPTER 3.5 OR PART 2, CHAPTER 3, ARTICLES 3 AND 4
RESPECTIVELY(COMMENCING WITH SECTION 75) OF THE REVENUE
AND TAXATION CODE OF THE STATE OF CALIFORNIA AS A RESULT OF
THE TRANSFER OF TITLE TO THE VESTEE NAMED IN SCHEDULE A; OR
AS A RESULT OF CHANGES IN OWNERSHIP OR NEW CONSTRUCTION
OCCURRING PRIOR TO DATE OF POLICY.

H. 6 MATTERS IN VARIOUS INSTRUMENTS OF RECORD WHICH CONTAIN
AMONG OTHER THINGS EASEMENTS AND RIGHTS OF WAY IN, ON,
OVER AND UNDER THE COMMON AREA FOR THE PURPOSE OF
CONSTRUCTING, ERECTING, OPERATING OR MAINTAINING THEREON
OR THEREUNDER OVERHEAD OR UNDERGROUND LINES, CABLES,
WIRES, CONDUITS, OR OTHER DEVICES FOR ELECTRICITY,
TELEPHONE, STORM WATER DRAINS AND PIPES, WATER SYSTEMS,
SPRINKLING SYSTEMS, WATER, HEATING AND GAS LINES OR PIPES,
AND SIMILAR PUBLIC OR QUASI-PUBLIC IMPROVEMENTS OR
FACILITIES.

ALSO THE RIGHT OF USE AND ENJOYMENT IN AND TO AND THROUGHOUT THE
COMMON AREA AS WELL AS THE NON-EXCLUSIVE EASEMENTS AND
RIGHTS FOR INGRESS, EGRESS TO THE OWNER HEREIN DESCRIBED.

REFERENCE IS HEREBY BEING MADE TO VARIOUS DOCUMENTS AND MAPS OF
RECORD FOR FULL AND FURTHER PARTICULARS.

AFFECTS THE COMMON AREA.

I. 7 THE MATTERS SET FORTH IN THE DOCUMENT SHOWN BELOW WHICH,
AMONG OTHER THINGS, CONTAINS OR PROVIDES FOR: CERTAIN
EASEMENTS; LIENS AND THE SUBORDINATION THEREOF;
PROVISIONS RELATING TO PARTITION; RESTRICTIONS ON
SEVERABILITY OF COMPONENT PARTS; AND COVENANTS,
CONDITIONS AND RESTRICTIONS, (BUT OMITTING THEREFROM ANY
COVENANT OR RESTRICTION BASED ON RACE, COLOR, RELIGION,
SEX, HANDICAP, FAMILIAL STATUS OR NATIONAL ORIGIN, IF ANY,
UNLESS AND ONLY TO THE EXTENT THAT SAID COVENANT (A) IS
EXEMPT UNDER CHAPTER 42, SECTION 3607 OF THE UNITED STATES
CODE OR (B) RELATES TO HANDICAP BUT DOES NOT DISCRIMINATE
AGAINST HANDICAPPED PERSONS).

RECORDED:NOVEMBER 28   1989 AS INSTRUMENTK NO.89-646298,
OFFICIAL RECORDS

SCHEDULE B (CONTINUED)

Title Order No..6805790

J. SAID COVENANTS, CONDITIONS AND RESTRICTIONS PROVIDE THAT A VIOLATION THEREOF SHALL NOT DEFEAT THE LIEN OF ANY MORTGAGE OR DEED OF TRUST MADE IN GOOD FAITH AND FOR VALUE.

K. THE PROVISIONS OF SAID COVENANTS, CONDITIONS AND RESTRICTIONS WERE EXTENDED TO INCLUDE THE HEREIN DESCRIBED LAND BY AN INSTRUMENT.

RECORDED   JANUARY 25, 1990 AS INSTRUMENT
                                  NO: 90-045127, OFFICIAL RECORDS

L. 8. THE MATTERS SET FORTH IN THE DOCUMENT SHOWN BELOW WHICH, AMONG OTHER THINGS, CONTAINS OR PROVIDES FOR: CERTAIN BASEMENTS; LIENS AND THE SUBORDINATION THEREOF; PROVISIONS RELATING TO PARTITION; RESTRICTIONS ON SEVERABILITY OF COMPONENT PARTS; AND COVENANTS, CONDITIONS AND RESTRICTIONS (BUT OMITTING THEREFROM ANY COVENANT OR RESTRICTION BASED ON RACE, COLOR, RELIGION, SEX, HANDICAP, FAMILIAL STATUS OR NATIONAL ORIGIN, IF ANY, UNLESS AND ONLY TOTHE EXTENT THAT SAID COVENANT (A) IS EXEMPT UNDER CHAPTER 42, SECTION 3607 OF THE UNITED STATES CODE OR (B) RELATES TO HANDICAP BUT DOES NOT DISCRIMINATE AGAINST HANDICAPPED PERSONS.)

RECORDED   NOVEMBER 28, 1989 AS INSTRUMENT
                                  NO. 89-646299, OFFICIAL RECORDS

M. SAID COVENANTS, CONDITIONS AND RESTRICTIONS PROVIDE THAT A VIOLATION THEREOF SHALL NOT DEFEAT THE LIEN OF ANY MORTGAGE OR DEED OF TRUST MADE IN GOOD FAITH AND FOR VALUE.

N. THE PROVISIONS OF SAID COVENANTS, CONDITIONS AND RESTRICTIONS WERE EXTENDED TO INCLUDE THE HEREIN DESCRIBED LAND BY AN INSTRUMENT.

RECORDED: JANUARY 25, 1990 AS INSTRUMENT
                                  NO. 90-045128, OFFICIAL RECORDS

O. 9. AN EASEMENT FOR THE PURPOSE SHOWN BELOW AND RIGHTS INCIDENTAL THERETO AS SET FORTH IN A DOCUMENT

GRANTED TO: SAN DIEGO GAS & ELECTRIC
PURPOSE: PUBLIC UTILITIES
RECORDED: DECEMBER 1, 1989 AS INSTRUMENT
                                  NO. 89-653629, OFFICIAL RECORDS
AFFECTS: THE NORTHEASTERLY 3 FEET OF
                                  PARCEL 1 AND ALL OF PARCEL 2

SCHEDULE B (CONTINUED)

Title order-No. 6805790

P. 10. AN EASEMENT FOR THE PURPOSE SHOWN BELOW AND RIGHTS
INCIDENTAL THERETO AS SET FORTH IN A DOCUMENT GRANTED TO:

GRANTED TO: RANCHO DEL RIO MASTER
ASSOCIATION
PURPOSE: REASONABLE INGRESS AND EGRESS
OVER LOT 16 FOR THE PURPOSES OF
MAINTENANCE, REPAIR OR
REPLACEMENT OF THE MASONRY
WALL, AS SAID WALL IS SHOWN AS
"PERIMETER WALL" ON EXHIBIT "A"
ATTACHED THERETO AND
INCORPORATED THEREIN
RECORDED: AUGUST 26, 1992 AS INSTRUMENT NO.
92-567937, OFFICIAL RECORDS
AFFECTS: SAID LAND

Q. 11 A DEED OF TRUST TO SECURE AN INDEBTEDNESS IN THE ORIGINAL
AMOUNT SHOWN BELOW:

AMOUNT: $222,000.00
DATED: APRIL 21, 1995
TRUSTOR: LARRY AND NOBUKO WILD
TRUSTEE: CAL FED SERVICE CORPORATION
BENEFICIARY: CALIFORNIA REDERAL BANK, FSA
RECORDED: MAY 1, 1995 AS INSTRUMENT NO.
950184380, OFFICIAL RECORDS
ORIGINAL LOAN NUMBER: 0206470049

R. 12. A DEED OF TRUST TO SECURE AN INDEBTEDNESS IN THE ORIGINAL
AMOUNT SHOWN BELOW:

AMOUNT: $225,500.00
DATED: JULY 20, 1995
TRUSTOR: LARRY AND NOBUKO WILD
TRUSTEE: AMERICAN SECSURITIES COMPANY
BENEFICIARY: WELLS FARGO BANK
RECORDED: JULY 19,1995 AS INSTRUMENT NO. 95-
0030762, OFFICIAL RECORDS
ORIGINAL LOAN NUMBER: NOT SHOWN

S. THE ABOVE DEED OF TRUST APPEARS TO SECURE A HOME EQUITY TYPE OF
LOAN.IF THIS LOAN IS TO PAID OFF AND RECONVEYED THROUGH
THIS
TRANSACTION, CHICAGO TITLE WILL REQUIRE A WRITTEN STATEMENT FROM
THE BENEFICIARY THAT A FREEZE IS IN EFFECT ON THE ACCOUNT
AND
THE DEMAND FOR PAY OFF MUST PROVIDE THAT A RECONVEYANCE WILL BE
ISSUED UPON PAYMENT OF THE AMOUNTS SHOWN THEREIN.

T. **END OF SCHEDULE B**

Title Order-No. 6805790

U. NOTE NO.1: IF A 1970 ALTA OWNER'S OR LENDER'S OR 1975 ALTA LEASEHOLD OWNER'S OR LENDER'S POLICY FORM HAS BEEN REQUESTED, WHEN APPROVED FOR ISSUANCE, WILL BE ENDORSED TO ADD THE FOLLOWING TO THE EXCLUSIONS FROM COVERAGE CONTAINED THEREIN:

LOAN POLICY EXCLUSION:

ANY CLAIM, WHICH ARISES OUT OF THE TRANSACTION CREATING THE INTEREST OF THE MORTGAGEE INSURED BY THIS POLICY, BY REASON OF THE OPERATION OF FEDERAL BANKRUPTCY, STATE INSOLVENCY, OR SIMILAR CREDITORS' RIGHTS LAWS.

OWNER'S POLICY EXCLUSION:

ANY CLAIM WHICH ARISES OUT OF THE TRANSACTION VESTING IN THE INSURED, THE ESTATE OF INTEREST INSURED BY THIS POLICY, BY REASON OF THE OPERATION OF FEDERAL BANKRUPTCY, STATE INSOLVENCY OR SIMILAR CREDITOR'S RIGHTS LAWS.

V. NOTE NO. 2: THE CHARGE FOR A POLICY OF TITLE INSURANCE WHEN ISSUED THROUGH THIS TITLE ORDER, WILL BE BASED ON THE SHORT-TERM RATE.

W. NOTE NO. 3: IF THIS COMPANY IS REQUESTED TO DISBURSE FUNDS IN CONNECTION WITH THIS TRANSACTION, CHAPTER 598, STATUES PF 1989 MANDATES HOLD PERIODS FOR CHECKS DEPOSITED TO ESCROW OR SUB-ESCROW ACCOUNTS. THE MANDATORY HOLD PERIOD FOR CASHIER'S CHECKS, CERTIFIED CHECKS AND TELLER'S CHECKS IS ONE BUSINESS DAY AFTER THEDAY DEPOSITED. OTHER CHECKS REQUIRE A HOLD PERIOD OF FROM TWO TO FIVE BUSINESS DAYS AFTER THE DAY DEPOSITED.   IN THE EVENT THAT THE PARTIES TO THE CONTEMPLATED TRANSACTION WISH TO RECORD PRIOR TO THE TIME THAT THE FUNDS ARE AVAILABLE FOR DISBURSEMENT (AND SUBJECT TO COMPANY APPROVAL), THE COMPANY WILL REQUIRE THE PRIOR

WRITTEN CONSENT OF THE PARTIES. UPON REQUEST, A FORM ACCEPTABLE TO THE COMPANY AUTHORIZING SAID EARLY RECORDING MAY BE PROVIDED TO ESCROW FOR EXECUTION.

WIRE TRANSFERS

THERE IS NO MANDATED HOLD PERIOD FOR FUNDS DEPOSITED BY CONFIRMED WIRE TRANSFER. THE COMPANY MAY DISBURSE SUCH FUNDS THE SAME DAY.

CHICAGO TITLE WILL DISBURSE BY WIRE (WIRE-OUT) ONLY COLLECTED FUNDS OR FUNDS RECEIVED BY CONFIRMED WIRE (WIRE-IN). THE FEE FOR EACH WIRE-OUT IS $25.00. THE COMPANY'S WIRE-IN INSTRUCTIONS ARE:

Title Order-No.6805790

WIRE-IN INSTRUCTIONS FOR BANK OF AMERICA:

BANK: BANK OF AMERICA
                                         1811 EL CAMINO REAL
                                         SAN CLEMENTE, CA 92672
BANK ABA: 121000359
ACCOUNT NAME: CHICAGO TITLE COMPANY
title order 6805790   1258972

ACCOUNT NUMBER:

                                         CHICAGO TITLE COMPANY
FOR CREDIT TO: 16969 VAN DARMAN
                                         IRVINE, CA 92714
FURTHER CREDIT TO: ORDER NO: 01689258

X. NOTE NO. 4: THERE ARE NO CONVEYANCES AFFECTING SAID LAND,
        RECORDED WITHIN SIX (6) MONTHS OF THE DATE OF THIS REPORT.

    Y. NOTE NO.5: NONE OF THE ITEMS SHOWN IN THIS REPORT WILL
    CAUSE THECOMPANY TO DECLINE TO ATTACH CLTA INDORSEMENT
    FORM100 TO AN ALTA LOAN POLICY, WHEN ISSUED.

Z. NOTE NO. 6: THERE IS LOCATED ON SAID LAND A SINGLE FAMILY
        RESIDENCE KNOWN AS : 1459 AVENIDA GAVIOTA, IN THE CITY OF
        SANCLEMENTE, COUNTY OF ORANGE, STATE OF CALIFORNIA

PRINTED EXCEPTIONS AND EXCLUSIONS

CALIFORNIA LAND TITLE ASSOCIATION STANDARD COVERAGE POLICY-1990

EXCLUSIONS FROM COVERAGE

The following matters are expressly excluded from the coverage of this policy and the Company will not pay loss or damage, costs, attorney's fees or expenses which arise by reason of:

1.
(a) Any law, ordinance or governmental regulation (including but not limited to building and zoning laws, ordinances or regulations) restricting, regulating, prohibiting or relating to the occupancy, use or enjoyment of the land; the character, dimensions or location of any improvement now or hereafter erected on the land; a separation in ownership or a change in the dimensions or area of the land or any parcel of which the land is or was a part; or environment protection, or the effect of any violation of these laws, ordinances or governmental regulations, except to the extent that a notice of the enforcement thereof or a notice of a defect, lien or encumbrance resulting from a violation or alleged violation affecting the land has been recorded in the public records at Date of Policy.

(b) Any governmental police power not excluded by (a) above, except to the extent that a notice of the exercise thereof or a notice of a defect, lien or encumbrance resulting from a violation or alleged violation affecting the land has been recorded in the public records at Date of Policy.

2.
Rights of eminent domain unless notice of the exercise thereof has been recorded in the public records at Date of Policy, but not excluding from coverage any taking which has occurred prior to Date of Policy which would be binding on the rights of a purchaser for value with knowledge,

3.
Defects, liens, encumbrances, adverse claims or other matters:
(a) whether or not recorded in the public records at Date of Policy, but created, suffered, assumed or agreed to by the insured claimant;
(b) not known to the Company, not recorded in the public records at Date of Policy, but known to the insured claimant and not disclosed.
(c) resulting in no loss or damage to the insured claimant;
(d) attaching or created subsequent to Date of Policy; or
(e) resulting in loss or damage which would not have been sustained if the insured claimant had paid value for the insured mortgage or the estate or interest insured by this policy.

4.

Unenforceability of the lien of the insured mortgage because of the ability or failure of the insured at Date of Policy, or the inability or failure of any subsequent owner of the indebtedness, to comply with applicable doing business laws of the state in which the land is situated.

5.

Invalidity or unenforceability of the lien of the insured mortgage, or claim thereof, which arises out of the transaction evidenced by the insured mortgage and is based upon usury or any consumer credit protection or truth-in-lending law.

6.

Any claim, which arises out of the transaction vesting in the insured the estate or interest insured by this policy or the transaction creating the interest of the insured lender, by reason of the operation of federal bankruptcy, state insolvency or similar creditor' rights laws.

EXCEPTIONS FROM COVERAGE

This policy does not insure against loss or damage (and the Company will not pay cost, attorneys' fees or expenses) which arise by reason of:

1. Taxes or assessments which are not shown as existing liens by the records of any taxing authority that levies taxes or assessments on real property or by the public records.

2. Proceedings by a public agency which may result in taxes or assessments, or notices of such proceedings, whether or not shown by the records of such agency or by the public records.

3. Any facts, rights, interests or claims which are not shown by the public records but which could be ascertained by an inspection of the land or which may be asserted by persons in possession thereof.

4. Easements, liens, or encumbrances, or claims thereof, which are not shown by the public records.

5. Discrepancies, conflicts in boundary lines, shortage in area, encroachments, or any other facts which a correct survey would disclose, and which are not shown by the public records.

6. (a) Unpatented mining claims; (b) reservations or exceptions in patents or in Acts authorizing the issuance thereof; (c) water rights, claims or title to water, whether or not the matters excepted under (a), (b) or (c) are shown by the public records.

AMERICAN LAND TITLE ASSOCIATION RESIDENTIAL TITLE INSURANCE POLICY

EXCLUSIONS FROM COVERAGE

In addition to the exceptions in Schedule B, you are not insured against loss, costs, attorney's fees and expenses resulting from:

1. Government police power, and the existence or violation of any law or government regulation. This includes building and zoning ordinances and also laws and regulations concerning:

- land use
- improvements on the land
- land division
- environmental protection

This exclusion does not apply to the violations or the enforcement of these matters which appear in the public records at Policy Date. This exclusion does not limit the zoning coverage described in Items 12 and 13 of Covered Title Risks.

2. The right to take the land by condemning it, unless:
- a notice of exercising the right appears in the public records on Policy Date
- the taking happened prior to the Policy Date and is binding on you if you bought the land without knowing of the taking.

3. Title Risks:
- that are created, allowed, or agreed to by you
- that are known to you, but not to us, on the Policy Date unless they appeared in the public records
- that result in no loss to you
- that first affect your title after the Policy Date-this does not limit the labor and material
- lien coverage in item 8 of Covered Title Risks

4. Failure to pay value for your title

5. Lack of a right:
- to any land outside the area specifically described and referred to item 3 of Schedule A, or
- in streets, alleys, or waterways that touch your land

This exclusion does not limit the access coverage in Item 5 of Covered Title Risks

EXCEPTIONS FROM COVERAGE

In addition to the Exceptions, you are not insured against loss, costs, attorneys' fees and expenses resulting from:

1. Someone claiming an interest in your land by reason of:
    A. Easements not shown in the public records
    B. Boundary disputes not shown in the public records
    C. Improvements owned by your neighbor placed on your land

2. If, in addition to a single family residence, your existing structure consists of one or more Additional Dwelling Units, Item 12 of Covered Title Risks does not insure you against loss, costs, attorneys' fees, and expenses resulting from:

    A. The forced removal of any Additional Dwelling Unit, or

    B. The forced conversion of any Additional Dwelling Unit back to its original use.

    If said Additional Dwelling Unit was either constructed or converted to use as a dwelling unit in violation of any law or government regulation

AMERICAN LAND TITLE ASSOCIATION LOAN POLICY WITH ALTA ENDORSEMENT - FORM 1 COVERAGE
and
AMERICAN LAND TITLE ASSOCIATION LEASEHOLD LOAN POLICY WITH ALTA ENDORSEMENT - FORM 1 COVERAGE

EXCLUSIONS FROM COVERAGE

The following matters are expressly excluded from the coverage of this policy and the Company will not pay loss or damage, costs, attorney's fees or expenses which arise by reason of:

1.
(a) Any law, ordinance or governmental regulation (including but not limited to building and zoning laws, ordinances, or regulations) restricting, regulating, prohibiting or relating to (i) the occupancy, use, or enjoyment of the land; (ii) the character,
dimensions or location of any improvement now or hereafter erected on the land; (iii)a separation in ownership or a change in the dimensions or area of the land or any parcel of which the land is or was a part; or (iv) environmental protection, or the effect of any violations of these laws, ordinances or governmental regulations, except to the extent that a notice of the enforcement thereof or a notice of a defect, lien or encumbrance resulting from a violation or alleged violation or alleged violation affecting the land has been recorded in the public records at Date of Policy.

(b) Any governmental police power not excluded by (a) above, except to the extent that a notice of the exercise thereof or a notice of a defect, lien or encumbrance resulting from a violation or alleged violation affecting the land has been recorded in the public records at Date of Policy.

2. Rights of eminent domain unless notice of the exercise thereof has been recorded the public records at Date of Policy, but not excluding from coverage any taking which has occurred prior to Date of Policy which would be binding on the rights of a purchaser for value without knowledge.

3. Defects, liens, encumbrances, adverse claims or other matters:
(a) created, suffered, assumed or agreed to by the insured claimant;
(b) not known to the Company, not recorded in the public records at Date of Policy but known to the insured claimant and not disclosed in writing to the Company by the insured claimant prior to the date the insured claimant became an insured under this policy;
(c) resulting in no loss or damage to the insured claimant;
(d) attaching or created subsequent to Date of Policy (except to the extent that this policy insures the priority of the lien of the insured mortgage over any statutory lien for services, labor or material or to the extent insurance is afforded herein as to assessments for street improvements under construction or completed at Date of Policy);

(e) resulting in loss or damage which would not have been sustained if the insured claimant had paid value for the insured mortgage

4. Unenforceability of the lien of the insured mortgage because of the inability or failure of the insured at Date of Policy, or the inability or failure of any subsequent owner of the indebtedness, to comply with applicable doing business laws of the state in which the land is situated.

5. Invalidity or unenforceability of the lien of the insured mortgage, or claim thereof, which is based upon usury or any consumer credit protection or truth in lending law.

6. Any statutory lien for services, labor or materials (or priority of any statutory lien for services, labor or materials over the lien of the insured mortgage) arising from an improvement or work related to the land which is contracted for and commenced subsequent to Date if Policy and is not financed in whole or in part by proceeds of the indebtedness secured by the insured mortgage which at Date of Policy the insured has advanced or is obligated to advance.

7. Any claim, which arises out of the transaction creating the interest of the mortgagee
insured by this policy, by reason of the operation of federal bankruptcy, state insolvency, or similar creditors' rights laws, that is based on:

(i) the transaction creating the interest of the insured mortgagee being deemed a fraudulent conveyance or fraudulent transfer; or
(ii) the subordination of the interest of the insured mortgagee as a result of the application of the doctrine of equitable subordination; or
(iii) the transaction creating the interest of the insured mortgagee being deemed a referential transfer except where the preferential transfer results from the failure:
(a) to timely record the instrument of transfer; or
(b) of such recordation to impart notice to purchaser for value or a judgment or lien creditor.

The above policy forms be issued to afford either Standard Coverage or Extended Coverage. In addition to the above Exclusions from Coverage, the Exceptions from Coverage in a Standard Coverage policy will also include the following General Exceptions:

EXCEPTIONS FROM COVERAGE

This policy does not insure against loss or damage (and the Company will not pay costs, attorneys' fees or expenses) which arise by reason of:

1. Taxes or assessments which are not shown as existing liens by the records of any taxing authority that levies taxes or assessments on real property or by the public records.

2. Proceedings by a public agency which may result in taxes or assessments, or notices of such proceedings, whether or not shown by the records of such agency or by the public records.

3. Any facts, rights, interests or claims which are not shown by the public records but which could be ascertained by an inspection of the land or by making inquiry of persons in possession thereof.

4. Easements, liens, or encumbrances, or claims thereof, which are not shown by the public records.

5. Discrepancies, conflicts in boundary lines, shortage in area, encroachments, or any other facts which a correct survey would disclose, and which are not shown by public records.

6. (a) Unpatented mining claims; (b) reservations or exceptions in patents or in Acts authorizing the issuance thereof: (c) water rights, claims or title to water, whether or not the matters excepted under (a), (b) or (c) are shown by the public records

AMERICAN LAND TITLE ASSOCIATION
OWNER'S POLICY
and
AMERICAN LAND TITLE ASSOCIATION LEASEHOLD
OWNER'S POLICY

EXCLUSIONS FROM COVERAGE

The following matters are expressly excluded from the coverage of this policy and the Company will not pay loss or damage, costs, attorney's fees or expenses which arise by reason of:

1.

> (a) Any law, ordinance or governmental regulation (including but not limited to building and zoning laws, ordinances or regulations) restricting, regulating, prohibiting or relating to (i) the occupancy, use, or enjoyment of the land; (ii) the character, dimensions or location of any improvement now or hereafter erected on the land; (iii) a separation in ownership or a change in the dimensions or area of the land or any parcel of which the land is or was a part; or (iv) environmental protection, or the effect of any violations of these laws, ordinances or governmental regulations, except to the extent that a notice of the enforcement thereof or a notice of a defect, lien or encumbrance resulting from a violation or alleged violation affecting the land has been recorded in the public records at Date of Policy.

> (b) Any governmental police power not excluded by (a) above, except to the extent that a notice of the exercise thereof or a notice of a defect, lien or encumbrance resulting from a violation or alleged violation affecting the land has been recorded in the public records at Date of Policy.

2. Rights of eminent domain unless notice of the exercise thereof has been recorded in the public records at Date ofPolicy, but not excluding from coverage any taking which has occurred prior to Date of Policy which would be binding on the rights of a purchaser for value without knowledge.

3. Defects, liens, encumbrances, adverse claims or other matters:
    (a) created, suffered, assumed or agreed to by the insured claimant;
    (b) not known to the Company, not recorded in the public records at Date of Policy, but known to the insured claimant and not disclosed in writing to the Company by the insured claimant prior to the date the insured claimant became an insured under this policy.
    (c) resulting in no loss or damage to the insured claimant
    (d) attaching or created subsequent to Date of Policy; or
    (e) resulting in loss or damage which would not have been sustained if the insured claimant had paid value for the estate or interest insured by this policy.

4. Any claim, which arises out of the transaction vesting in the insured the estate or interest insured by this policy, by reason of the operation of federal bankruptcy, state insolvency, or similar creditors' rights laws, that is based on:

   (i) the transaction creating the estate or interest insured by this policy being deemed a fraudulent conveyance or fraudulent transfer; or

   (ii) the transaction creating the estate or interest insured by this policy being deemed a preferential transfer except where the preferential transfer results from the failure:

   (a) to timely record the instrument of transfer; or

   (b) of such recordation to impart notice to a purchaser for value or a judgment or lien creditor.

The above policy forms may be issued to afford either Standard Coverage or Extended Coverage. In addition to the above Exclusions from Coverage, the Exceptions from Coverage in a Standard Coverage policy will also include the following General Exceptions:

EXCEPTIONS FROM COVERAGE

This policy does not insure against loss or damage (and the Company will not pay costs, attorney's fees or expenses) which arise by reason of:

1. Taxes or assessments which are not shown as existing liens by the records of any taxing authority that levies taxes or assessments on real property or by the public records.
Proceedings by a public agency which may result in taxes or assessments, or notices of such proceedings, whether or not shown by the records of such agency or by the public records.

2. Any facts, rights, interests or claims which are not shown by the public records but which could be ascertained by an inspection of the land or by making inquiry of persons in possession thereof.

3. Easements, liens, or encumbrances, or claims thereof, which are not shown by the public records.

4. Discrepancies, conflicts in boundary lines, shortage in area, encroachments, or any other facts which a correct survey would disclose, and which are not shown by the public records.

5. (a) Unpatented mining claims; (b) reservations or exceptions in patents or in Acts authorizing the issuance thereof; (c) water rights, claims or title to water, whether or not the matters excepted under (a), (b) or (c) are shown by the public records.

Post Test

The following self test repeats the one you took at the beginning of this chapter. Now take the exam again--since you have read all the material-- and check your knowledge of escrow closing procedures.

True/False

1. Title insurance is a contract to protect against losses arising through defects in title to real estate.

2. The foundation of real property ownership is title.

3. Title officers today are called conveyancers.

4. Standard coverage insures against matters not of record.

5. A CLTA policy of title insurance is designed primarily for the lender.

6. An extended policy of title insurance protects only against matters of record.

7. A basic policy of title insurance may be expanded or modified by special endorsements.

8. Title insurance covers defects known by the parties prior to the transfer, even though not disclosed.

9. The preliminary title report contains all encumbrances against the property in question.

10. If an untrue statement about the quality of the title to a property is made, the insurance is not valid.

chapter 12

COMPUTERIZED ESCROW

Focus

- **Introduction**
- **Computer tasking**
- **Title insurance**
- **Title examination**
- **Automated escrow**

Pre-Test

The following is a self test to determine how much you know about computerized escrows before reading this chapter. Take it without studying, then read the material presented in the text. At the end of the chapter you will find a repeat of this exam. Test your knowledge by answering the questions again, then check your improvement. (The answers are found at the end of the book.) Good luck.

True/False

1. Traditional methods of conducting escrows have been replaced by computer technology.

2. The title industry does not use computer technology.

3. Title research is still done by manual methods.

4. The job of a title searcher is that of recovery of information about a specific property.

5. Legal opinions are sought by title examiners on some matters in the chain of title, rather than getting the information by computer search.

6. Accounting is one of the main uses for computers in escrow offices.

7. A start card places information in a computer at the end of a transaction.

8. An audit trail is created with an escrow receipt which is generated by a computer.

9. Mistakes made when data is entered are corrected with an adjustment slip.

10. A report that keeps track of the balance between the trust bank account and the balance shown in the trust account system is a reconciliation report.

Introduction

Computer technology, for the most part, has replaced traditional methods of conducting escrows. In addition to software which provides conforming forms, word processing programs allow for quick and accurate input of information. Both escrow and title insurance rely heavily on saved information in computers and on reproduction of data.

Computer Tasking

Efficiency and accuracy of the escrow product have been refined as a byproduct of computer technology. In the last decade of the 20th Century, escrow and title officers have learned to use new software capability to create new models for forms and other documents.

Research capabilities also have been extended beyond what was possible before computer memory became available. Word processing software has allowed the timely and consistent storage and retrieval of data as well as faster and more accurate communication between parties to the escrow.

Title Insurance

Computer technology is most often used in the title industry for title searching and title examination. Untold hours have been spent in the past by researchers using archives as their only source to unravel the history of a piece of property. Technology has now supplied those researchers with the tools to make their jobs easier and quicker.

Title Research

The job of a title searcher is mainly to recover information about a specific property or parcel. The researcher uses various systems which classify real property by legal description or assessor's parcel number to find data that might affect the title. The information is accessed from computer storage files.

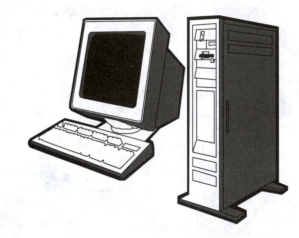

After the title search has been completed, the documents listed in the chain of title are copied for title examination. Computer communications and graphics may be used for this process.

There are certain items -- such as divorce, incompetence, parole proceedings, guardianship, probates, bankruptcy filings, judgments, tax liens, or powers of attorney -- that affect an owner or the property in question. If they cannot be found by legal description of the property in question, the information is gathered using the names of parties involved. These are indexed by grantor and grantee, alphabetically, in computer files.

Unfortunately, all steps necessary to complete a title search do not necessarily lend themselves to automation and the use of technology. Legal opinions still must be sought by the title examiner on matters in the chain of title, such as partition and quiet title actions, orders confirming sale, attachments and executions, divorces, probates and other legal matters.

Many times documents recorded prior to the transaction in question, or other documents in possession of a third party must be obtained. Commonly, copies of CC&R's on a property are required for extended coverage insurance or construction of new improvements.

Title Examination

After the title data is collected by the researcher the information gathered is interpreted by a person who specializes in examining chains of title, and a title report is assembled. This information is then entered into a computer and saved for printing the title report and writing the title policy when the title search process is complete.

At the closing, when the title policy is written, the information may be modified if there have been any new documents recorded, such as reconveyances, deeds of trust or liens, since the title search was completed. The final report is then presented to the insured parties.

Data Processing

Word processing supports the entire course of gathering and interpreting title data for the purpose of issuing title insurance. The speed with which information is input, stored or printed has allowed the title procedures needed to complete a real estate transaction to be much more efficient than in the past, with fewer mistakes or oversights because of human error.

In transactions where there is an institutional lender of record, the title insurer often is involved in a sub-escrow. The lender will send a demand for payoff of a loan to the title company rather than to the escrow holder for payment. Also, if a new loan is being funded, the net proceeds are always sent to the title company instead of to the escrow holder.

The complex task of accounting for all payoff funds, checks for payments to the seller or buyer, or any refunds to the escrow holder or other parties is accomplished by computer. Formerly, hours of the escrow holder's time were spent at accounting, tracking and processing the paperwork.

A special sub-escrow software program may be required to calculate exact figures needed for variations in transactions. Variable interest rate financing, graduated payments and negative amortization, prepayment fees, late charges, or lender fees for producing the demand for pay-off all require special accounting and handling.

Computer calculations are essential to the timely and successful closing of these escrows.

A total data processing system will contain applications for the processing of monetary data for financial statements, investments of surplus cash, maintenance and reconciliations of bank accounts, customer billing and accounting. In addition, a marketing support system of customer profiles, tracking customer activity, analysis of customer volume or other customer related activity supports automated escrow and title procedures.

Automated Escrow

Automated systems for an escrow office must be capable of managing a large extent of accounting and document processing. One of the most important charges to an escrow holder is the protection of money that flows through transactions. Suitable apportionment of charges to the responsible parties, as supported by clear escrow instructions, is an application of that duty.

Accounting Procedures

Each escrow office must decide what kind of accounting system it will use. The system must be appropriate to the size of the escrow operation, the number and type of transactions and the basic management and information requirement of the office.

The escrow office also must decide whether to use manual or automated methods for trust fund accounting and other accounting for which it is responsible.

Manual Accounting

All receipts and disbursements are posted to individual ledger cards by escrow number and then posted and balanced to the office escrow account with the manual bookkeeping method. The main source of information in this process is the ledger card, which is then used to prepare further reports. Manual accounting can be suitable for a small escrow office that keeps a steady but limited volume of business. It is a rare escrow office, however, which manages its accounts without the aid of computerized technology.

Automated Accounting

A small escrow office may use either a small personal computer for accounting or a bank's or title company's

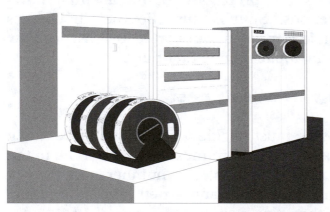

mainframe. The types of information and documents or reports generated will be determined by the type, amount and complexity of information put into the computer as well as the adequacy of the accounting software installed for bookkeeping purposes. Each office should assess its accounting needs before making a decision about the extent of automated bookkeeping it will use.

Once an escrow office has committed to using automated accounting rather than the manual method, there are a few basic documents with which to become familiar.

Start Card

The first data for entering a transaction into the system is provided by a start card. Information such as company number, names of buyer and seller, amount of consideration, date escrow opened, legal description or street address of property, type of escrow, escrow officer assigned, designated title company and any other useful information about the transaction is entered.

Escrow Receipt

The escrow receipt acts as an audit trail for money being processed through the computer system. When funds are deposited in the escrow account, a receipt for the amount deposited is generated for this purpose by the accounting program.

Adjustment Slip

If a mistake is made when data is entered into the system, an adjustment slip is used to correct the error.

Escrow Checks

As checks are written against deposited funds in the escrow account, data processing accounts for each individual check debit.

Fee Slips

As work is completed on individual escrow files, payment for services is drawn using a fee slip, and the amount earned is transferred to the bank's fee account.

Periodically, the escrow holder transfers funds, as needed, to its operations account.

Other Reports

Account Control

Report of new escrow
Receipt listing and
adjustments
Disbursement activity and
adjustments
Overdraft report
Fee report
Status reports
Master control and summary
of activity
Closed escrow report
List of missing start cards
Unprocessed and voided checks

Peripheral Data

Indices--cross references by escrow number, buyer, seller, broker, legal description, property address, type of escrow, or other meaningful index for the escrow office.

Trial Balance--monitors escrows open for a prolonged period.

Ledger Card--a permanent file record, produced monthly after final file disbursements.

Reconciliation--a report that keeps track of the balance between the trust bank account and the balance shown in the trust account system, making sure they conform with each other.

Checks Outstanding—a list of checks that are unpaid as yet by the bank.

Purged Escrow Listing—a list of the disbursement of all deposited funds, kept as escrows are removed from the system, either through closing or cancellation.

Roster of Escrow Officers—a list of escrow agents conducting each escrow.

Roster of Business Sources--client list.

Roster of Title Companies--sources most used by the escrow holder.

Audit Confirmation Letter--preprinted and addressed audit letters to the parties who deposit money in escrow to confirm the amounts in the trust account.

Customer Reports--a final file accounting with supporting disbursements.

Marketing Analysis

Escrow Activity--all escrows that have been opened, closed or canceled, listed by date and address.

Income Analysis by Officer—a list of fees earned by each escrow officer, thereby indicating strengths and weaknesses in productivity.

Income Analysis by Source--a marketing tool to indicate where market strengths lie.

Title Business Placement—a list of title orders placed by company.

SMS TITLE WORKS

Revolutionize the title business!

SMS Title Works represents a new concept in the title business business--true integration and sharing of information from one department or system to another. This eliminates the need to enter the same information over and over in numerous systems to process a title order.

Imagine entering your new title orders in your computer (just once)! And having that open order information automatically:

* order your title search
* pull the maps, recorded documents and starter file
* create an "Electronic title File" with all necessary paperwork
* prepare the preliminary title report or commitment

Your staff could actually do the examination right on the computer and have the preliminary title report or commitment prepared. All available on the same computer screen, with tracking information about each step. No need to make copies, print documents from the reader printer, or pass the paper file from one desk to another.

SMS Title Works is a suite of application systems offered by SMS including *TITLE/ESCROW/CLOSING production, DMS TITLE PLANT and IMAGE-PRO DOCUMENT IMAGING.* In addition to providing integration between our own systems, we have the ability to interface with competitive products that you may already have in place.

Our goal is to truly automate the process of a title order, from beginning to end. What will this mean to you? Improved productivity, better control, and a competitive advantage that all lead to increased revenue. And the best part...you don't have to radically change the way you currently do business. Simply let SMS Title Works do the work for you!

SMS

COMPANY: NEW

OFFICE: Demo

START CARD

Escrow Number	Opening Date	Officer	Title	Sales Price	Type
1111-Demo	7/8/99	JW	Fatco	$950,000.00	Sale

PROPERTY DESCRIPTION	EST. FEE	EST. COE	STATUS
1907 Elmhurst Costa Mesa, CA 92626	$680.00	9/06/99	

AGENT	BUYER'S NAME
	Frederick T. McBuyer

BUYER'S ADDRESS (audit letters)

1907 Elmhurst Avenue, Costa Mesa, CA 92626

AGENT	SELLER'S NAME
	Jonathan J. Sellerman, Jr.

SELLER'S ADDRESS (audit letters)

3445 Avenida de La Carlota, San Joan Capistrano, CA 92222

BAL. FRWD

❑YES ❑NO

COMMENTS

HOLD

Escrow to close concurrently with E#12341

❑YES ❑NO

FILE COPY

Listing Broker: WimbushRealty
Agent: Frank Allen

Selling Broker: Grubb & Ellis Company
Agent: Mary Allen

Title Company: First American Title Company
123 Marguerite Pkwy, Mission Viejo, CA 92692

Conversation Log

Date: 06-06-99   Page No: 1
Escrow: 1111-DEMO

Officer: Ella Escrowson   Opened: 4-06-99
Property: 8907 elmhurst   Closed: 6-06-99
Avenue
        Costa Mesa, CA 92626

Buyer: Seller:
Frederick McBuyer   Jonathan Sellerman
Josephine Buyertwo   Betty Sellerman

Entry: 06-06-99 2:47 PM By: jjw

This is a sample conversation log which you would use to type information on this particular escrow, then print a copy and attach in your escrow file.

Escrow No. 1111-Demo

Date Printed: June 6, 1999
Est. Close Date: June 6, 1999
Actual Close Date: June 6, 1999
Page 1

Reference:
8907 Elmhurst Avenue
Costa Mesa, CA 92626

SELLER:
Jonathan J. Sellerman, Jr.
Betty Jo Sellerman

BUYER:
Frederick T. McBuyere
Josephine P. Buyertwo

CHECK REGISTER

ISSUE DATE	RECEIPT NUMBER	PAYOR	AMOUNT
6/06/99	1234	Deposit: Buyer	2,000.00
6/06/99	01000	Deposit: Frederick T. Mcbuyer	36,700.00
6/06/99	1000	Draft: Fatco	4,311.08

ISSUE DATE	CHECK NUMBER	PAYEE	AMOUNT
6/06/99	1000	Jonathan J. Sellerman Jr.	26,536.97
6/06/99	1001	Fredereick T. Mcbuyer	359.93
6/06/99	1002	Wimbush Realty	2,555.00
6/06/99	1003	Frank Allen	2,500.00
6/06/99	1004	Grubb & Ellis Co.	600.00
6/06/99	1005	Mary Allen	4,200.00
6/06/99	1006	Allstate Insurance Company	460.00
6/06/99	1007	ACE Pest Control	50.00
6/06/99	1008	The Elms Homeowners Association	175.00
6/06/99	1009	California Proprty Management	125.00
6/06/99	1010	Home Warranty Company	245.00
6/06/99	1011	Discover Card	2,345.00
6/06/99	1013	Courier Express Services	45.00
6/06/99	1014	Jonathan J. Sellerman	160.27
6/06/99	1015	First American Title Company	1,553.91
6/06/99	1012	SMS	1,000.00

Deposits:		38,700.00
Drafts/Wires: +		4,311.08
Checks: -		43,011.08
Funds Held		.00
Balance		.00

Date: 02-20-1999

Preliminary Disbursement Report

Page 1

Time: 18:30:59

SMS SETTLEMENT SERVICES

User: SMS

Escrow No. 004861
Seller/Buyer: Getz/Trabuco

Open Date: 01/24/1999
Closed Date: 02/20/1999

I. RECEIPTS:

1. Bob Trabuco	002381 02/01/1999	$1,750.00		
				$1,750.00

A. RECEIPTS IN PROCESS:

Bank of America	002394 02/20/1999	$80,008.13		
Total receipts in process				$80,008.13
Total Receipts				$81,758.13

II. DISBURSEMENTS   0.00

  A. DISBURSEMENTS IN PROCESS:

Total disbursements in process	0.00
	0.00
Total Disbursements	

  B. PRELIMINARY DISBURSEMENTS:

ANDERSON SURVEYING
4475 SOUTHWIND LANE
YORBA LINDA, CA

Survey - Buyer	350.00	
Total Checks		350.00

BLUE LAGOON REAL ESTATE
1590 SOUTH COAST HIGHWAY
LAGUNA BEACH, CA

Commission	5,697.00	
Total Checks		5,697.00

COMMERCIAL CENTER BANK
2900 S. HARBOR BLVD.
SANTA ANA, CA

Interest	450.63	
Principal Balance	67,595.00	
Total Checks		68,045.63

D.L. BRUCE EXTERMINATING CO
100 SANTA ANA BLVD
SANTA ANA, CA

Pest Inspection-Buyer	200.00~	
Total Checks		200.00

<table>
<tr><td>Date: 02-20-1999</td><td></td><td>Page 2</td></tr>
</table>

Preliminary Disbursement Report

Time: 18:30:59   **SMS SETTLEMENT SERVICES**   User: SMS

Escrow No. 004861	Open Date: 01/24/1999	
Seller/Buyer: Getz/Trabuco	Closed Date: 02/20/1999	

GRUBB & ELLIS CO.
24200 ALICIA PARKWAY
MISSION VIEJO, CA

Commission	5,697.00	
Total Check		5,697.00

MARICOPA COUNTY
RECORDER

Recording Fees-Buyer	20.50	
Recording Fees-Seller	35.00	
Total Check	55.50	

SMS SETTLEMENT
SERVICES

Creditline Endorsement	75.00	
Escrow Fees-Buyer	225.00	
Escrow Fees-Seller	175.00	
Title Examination-seller	250.00	
Title Insurance-Buyer	50.00	
Title Insurance-Seller	813.00	
Transfer Fee	25.00	
Total Check		1613.00

STRACHEN AND GREEN

Attorney's Fees-Seller	85.00	
Total Check		85.00

TRW

Credit Report-Buyer	15.00	
Total Check		15.00

Total Preliminary Disbursements		81,758.13
Total disbursements		81,758.13-
Escrow Balance		0.00

Approved by_____

Approved by_____

```
┌─────────────────────────────────────────────────────────────────────────┐
│ Date: 02-20-1999                  Final                        Page 1     │
│                               Disbursement                                │
│                                  Report                                   │
│ ──────────────────────────────────────────────────────────────────────  │
│ Time: 18:33:44              SMS SETTLEMENT              User: SMS         │
│                                SERVICES                                   │
│                                                                           │
│ Escrow No.: 004861                         Open Date: 01/24/1999         │
│ Seller/Buyer:  Getz/Trabuco                Closed Date: 02/20/1999       │
│                                                                           │
│ I. RECEIPTS:                                                              │
│ 1. Bob Trabuco        002381 02/01/1999    $1,750.00                      │
│                                                          $1,750.00        │
│                                                                           │
│ A. RECEIPTS IN PROCESS:                                                   │
│ Bank of America       002394 02/20/1999    $80,008.13                     │
│ Total receipts in                                        $80,008.13       │
│ process                                                                   │
│                                                                           │
│ Total Receipts                                           $81,758.13       │
│                                                                           │
│ II. DISBURSEMENTS                                          0.00           │
│                                                                           │
│ A. DISBURSEMENTS IN PROCESS:                                              │
│ 1. Anderson Surveying        001223 02/20/1999      350.00                │
│ 2. Blue Lagoon Real Estate   001224 02/20/1999    5,697.00                │
│ 3. Commercial Center Bank    001225 02/20/1999   68,045.63                │
│ 4. D.L. Bruce Exterminating  001226 02/20/1999      200.00                │
│ 5. Grubb & Ellis Company     001227 02/20/1999    5,697.00                │
│ 6. Maricopa County Recorder  001228 02/20/1999       55.50                │
│ 7. SMS Settlement Services   001229 02/20/1999    1,613.00                │
│ 8. Strachen and Green        001230 02/20/1999       85.00                │
│ 9. TRW                       001231 02/20/1999       15.00                │
│                                                                           │
│ Total disbursements in process                           81,758.13        │
│                                                                           │
│ Total Disbursements                                      81,758.13        │
│                                                                           │
│ Escrow Balance                                            0.00            │
│                                                                           │
│                                                                           │
│ Approved by:                                                              │
│                                                                           │
└─────────────────────────────────────────────────────────────────────────┘
```

Lender Summary

Escrow Number	004859	Page 1
Escrow Officer:	Ted D. Gregory	User SMS
Borrower Name	Miller, George	

Lender Name	Bank of America
Type of Loan	New Loan

Amount of Loan	124,750.00
Amount withheld	2,428.50
Amount Due From Lender	122,321.50

Items Withheld From Loan

Description	Amount
Loan Origination Fee	180.00
Loan Discount	180.00
Appraisal Fee	350.00
Credit Line	200.00
Documentation Preparation	250.00
Tax Service	68.50
Hazard Insurance Premium	1,200.00

Post Test

The following self test repeats the one you took at the beginning of this chapter. Now take the exam again--since you have read all the material-- and check your knowledge of escrow closing procedures.

True/False

1. Traditional methods of conducting escrows have been replaced by computer technology.

2. The title industry does not use computer technology.

3. Title research is still done by manual methods.

4. The job of a title searcher is that of recovery of information about a specific property.

5. Legal opinions are sought by title examiners on some matters in the chain of title, rather than getting the information by computer search.

6. Accounting is one of the main uses for computers in escrow offices.

7. A start card places information in a computer at the end of a transaction.

8. An audit trail is created with an escrow receipt which is generated by a computer.

9. Mistakes made when data is entered are corrected with an adjustment slip.

10. A report that keeps track of the balance between the trust bank account and the balance shown in the trust account system is a reconciliation report.

chapter 13

DISCLOSURE & CONSUMER PROTECTION

Focus

- **Introduction**
- **Real property disclosures**
- **Subdivision disclosures**
- **Lending disclosures**

Pre-Test

The following is a self test to determine how much you know about disclosure and consumer protection before reading this chapter. Take it without studying, then read the material presented in the text. At the end of the chapter you will find a repeat of this exam. Test your knowledge by answering the questions again, then check your improvement. (The answers are found at the end of the book.) Good luck.

True/False

1. The escrow holder is responsible for making all real estate disclosures.

2. The Transfer Disclosure Statement is an optional disclosure.

3. Required disclosures must be made to the buyer as soon as practicable.

4. The Mello Roos Community Facilities Act is concerned with levying special taxes to finance public facilities.

5. The law requires a structural pest control inspection on all properties in escrow.

6. The Foreign Investment in Real Property Tax Act refers to withholding of taxes when sellers are not citizens.

7. In certain California real estate transactions, the buyer must withhold 3 1/3% of the total sales price as state income tax.

8. RESPA requires disclosure of good credit practice.

9. Truth in Lending Act promotes informed use of consumer credit.

10. Under the Real Property Loan Law, anyone negotiating a loan must have a real estate license.

Introduction

As the business of buying and selling real estate gets more complex, so do the required disclosures. What used to be a matter of a buyer's or seller's word, and simple honesty, is now elevated (or reduced, depending on your point of view) to multiple sworn copies of those same statements, with serious penalties for untruth or misrepresentation.

It is true that most of these disclosures are supplied through the real estate agent. The escrow holder is only concerned with carrying out the requirements of the escrow as they apply to the disclosures. The escrow agent, however, ultimately is the tally keeper, and must be aware of each of the requirements for disclosure as the escrow progresses.

Real Property Disclosures

As an escrow agent, one of your jobs is to guide the parties through the minefield of disclosure. Most of the disclosures are made by the real estate agent, with a small number made by the escrow holder. However, the practical escrow agent will make sure all disclosures have been made and all documents signed by the proper party.

Required Real Estate Disclosures

- Real Estate Transfer Disclosure Statement (TDS)
- Mello-Roos Disclosure
- Smoke Detector Statement of Compliance
- Lead Based Paint Disclosure
- State Responsibility Areas Disclosure
- Geological Hazard Disclosure
- Special Studies Zones Disclosure
- Secured Water Heater Disclosure
- Disclosure of Ordnance Location
- Environmental Hazard Disclosures
- Energy Conservation Retrofit Disclosure
- Flood Zone Disclosure
- City and County Ordinance Disclosure

Required Escrow Disclosures

- Foreign Investment in Real Property Tax Act
- Notice and Disclosure to Buyer of State Tax Withholding
- Controlling Documents and Financial Statement (condo)
- Notice of Advisability of Title Insurance
- Pest Control Inspection Disclosure

Real Estate Transfer Disclosure Statement (TDS)

Many facts about a residential property could materially affect its value and desirability. In the Real Estate Transfer Disclosure Statement, the seller reveals any information that would be important to the buyer regarding condition of the property. The seller states that-to his or her knowledge, everything pertinent, or in other words, anything that would significantly affect the value, has been disclosed. The escrow instructions then reflect the buyer's and seller's agreement about the disclosures.

Required TDS Disclosures

 Age, condition and any defects or malfunctions of the structural components and/or plumbing, electrical, heating or other mechanical systems

 Easements, common driveways or fences

 Room additions, structural alterations, repairs, replacements or other changes, especially those made without required building permits

 Flooding, drainage or soils problems on, near or in any way affecting the property

 Zoning violations, such as nonconforming uses or insufficient setbacks

 Homeowners' association obligations and deed restrictions or common area problems

 Citations against the property, or lawsuits against the owner or affecting the property

379

Location of the property within a known earthquake zone

 Major damage to the property from fire, earthquake or landslide

California law requires that a seller of one-to-four dwellings deliver to prospective buyers a Transfer Disclosure Statement about the condition of the property. This requirement extends to any transfer: by sale, exchange, installment land sale contract, lease with an option to purchase, any other option to purchase, or ground lease coupled with improvements.

<u>Exempt from the Obligation to Deliver the Statement are Various Transfers such as:</u>

- A foreclosure sale

- A court-ordered transfer by a fiduciary in the administration of a probate estate or a testamentary trust

- To a spouse or another related person resulting from a judgment of dissolution of marriage or of legal separation or from a property settlement agreement incidental to such a judgment

- From one co-owner to another

- By the state controller for unclaimed property

<u>Exempt from the Obligation to Deliver the Statement are Various Transfers such as:</u>
(continued)

- Result from the failure to pay taxes

- From or to any governmental entity

- The first sale of a residential property within a subdivision

The required disclosure must be made to the prospective buyer, by the real estate agent, as soon as practicable before transfer of title, or in the case of a lease option, sales contract, or ground lease coupled with improvements, before the execution of the contract.

Should any disclosure or amended disclosure be delivered after the required date, the buyer/transferee has three days after delivery in person or five days after delivery by deposit in the U.S. mail to terminate the offer or agreement to purchase. A written notice of termination is the instrument that must reach the seller/transferor or the seller's agent for that purpose.

The obligation to prepare and deliver disclosures is imposed on the seller and the seller's agent and any agent acting in cooperation with them. Should more than one real estate agent be involved in the transaction (unless otherwise instructed by the seller), the agent obtaining the offer is required to deliver the disclosures to the prospective buyer.

Delivery to the prospective buyer of a report or an opinion prepared by a licensed engineer, land surveyor, geologist, structural pest control operator, contractor or other expert (with a specific professional license or expertise) may limit the

liability of the seller and the real estate agents when making required disclosures. The overall intention is to provide meaningful disclosures about the condition of the property being transferred. A violation of the law does not invalidate a transfer; however, the seller may be liable for actual damages suffered by the buyer.

For information about the neighborhood or community, a city or county may require use of a Local Option Transfer Disclosure Statement disclosing special local facts.

Mello-Roos Disclosure

The Mello-Roos Community Facilities Act of 1982 authorizes the formation of community facilities districts, the issuance of bonds and the levying of special taxes which will finance designated public facilities and services. Effective July 1, 1993, the seller of a property consisting of one-to-four dwelling units subject to the lien of a Mello-Roos community facilities district must make a good faith effort to obtain from the district a disclosure notice concerning the special tax and give the notice to a prospective buyer. Exempt from this requirement are the various transfers listed earlier for the Transfer Disclosure Statement.

Smoke Detector Statement of Compliance

Whenever a sale or exchange of a single-family dwelling occurs, the seller must provide the buyer with a written statement representing that the property is in compliance with California law regarding smoke detectors. The state building code mandates that all existing dwelling units must have a smoke detector installed in a central location outside each sleeping area. In a two-story home with bedrooms on both floors, at least two smoke detectors would be required.

New construction, or any additions, alterations or repairs exceeding $1,000 and for which a permit is required, must include a smoke detector installed in each bedroom and also at a point centrally located in a corridor or area outside the bedrooms. This standard applies for the addition of one or more bedrooms, no matter what the cost.

In new home construction, the smoke detector must be hard-wired, with a battery backup. In existing dwellings, the detector may be only battery operated.

Disclosure Regarding Lead-Based Paint Hazards

When an FHA-insured mortgage will be involved in the transfer of a dwelling built before 1978, the prospective buyer/borrower must, prior to signing the offer to purchase, receive and sign a prescribed notice concerning lead-based paint hazards. If this is not done, the buyer/borrower will have to receive and sign the notice and then execute a new offer to purchase. When implementing regulations have been adopted, a

383

similar notice requirement will apply to such transactions when any other federally-related mortgage is involved.

Disclosures Regarding State Responsibility Areas

The Department of Forestry and Fire Protection has produced maps identifying rural lands classified as state responsibility areas. In such a region, the state (as opposed to a local or federal agency) has the primary financial responsibility for the prevention and extinguishing of fires. Maps of these state responsibility areas and any changes (including new maps to be produced every five years) are to be provided to assessors in the affected counties.

Should the seller know his or her real property is located in a state responsibility area, or if the property is included on a map given by the department to the county assessor, the seller must disclose the possibility of substantial fire risk in such wild land area and the fact that the land is subject to certain preventive requirements.

With the department's agreement, and by ordinance, a county may assume responsibility for all fires, including those occurring in state responsibility areas. If there is such an ordinance, the seller of property located in the area must disclose to the buyer that the state is not obligated to provide fire protection services for any building or structure unless such protection is required by a cooperative agreement with a county, city or district.

Disclosure of Ordnance Location

Federal and state agencies have identified certain areas once used for military training and which may contain live ammunition as part of the ordnance--or military supplies--from past activity. A seller of residential property located within one mile of such a hazard must give the buyer written notice as soon as practicable before transfer of title. This obligation depends upon the seller having actual knowledge of the hazard.

Delivery of Structural Pest Control Inspection and Certification Reports

The law does not require that a structural pest control inspection be performed on real property prior to transfer. Should an inspection report and certification be required as a condition of transfer or obtaining financing, however, it must be done as soon as possible. Before transfer of title or before executing a real property sales contract, the seller or the seller's agent (and any agent acting in cooperation) must deliver or have delivered to the buyer a copy of the report. There must also be written certification attesting to the presence or absence of wood-destroying termites in the visible and accessible areas of the property. Such an inspection report and written certification must be prepared and issued by a registered structural pest-control company.

385

Upon request from the party ordering such a report, the company issuing same must divide it into two categories: one part to identify the portions of the property where existing damage, infection or infestation are noted; and the other to point out areas that may have impending damage, infection or infestation.

Generally, if there is more than one real estate agent in the transaction, the agent who obtained the offer is responsible for delivering the report unless the seller has given written directions regarding delivery to another agent involved. Delivery of the required documents may be in person or by mail to the buyer. In reality, the escrow holder in most cases sends the termite report to all parties. The real estate agent responsible for delivery, however, must retain for three years a complete record of the actions taken to effect delivery.

Disclosure of Geological Hazards and Special Studies Zones

Geologists describe the surface of the earth as always changing. Some of these geological changes are relatively unimportant--not requiring a disclosure. Other changes are apparent by casual inspection--of a nature that a potential buyer should be able to judge the impact of the existing geological condition on the intended property's use.

In some cases, disclosure of a geological condition must be made. This is true of potential hazards from earthquakes, flooding, landslides, erosion and expansive soils. One condition requiring such disclosure is "fault creep," caused by stress and/or earthquake shaking.

Geology in the context of the required disclosures refers to the type of soil and how that soil will respond to earthquakes. Soft sediments tend to amplify shaking, whereas bedrock soils tend to lessen the shaking.

Generally, the closer in location to the fault, the more intense the shaking will be. However, soils types and conditions may be more important than distance from the epicenter.

The state geologist is in the process of identifying areas susceptible to "fault creep," to be shown on maps prepared by the State Division of Mines and Geology.

These maps also identify known historic landslides. The seller or the seller's agent and any agent acting in cooperation with such agent usually may rely on the identification of the special studies zones by the state geologist for disclosure purposes. In some instances, additional investigation may be required. Construction on real property of any structure for human occupancy may be subject to the findings and recommendations of a geologic report prepared by a geologist or soils engineer registered in or licensed by the state of California.

A seller of real property situated in a special studies zone, or the agent of the seller and any agent acting in cooperation with such agent, must disclose to the buyer that the property is or may be situated in such a zone as designated under the Alquist-Priolo Special Studies Zones Act.

This disclosure must be made on either the Real Estate Transfer Disclosure Statement or the Local Option Real Estate Transfer Disclosure Statement or in the purchase agreement.

The escrow holder is not responsible for this disclosure, but should be aware of the requirement.

<u>Excluded from Requirements of the</u>
<u>Special Studies Zones Act:</u>

- Structures in existence prior to May 4, 1975

- Single family wood-frame or steel-frame dwellings for which geologic reports have been approved, to be built in subdivisions authorized by the Subdivision Map Act

- Single family wood-frame or steel dwellings not over two stories, provided the dwelling is not part of a development of four or more dwellings (includes mobile homes over eight-feet wide)

- Conversions of existing apartments into condominiums, except it must be disclosed that the property is located within a delineated special-studies zone

- Alterations under 50% of the value of the structure

In addition, under the California Legislature's authorization, the Seismic Safety Commission developed a *Homeowner's Guide to Earthquake Safety* for distribution to real estate licensees and the general public. The guide includes information on geologic and seismic hazards for all areas, explanations of related structural and nonstructural hazards, and recommendations for mitigating the hazards of an earthquake.

The guide states that safety or damage prevention cannot be guaranteed with respect to a major earthquake and that only precautions such as retrofitting can be undertaken to reduce the risk of various types of damage.

Should a buyer of real property receive a copy of the Homeowner's Guide, neither the seller nor the agent are required to provide additional information regarding geologic and seismic hazards. Sellers and real estate agents must disclose that the property is in a special studies zone, however, and that there are known hazards affecting the real property being transferred.

Delivery of the *Homeowner's Guide to Earthquake Safety* is required in the following transactions:

- Transfer of any real property with a residential dwelling built prior to January 1, 1960, and consisting of one-to-four units, any of which are of conventional light-frame construction

- Transfer of any masonry building with wood-frame floors or roofs built before January 1, 1975

In a transfer subject to the first item above, the following structural deficiencies and any corrective measures taken that are within the transferor's actual knowledge, are to be disclosed to prospective buyers.

389

Required Disclosures:

- Absence of foundation anchor bolts
- Unbraced or inappropriately braced perimeter cripple walls
- Unbraced or inappropriately braced first-story wall/walls
- Unreinforced masonry perimeter foundation
- Unreinforced masonry dwelling walls
- Habitable room or rooms above a garage
- Water heater not anchored, strapped or braced

Certain exemptions apply to the obligation to deliver the booklet when transferring either a dwelling of one-to-four units or a reinforced masonry building. These exemptions are essentially the same as those that apply to delivery of the Real Estate Transfer Disclosure Statement described earlier in this section.

The buyer and/or agent may be responsible for making further inquiries of appropriate governmental agencies. The obligation of the buyer and/or agent to make further inquiry does not eliminate the duty of the seller's agent to do the following: make a diligent inquiry to identify the location of the real property in relationship to a defined special studies zone and to determine whether the property is subject to any local ordinance regarding geological and soils conditions. Full and complete disclosure is required of all material facts regarding a special studies zone, local ordinances or known structural deficiencies affecting the property.

Finally, the state geologist is responsible for the long-term project of mapping California's Seismic Hazard Zones, identifying areas susceptible to strong ground shaking, liquefaction, landslides or other ground failure and other seismic hazards caused by earthquakes. The seller's duty to disclose that the property is in a special-studies zone or a seismic-hazard zone may be limited by the availability of the maps at locations specified by local county officials.

Environmental Hazard Disclosures

Numerous federal, state and local laws have been enacted to address the problems created by environmental hazards. Responsible parties, or persons deemed responsible, for the improper disposal of hazardous waste and owners of contaminated property may be held liable for contamination cleanup.

Several disclosure laws relating to the transfer of land affected by hazardous waste contamination also have been enacted. The California Real Estate Transfer Disclosure Statement now requires sellers to disclose whether they are aware of the presence of hazardous substances, materials or products including--but not limited to--asbestos, formaldehyde, radon gas, lead-based paint, fuel or chemical storage tanks and contaminated soil or water.

ASBESTOS WASTE DISPOSAL SITE

BREATHING ASBESTOS DUST MAY CAUSE LUNG DISEASE AND CANCER

Any owner of nonresidential property who knows or suspects that there has been a release of a hazardous substance or that it may occur on or beneath the property must notify a buyer, lessee or renter of that condition prior to the sale, lease, or rental of that property. Failure to give written notice may subject the owner to actual damages and/or civil penalties.

Under Proposition 65, certain businesses may not knowingly and intentionally expose any individual to a cancer-causing chemical or reproductive toxin without first giving clear, reasonable warning to such individuals. Recently, the law also has imposed extensive asbestos disclosure requirements on owners of commercial buildings constructed prior to January 1, 1979.

The Department of Real Estate and Office of Environmental Health Hazard Assessment have developed a booklet to help educate and inform consumers about environmental hazards that may affect real property. The booklet identifies common environmental hazards, describes the risks involved with each, discusses mitigation techniques and provides lists of publications and sources from which consumers can obtain more detailed information.

Hazards Discussed in the Environmental Hazard Booklet

- Asbestos
- Radon
- Lead
- Formaldehyde

Once the booklet is provided to a prospective buyer of real property, neither the seller nor a real estate agent involved in the sale has a duty to provide further information on such hazards. If the seller or agent has actual knowledge of environmental hazards on or affecting the subject property, that information must be disclosed.

Energy Conservation Retrofit and Thermal Insulation Disclosure

State law prescribes a minimum energy conservation standard for all new construction, without which a building permit may not be issued. Local governments also have ordinances that impose additional energy conservation measures on new and/or existing homes. Some local ordinances impose energy retrofitting as a condition of selling an existing home. The requirements of the various ordinances, as well as who is responsible for compliance, may vary among local jurisdictions. The existence and basic requirements of local energy ordinances should be disclosed to a prospective buyer by the seller and/or the seller's agent and any agent cooperating in the deal.

Federal law requires a "new home" seller to disclose in every sales contract the type, thickness and R-value of the insulation which has been or will be installed in each part of the house, including the ceiling and interior and exterior walls. This law also applies to developers of "new home" subdivisions.

Special Flood Hazard Area Disclosure and Responsibilities of the Federal Emergency Management Agency (FEMA)

Flood Hazard Boundary Maps identify the general flood hazards within a community. They are also used in flood plain management and for flood insurance purposes.

These maps, developed by the Federal Emergency Management Agency (FEMA) in conjunction with communities participating in the National Flood Insurance Program (NFIP) show areas within 100-year flood boundary,  termed "special flood zone areas." Also identified are areas between 100 and 500-year levels termed "areas of moderate flood hazards" and the remaining areas above the 500-year level termed "areas of minimal risk."

A seller of property located in a special flood hazard area, or the seller's agent and/or any agent cooperating in the deal, must disclose that fact to the buyer and that federal law requires flood insurance as a condition of obtaining financing on most structures located in a special flood hazard area. Since the cost and extent of flood insurance coverage may vary, the buyer should contact an insurance carrier or the intended lender for further information.

Local Requirements Resulting from City and County Ordinances

Residential properties in cities and counties throughout California are typically subject to specific local ordinances on occupancy; zoning and use; building code compliance; fire, health and safety code regulations; and land subdivision descriptions. The various requirements for compliance as well as who and what is affected thereby should be disclosed to the prospective buyer of the

property by the seller or the seller's agent and any agent acting in cooperation with such agent.

Foreign Investment in Real Property Tax Act

Federal law requires that a buyer of real property must withhold and send to the Internal Revenue Service (IRS) 10% of the gross sales price if the seller of the real property is a foreign person.

<u>Primary Grounds for Exemption from this Requirement are:</u>

- Seller's non-foreign affidavit and U.S. taxpayer identification number

- A qualifying statement obtained through the IRS saying arrangements have been made for the collection of or exemption from the tax

- Sales price does not exceed $300,000

- Buyer intends to reside on the property

Because of the number of exemptions and other requirements relating to this law, it is recommended that the IRS be consulted for more detailed information.

Sellers and buyers and the real estate agents involved who desire further advice should consult an attorney, CPA or other qualified tax advisor.

Notice and Disclosure to Buyer of State Tax Withholding on Disposition of California Real Property

In certain California real estate sales transactions, the buyer must withhold 3 1/3% of the total sale price as state income tax and deliver the sum withheld to the state Franchise Tax Board. The escrow holder, in applicable transactions, is required by law to notify the buyer of this responsibility.

A buyer's failure to withhold and deliver the required sum may result in penalties. Should the escrow holder fail to notify the buyer, penalties may be levied against the escrow holder.

Transactions Subject to the Law:

- The seller shows an out-of-state address, or sale proceeds are to be disbursed to the seller's financial intermediary

- The sales price exceeds $100,000

- The seller does not certify that he or she is a California resident, or that the property being conveyed is his or her personal residence

---

Furnishing Controlling Documents and a Financial Statement

The owner (other than a subdivider) of a separate legal share in a common interest development (community apartment project, condominium project, planned development or stock cooperative) must provide a prospective buyer with the following:

<u>Required Disclosures:</u>

- A copy of the governing documents of the development

- Should there be an age restriction not consistent with the law, a statement that the age restriction is only enforceable to the extent permitted by law; and applicable provisions of the law

- A copy of the homeowners association's most recent financial statement

- A written statement from the association specifying the amount of current regular and special assessments as well as any unpaid assessment, late charges, interest and costs of collection which are or may become a lien against the property

- Information on any approved change in the assessments or fees not yet due and payable as of the disclosure date

Notice Regarding the Advisability of Title Insurance

In an escrow for a sale (or exchange) of real property where no title insurance is to be issued, the buyer (or both parties to an exchange) must receive and sign the following notice as a separate document in the escrow:

Important:

In a purchase or exchange of real property, it may be advisable to obtain title insurance in connection with the close of escrow where there may be prior recorded liens and encumbrances which affect your interest in the property being acquired. A new policy of title insurance should be obtained in order to ensure your interest in the property that you are acquiring.

While the law does not expressly assign the duty, it is reasonable to assume that the escrow holder is obligated to deliver the notice. A real estate agent conducting an escrow also would be responsible for delivering the notice.

Subdivision Disclosures

A subdivision is the division of land into five or more lots for the purpose of sale, lease or financing. Because of abuses in the early years of development, the division and resale of real property has received significant legislative attention. The escrow officer must be aware of special laws regulating subdivisions and the requirements and time periods involved in the resale of subdivided land.

Subdivision Map Act

This act authorizes city and county governments to enact and carry out subdivision laws according to the regulations set down in the Subdivision Map Act. All division of land into two or more parcels falls under this law.

The main objective of the Subdivision Map Act is to define the rules and procedures for filing maps to create subdivisions. It is directly controlled by local authorities (city and county) and is concerned with the physical aspects of a subdivision--such as building design, streets and environmental impact.

As a result of the Subdivision Map Act, the direct control of the kind and type of subdivisions to be allowed in each community and the physical improvements to be installed are left to local jurisdictions (city and county) within certain general limits specified in the act.

Subdivision Map Act has Two Major Objectives:

1. To coordinate the subdivision plans and planning, including lot design, street patterns, right-of-way for drainage and sewers, etc., with the community pattern and plan, as laid out by the local planning authorities

2. To ensure initial proper improvement of areas dedicated for public purposes by filing subdivision maps, including public streets and other public areas, by the subdivider so that these necessities will not become an undue burden in the future for taxpayers in the community

---

The Subdivision Map Act requires every city and county to adopt a law to regulate subdivisions for which a tentative and final map, or a parcel map, is required. Also, the act allows cities and counties to adopt laws for subdivisions for which no map is required.

State and local requirements for processing subdivision maps must be acknowledged by the escrow agent while working with the title company which will be principally responsible for map processing and recording.

The approval process for a subdivision starts at the preliminary planning stage, moving along to satisfy the requirements of the state, local government, title company and lender

If the transaction includes a map filing, the escrow holder should be practical when calculating the closing time for the escrow. The filing of a parcel map can take six to nine months, and a formal tract map filing process involves 12 to 18 months.

Subdivided Lands Act

In California, the Subdivided Lands Act is administered directly by the Real Estate Commissioner. Its objective is to protect buyers of property in new subdivisions from fraud, misrepresentation or deceit in the marketing of subdivided lots, parcels, units and undivided interests.

The Real Estate Commissioner must issue a subdivision public report before any subdivision can be offered for sale in California. This even applies to lands outside the state, if they are being marketed in California. The public report is a document disclosing all important facts about the marketing and financing of the subdivision.

The public report must show that the subdivider (developer) can complete and maintain all improvements and that the lots or parcels can be used for the purpose for which they are being sold.

Before a developer can sell each lot in the project, he or she must give a copy of the commissioner's final report to the buyer for approval. The buyer signs a receipt for the report stating it has been read. The seller (developer) must keep a copy of the statement for three years.

The public report is valid for five years, with any material changes in the development reported to the commissioner, who then can issue an amendment to the original report.

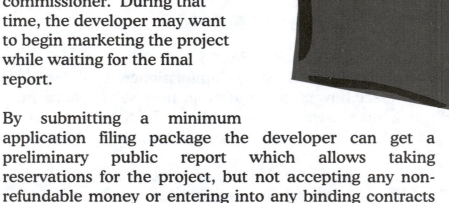

It can take many months for a developer to get project approval, once all the proper paperwork is submitted to the commissioner. During that time, the developer may want to begin marketing the project while waiting for the final report.

By submitting a minimum application filing package the developer can get a preliminary public report which allows taking reservations for the project, but not accepting any non-refundable money or entering into any binding contracts until receiving the final report from the commissioner.

Lending Disclosures

Along with the need for real property disclosures came a need for consumer protection in lending. Borrowers wanted to know what the real cost of borrowing money was and demanded to be protected from less than honest loan brokers. Thus, disclosures regarding loans and consumer credit and laws governing loan brokers became part of the rapidly growing consumer protection movement.

The Real Estate Settlement Procedures Act (RESPA)

The Real Estate Settlement Procedures Act (RESPA) applies to all federally related mortgage loans. The act requires special disclosures for certain lenders who provide loan funds for transactions involving one-to-four residential units.

Special procedures and forms for settlements (closing costs) must be used for most home mortgage loans, including FHA and VA loans, and those from financial institutions with federally-insured deposits.

The lender must furnish a copy of a Special Information Booklet, together with a Good Faith Estimate of the amount or range of closing costs to every person from whom the lender receives a written application for any federally related loan.

Truth-in-Lending Act (Regulation Z)

The Truth-in-Lending Act became effective July 1, 1969. The main purpose of the law is to promote the informed use of consumer credit by requiring creditors to disclose credit terms so consumers can make comparisons between various credit sources. To accomplish the objectives of the act the Board of

403

Governors of the Federal Reserve System issued a directive known as Regulation Z.

Later, the Federal Reserve Board adopted model disclosures for closed-end transactions such as the purchase of real property and model language for certain other disclosures. The Federal Reserve Board also announced that its staff would no longer provide written answers to individuals requesting interpretations of Regulation Z, but would issue general statements from time to time to answer questions of interpretation.

Real Property Loan Law

The Real Estate Law requires anyone negotiating a loan to have a real estate license. In the past, abuses have occurred in the form of excessive commissions, inflated costs and expenses, the negotiating of short-term loans with large balloon payments, and misrepresentation or concealment of material facts by licensees negotiating these loans.

As a result of this mistreatment of consumers by corrupt agents, legislation was passed to correct the situation. The Real Property Loan Law now applies to loans secured by first trust deeds under $30,000 and by junior trust deeds under $20,000.

The law requires anyone negotiating a loan to provide a Mortgage Loan Broker's Statement (sometimes called a Mortgage Loan Disclosure Statement) to a prospective borrower, with information concerning all important features of a loan to be negotiated for the borrower.

From time to time, a real estate agent, as part of a transaction, will be involved in negotiating a loan for the borrower. A completed Mortgage Loan Disclosure Statement must be presented to the prospective borrower, and the borrower must sign the statement prior to signing loan documents.

Professionalism and Ethics

Staying informed is probably the most important task left to the escrow agent. Those who make continuing efforts to learn and stay current on real estate industry changes will be the ones to compete successfully in the future.

Increasingly, escrow agents must know what and how to disclose--as well as when, where, why, by and to whom. The uninformed escrow agent is highly vulnerable to court action in our consumer-oriented society.

Post Test

The following self test repeats the one you took at the beginning of this chapter. Now take the exam again--since you have read all the material-- and check your knowledge of escrow closing procedures.

True/False

1. The escrow holder is responsible for making all real estate disclosures.

2. The Transfer Disclosure Statement is an optional disclosure.

3. Required disclosures must be made to the buyer as soon as practicable.

4. The Mello Roos Community Facilities Act is concerned with levying special taxes to finance public facilities.

5. The law requires a structural pest control inspection on all properties in escrow.

6. The Foreign Investment in Real Property Tax Act refers to withholding of taxes when sellers are not citizens.

7. In certain California real estate transactions, the buyer must withhold 3 1/3% of the total sales price as state income tax.

8. RESPA requires disclosure of good credit practice.

9. Truth in Lending Act promotes informed use of consumer credit.

10. Under the Real Property Loan Law, anyone negotiating a loan must have a real estate license.

chapter 14

OTHER TYPES OF ESCROWS

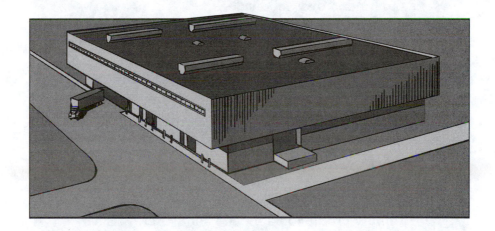

Focus

- **Introduction**
- **Holding escrow**
- **Loan escrow**
- **Trust deed sale**
- **Subdivision escrow**
- **Leasehold escrow**
- **Mobile home escrow**
- **Bulk transfer**
- **1031 exchange**

Pre-Test

The following is a self test to determine how much you know about other types of escrows before reading this chapter. Take it without studying, then read the material presented in the text. At the end of the chapter you will find a repeat of this exam. Test your knowledge by answering the questions again, then check your improvement. (The answers are found at the end of the book.) Good luck.

True/False

1. Only sale escrows may be conducted by private escrow companies.

2. A loan escrow is used to transfer property which is being sold and funded by a subdivider.

3. A trust deed is sold whenever property transfers ownership.

4. An escrow can be required where fee title is not transferred.

5. Typical leasehold escrows will be a land lease or a space lease.

6. In commercial leasing, title insurance is never used.

7. The primary product in a mobile home escrow is considered personal property.

8. A mobile home never becomes real property.

9. Bulk transfer refers to the sale of a business.

10. Capital gains are deferred when a seller completes a 1031 tax-free exchange.

Introduction

As you have journeyed through this text, the sale escrow has been used as the basic teaching tool for the beginning escrow student. It is desirable, however, for every escrow student to be familiar with other varieties.

Each type of escrow has its own terminology, special requirements and personality. As you read through this chapter you will see the myriad ways escrow serves the real estate industry beyond the common sale escrow.

A description of each type of escrow that may be encountered in the course of a career in escrow follows.

Holding Escrow

The escrow agent, acting in the capacity of a neutral "stake-holder," holds money, documents or something else of value until directed to release them upon performance of conditions specified by the principals.

Subdivision Pre-Sale

Reservations on a subdivision may be taken by a developer who has received a Preliminary Public Report from the Real Estate Commissioner. Parcels may be reserved by placing them in an escrow until the developer is issued a final report, at which time a sale escrow can be opened.

Construction Funding

A builder may receive funds from a construction loan by "draw." The lender deposits the proceeds from the loan in an escrow, with instructions about how the funds are to be released to the builder.

Stock Distribution

When stock representing a majority interest in a corporation is transferred, many times an escrow is required. An escrow agent must be totally familiar with the needs of the parties and the complexity of the process to be involved in these kinds of transactions. The specialized types of documents and procedures along with government regulatory involvement make a stock transfer complicated and demanding for the escrow officer.

Loan Escrow

Separate instructions may be prepared for a loan escrow, depending upon the structure of the sale escrow directions. Typically, a loan escrow would be prepared for a refinance of an existing loan. In some instances, however, a sub-escrow opened specifically as a loan escrow may be connected to a sale transaction.

In most cases where there is an open sale escrow, the sale instructions include directions for the escrow officer regarding the financing. A separate loan escrow is not commonly opened.

If the lender is a private party, the escrow holder is responsible for preparing the loan documents, usually a promissory note and trust deed. If a transaction requires other types of loan documents, such as a contract of sale or an all inclusive trust deed (AITD), the principals are encouraged to use the services of an attorney to prepare the instruments of finance.

If the transaction calls for a loan to be funded by an institutional lender, the loan documents are prepared by the lender and sent to the escrow holder for signing by the borrower. The promissory note and a copy of the trust deed are then returned to the lender. The original notarized trust deed is held by the escrow officer until the escrow is ready to close. When the title company receives the signed, notarized trust deed from the escrow holder, loan funds are released to the escrow officer for disbursement and closing, and the trust deed is recorded.

Trust Deed Sale

A loan may be sold many times during its life, whether it was originated by an institutional lender or a private party. A loan can be bought and sold in the secondary mortgage market or privately, and in the course of the sale, go through an escrow.

The primary instrument in the sale of a loan is the trust deed, just as a grant deed is the primary instrument in the sale of real property. As you recall, the evidence of the debt is the promissory note, with the deed of trust as collateral or security for the loan.

When the holder of a note secured by a deed of trust wants to sell his or her interest, the instrument of transfer is an assignment of trust deed. The buyer may require an escrow and title insurance to confirm clear title to the indebtedness (the trust deed).

SMS - SETTLEMENT SERVICES DIVISION, A CALIFORNIA CORPORATION IS LICENSED AS AN ESCROW AGENT BY THE DEPARTMENT OF CORPORATIONS OF THE STATE OF CALIFORNIA.

LOAN ESCROW INSTRUCTIONS

TO: **SMS - Settlement Services Division** Date: **July 8, 1999**
Escrow Number: DEMOREFI
Escrow Officer: **Ella Escrowson**
Page 1 of 5

The undersigned Borrower(s) is obtaining a loan on the property hereinafter described and will cause Lender to hand you the proceeds of a new First Trust Deed in the amount of **$171,000.00**, less Lender's normal costs and charges, which you are authorized to use on or before **September 6, 1999**, providing upon recordation of the securing Deed of Trust, you obtain an ALTA Lender's Policy of Title insurance, per Lender's requirements covering real property in the County of **Orange**, State of California, as follows:

Lot 123 of Tract 12345, in the City of Lake Forest, County of Orange as per map recorded in Book 324, Page(s) 12-13, of Miscellaneous Maps in the Office of the County Recorder of said County.

COMMONLY KNOWN AS: **22177 Oakwood Lane, Lake Forest, CA 92222**

The title policy is to show the title to the property to be vested in:

John J. Borrower and Linda K. Borrower, Husband and Wife as Joint Tenants

The policy is to be free of encumbrances except as follows:

(1) Any General and Special Taxes and Special District Levies not due or delinquent; this will include the lien of supplemental taxes, if any, assessed pursuant to Chapter 498, 1983 Statutes of the State of California.
(2) All Taxes, Bonds and Assessments levied or assessed subsequent to the date of these instructions.
(3) Covenants, conditions, reservations (including exceptions of oil, gas minerals, hydrocarbons, and/or lease without right of surface entry), restrictions, right of way, and easements for public utilities, districts, water companies, alleys, and streets.
(4) First Trust Deed to file, securing a note in the principal amount of **$171,000.00** in favor of **Bank of America** at the best prevailing rate and terms per lenders instructions to be deposited into escrow.

DEPOSIT OF FUNDS INTO ESCROW: Each of the undersigned acknowledges and understands that pursuant to State of California Assembly Bill ("Good Funds Legislation") which became effective January 1, 1990, funds deposited into escrow and/or deposited with the Title Company for use in this escrow by the Property Owner, Buyer and New Lender in any form other than a wire transfer may cause a delay in the closing of this escrow and/or disbursement of funds at the time of closing. Each of the undersigned hereby indemnifies and holds SMS - Settlement Services Division and its officers and/or Employees harmless with the respect to any delay in closing and/or disbursement of funds due to compliance with the Provisions of "AB512".

NOTICE REGARDING CLOSING FUNDS: In the event Borrower elects to deposit closing funds by Cashier's Check, said funds MUST be deposited not later than 48 hours prior to the anticipated date of close of escrow, pursuant to AB512 Good Funds Law.

CONDITION OF TITLE: Escrow Holder is authorized and instructed to pay any encumbrance necessary to place title in the condition called for herein and Borrower will hand you any instruments and/or funds as required for such purpose.

LOAN ESCROW INSTRUCTIONS

TO: **SMS - Settlement Services Division**

Date: **July 8, 1999**
Escrow Number: DEMOREFI
Escrow Officer: **Ella Escrowson**
Page 2 of 5

OBTAIN DEMAND: Escrow holder is hereby authorized and instructed to obtain demand from lender(s) of record and to pay for same from Borrower's proceeds at the close of escrow, including prepayment penalties, interest and such other costs, if applicable.

FIRE INSURANCE: Secure for Lender an endorsement on existing insurance policy naming lender as First Trust Deed Holder and providing for replacement cost guarantee, as required by Lender. Charge account of Borrower at close of escrow and pay premiums as may be required for same, per billing to be deposited herein prior to close of escrow.

CLOSING COSTS/CHARGES: Pay escrow charges and proper recording fees, also charges for evidence of title called for above (whether or not this escrow is consummated) and you are authorized to pay off any bonds, assessments and/or taxes, also any encumbrances of record, plus accrued interest, charges and bonus, if any, to show title as called for above and/or necessary to comply with same. Instruct the title company to begin search of title at once.

ADVANCE RELEASE OF DEMAND FEES: In the event the Existing Lienholder(s) requires payment to demand statement fees in advance of issuing their demand statement. Borrower shall deposit sufficient funds as called for by Escrow Holder for payment of same and authorizes Escrow Holder to release said funds to Existing Leinholder(s) prior to close of escrow. Borrower acknowledges and agrees that said funds are NON-REFUNDABLE in the event this escrow is not consummated.

CANCELLATION FEE: Borrower is aware that in the event this escrow is canceled. Borrower shall pay a cancellation fee of $100.00 to Escrow Holder. Said cancellation fee to be deducted from funds on deposit upon written and/or verbal notice of cancellation by Lender or Borrower.

HOLD OPEN FEE: It is agreed that if, for any reason, this escrow is not closed within NINETY (90) days of the established date for closing as shown herein. Escrow Holder may at their option charge a hold-open fee against funds then on deposit in the amount of $25.00 for each month, or fraction thereof, that this escrow remains unclosed.

CLOSE OF ESCROW: The close of escrow shall be the day documents deposited in this escrow are recorded pursuant to these instructions.

EXTENSION OF TIME FOR CLOSING: If the condition of this escrow have not been complied with at the time provided for in these instructions, you are nevertheless to complete this escrow as soon as the conditions (except as to time) have been complied with, unless a written demand for the return of money and/or instruments by a party to his escrow is received by you prior to the recording of any instrument provided for in these instructions.

NECESSITY FOR WRITTEN INSTRUCTIONS: No notice, demand or change or instructions shall be of any effect unless given to you in writing and approved in writing by all parties affected by same.

DEPOSITS AND DISBURSEMENTS: All funds delivered to you by parties to this escrow shall be deposited in any non-interest bearing account designated as a "Trust Account" with any bank or depository authorized by the Federal or State Government, and may be transferred to, and co-mingled with, other such trust accounts. You shall not be obligated to identify or to guarantee the signature of any payee on said checks.

LOAN ESCROW INSTRUCTIONS

TO: **SMS - Settlement Services Division**

Date: **July 8, 1999**
Escrow Number: DEMOREFI
Escrow Officer: **Ella Escrowson**
Page 3 of 5

SUB-ESCROW AGENTS: As you deem reasonably necessary to the closing of this escrow, you may deposit any funds or documents received by you herein, with any bank, title insurance company, savings and loan association, trust company, industrial loan company, credit union, admitted insurer or licensed escrow agent and any such deposit shall be deemed in accordance herewith. In this regard, you are authorized to utilize the services of one or more sub-escrow agents as defined under the California Financial Code and/or documents prior to close of escrow, if reasonable necessary in your discretion.

ADJUSTMENTS AND PRORATIONS: All adjustments shall be made upon the basis of a thirty day month, including, but not necessarily limited to the following: A. Taxes for the current year, based on tax amounts disclosed on last available tax bill; B. Premiums on fire insurance policies as handed you; C. Interest on loans of record, based on statement from the lender.

RECORDING AND TRANSFER FEES: To facilitate the recording of any documents delivered into or through this escrow, you may pay all required fees; all of the costs of which shall be deemed to constitute an authorized expenditure to be paid or charged to the party responsible therefore.

EFFECT OF CONFLICT: If, before or after recording documents, you receive or become aware of any conflicting demands or claims (hereinafter "conflicts") with respect to this escrow, the rights or obligations of any of the parties of any money or property deposited or affected, you shall have the right to discontinue further performance on your part until the conflict is resolved to your satisfaction. In addition, you shall have the right to commence or defend any action or proceeding you deem necessary for the determination of the conflict. A conflict shall be deemed to include, but is not necessarily limited to, your receipt of unilateral instructions or instructions from some, but not all of the escrow. In the event of a conflict, you shall not be liable to take any action of any kind, but may withhold all moneys, securities, documents or other things deposited into escrow, until such conflict has been determined by agreement of the parties or by legal process.

In the event any action is commenced to determine a conflict or otherwise to enforce or declare the provisions of these instructions or to rescind them, including, but not limited to, a suit in inter pleader (whether or not the action is prosecuted to final judgment, voluntarily dismissed or settled, and irrespective of whether you are the prevailing party in any such action) and it becomes necessary or desirable for you to obtain legal advice with respect to a conflict or on account of any matter or thing arising out of or in any way related to these instructions, whether or not suit is actually commenced, the parties to this escrow jointly and severally agree to pay all of your costs, damages, judgments and expenses, including attorney's fees, incurred by you in connection with the same.

PAYMENT OF FEES AND CHARGES: It is understood that the fees agreed to be paid for your services are for ordinary and usual services only, and should there be any extraordinary or unusual services rendered by you, the undersigned agree to pay reasonable compensation to you for such extraordinary or unusual services, together with any costs and expenses which may be incurred by you in connection with same. Upon the close of the escrow, you may retain, on your own behalf, your charges, costs and fees and charge the same in your accounting against the person responsible therefore.

IT IS UNDERSTOOD THAT, IN THE EVENT THIS ESCROW IS CANCELED OR TERMINATED, YOU WILL RECEIVE COMPENSATION FOR SUCH SERVICES AS YOU HAVE RENDERED IN CONNECTION WITH THIS ESCROW.

LOAN ESCROW INSTRUCTIONS

TO: **SMS - Settlement Services Division**

Date: **July 8, 1999**
Escrow Number: DEMOREFI
Escrow Officer: **Ella Escrowson**
Page 4 of 5

LIMITATIONS ON DUTIES AND LIABILITIES: YOU SHALL NOT, IN ANY MANNER OR UNDER ANY THEORY OF LAW OR EQUITY, HAVE ANY RESPONSIBILITY OR LIABILITY FOR ANY OR ALL OF THE FOLLOWING ACTS, EVENTS, KNOWLEDGE OR CIRCUMSTANCES:

1. Determining the sufficiency, genuineness or validity of any document, instrument or writing deposited with you herein or the form of content, or the identity or authority of the person executing or depositing any of the same;

2. Ascertaining the terms, covenants or conditions of any document, instrument or writing deposited with you, or to investigate or examine the circumstances under which it was executed and/or delivered to you;

3. The failure to notify any person, including but not limited to the parties herein, of any sale, resale, loan, exchange or other transaction involving the property or rights that are the subject hereof or incidental thereto, or any profit or advantage to any person, firm or corporation, including by not limited to any broker or agent of any party hereto, regardless of the fact that such other transaction(s) may be directly or indirectly handled by you in connection with the within escrow or any other escrow, or come to your knowledge, in any form whatsoever;

4. The payment, examination as to amount, propriety or validity of any tax, including but not limited to personal property, corporate, business or license tax or any description, assessed against, chargeable or payable by either of the parties hereto;

5. Your failure or refusal to comply with any amendments, supplements and/or notation hereof or hereto which are not signed by all parties hereto and actually delivered to you;

6. Your failure or refusal to terminate or cancel the within escrow, without full and complete compliance, to your satisfaction, with the provisions of paragraph "Necessity for Written Instructions" herein;

7. For any liability predicated upon any relationship other than that of an escrow holder, it being specifically irrevocably and conclusively understood, agreed and deemed no other legal relationship is hereby created or shall be implied, assumed or come into being;

8. For failure of any party to this escrow with any of the provisions of any agreement, contract, or other instrument, contract or other instrument filed or referred to in these instructions;

9. Any duties beyond that of an escrow holder, which are expressly limited to the safekeeping of money, instruments or other document received by escrow holder and for the disposition of them in accordance with the written instructions accepted by you.

10. Your knowledge of matters affecting the property which is the subject hereof shall not, and does not, create any liability or duty in addition to the responsibility of escrow holder under these instructions;

11. You shall not be obligated to make any physical examination of any real or personal property described in any document deposited into this escrow, and the parties agree that you have not made, and will not make, any representations whatsoever regarding said property;

415

LOAN ESCROW INSTRUCTIONS

TO: **SMS - Settlement Services Division**

Date: **July 8, 1999**
Escrow Number: DEMOREFI
Escrow Officer: **Ella Escrowson**
Page 5 of 5

12. You shall not be concerned with, nor responsible for, the giving of any disclosures required by Federal or State law, including but not limited to, any disclosures required under Regulation Z, pursuant to the Federal Consumer Credit Protection Act, the effect of any zoning laws, ordinances or regulations affecting any other property described in this escrow. The undersigned jointly and severally agree to indemnify and hold you harmless by reason of any misrepresentation of omission by either party or their respective agents, or the failure of the parties to this escrow to comply with the rules and/or regulations of any governmental agency, state, federal, county, municipal or otherwise. Parties to this escrow have satisfied themselves outside of escrow that this transaction is not in violation of the Subdivision Map Act or any other law relating to land division, and you are relieved of all responsibility and/or liability in connection with same, and are not to be concerned with the enforcement of said laws;

13. Any loss that may occur by reasons of (i) forgeries or false representations; (ii) the exercise of your discretion in any particular manner, (iii) for any act, duty requirement or obligation not expressly required of you hereunder or specifically state herein; or, (iv) for any reason whatsoever except your gross neglect or willful misconduct.

AUTHORITY OF BUSINESS ENTITY: As to any corporation, partnership or other entity which may be a party hereto, it shall be conclusively presumed that any document executed by any officer or general partner of such entity was made upon due, full, legal and complete authority of the governing body of such entity, and you shall have no responsibility to independently investigate or verify such authority.

AUTHORITY TO RELEASE INFORMATION: You are authorized and instructed to furnish information from this escrow to lender and/or brokers as may be requested by them, including, but not limited to copies of all instructions and closing statement(s) in this escrow. You are authorized to accept funds deposited to a party's broker or agent without further authorization.

SUCCESSORS AND ASSIGNS: The provisions hereof shall bind each party hereto and his respective heirs, administrators, executors, assigns, trustees, guardians, conservators, receivers and successors in interest.

DESTRUCTION OF DOCUMENTS: You are authorized to destroy or otherwise dispose of all documents, instruments or writings received by you herein and accounting or disbursement records pertaining hereto at the expiration of five ((5) years from and after the initial date hereof, regardless of any subsequent notations thereto or the date of close of escrow, without liability or further notice to any parties hereto.

EFFECT OF EXECUTION: The signatures of the undersigned hereon and on any document(s) and instrument(s) pertaining to this escrow indicates their unconditional acceptance of the same and constitutes acknowledgment of their receipt oa copy of the same.

ESCROW COMPANIES ARE NOT AUTHORIZED TO GIVE LEGAL ADVICE, IF YOU DESIRE LEGAL ADVICE, CONSULT YOUR ATTORNEY BEFORE SIGNING.

We, the undersigned, jointly and severally, acknowledge receipt of a complete copy of the within escrow instructions and by our signature set forth below, acknowledge that we have read, understand and agree to the same in their entirety.

John T. Borrower	Linda K. Borrower

Subdivision Escrow

A subdivision escrow is a specialized subject that is conducted exclusively by certain escrow holders as their sole business.

The subdividing of land parcels by a developer is a time consuming and complex activity. It involves planning and close work between the builder and the escrow holder.

The first step for the builder is acquiring the land and entering into an escrow for the sale of the large parcel to be subdivided.

The next steps require conforming with the regulations of subdivision laws, obtaining approval of a subdivision map, and recording the activity --after the builder receives a final public report from the Real Estate Commissioner. Other state or local requirements may be involved before the developer is allowed to start selling parcels in the subdivision.

At this point, an escrow for the sale of lots in a subdivision involves the basic sale escrow instructions with adaptations to meet specific requirements for the sale of subdivided land.

Leasehold Escrow

An escrow can be required for transactions where fee title is not transferred. In certain instances, a leasehold interest in real property may be transferred from a lessor to a lessee. There are two forms of leases that can be involved in an escrow.

Types of Leaseholds

Land Lease

A land lease conveys the right to use a certain parcel of land and improvements, for a specified number of years, under the terms and conditions described in the lease.

Space Lease

A space lease conveys the right to use a certain suite or unit located on the land. Apartment leases, office space and other commercial uses are common.

In commercial leasing, a large financial investment is usually involved. Because of that, title insurance is particularly important. Leases can be very complex, and determining the validity of a lease can involve many factors. Title insurance is commonly required to protect the investment by assuring the condition of title and providing for a transfer according to the desires of the parties.

Mobile Home Escrow

The primary product in a mobile home escrow is considered personal property. Mobile home escrows can be complicated because of the many regulatory laws and agencies involved in the transfer.

The Mobile Homes Manufactured Housing Act of 1980 is the primary law governing the transfer of mobile homes. It is enforced by the Department of Housing and Community Development.

Certain requirements must be met when a mobile home is sold in California to comply with the law.

Requirements for Escrow to Transfer Ownership in a Mobile Home

- In most cases, an escrow must be used
- A notice of escrow opening must be filed with the Housing and Community Development Department
- The legal owner and any junior lien holders must receive a demand for statements of lien release or assumption
- A demand for a tax clearance certificate must be sent to the county tax collector
- If a part of the consideration is for accessories, that part shall not be released until the accessories are actually installed
- The escrow holder may not be an agency under the Department of Corporations in which the mobile home dealer or seller holds more than 5% ownership interest.
- If the mobile home is to be permanently installed on a foundation, it becomes real property. In that case, the registration requirements and other escrow requirements are changed. A document showing delivery and placement on a foundation must be given to the escrow holder for recording upon close of escrow.

Bulk Transfer

The sale of a business, or business opportunity as it is known, is another personal property escrow transaction.

This type of transaction is known as a bulk sale or bulk transfer, subject to regulations in the Uniform Commercial Code.

The primary reason for the regulation of the sale of a business is to protect creditors of the business, so they can submit unpaid bills for payment before the business is sold to a new owner. The sale must be advertised in local publications to notify creditors and give them time to present a final bill.

BULK ESCROW Standard Documents

Opening Documents

Instruction: Bulk w/Liquor
Instruction: Bulk Sale
Buyer/Seller Information Form
Exhibit "A": Bulk Sec 24074

Exhibit "A": Bulk Sec 6106.2

Commission Inst.: Bulk Sale

Buyer Open Letter: Bulk Sale
Buyer Information: Bulk Sale
Seller Open Letter: Bulk Sale
Seller Information: Bulk Sale
Inventory Form

Landlord Letter

Statement of Information
Bill of Sale
Demand Request
Demand Note
Demand Note: unsecured
Demand Note: Sec. Agreement
Security Agreement
Security Agreement: Str. Note
Security Agreement: Inst. Note
ABC 226: Consideration
ABC 227: Transfer License
Assignment of Lease
Assumption of Lease
Consent to Lease
Assign of Lease-Collateral
Assumption Agreement
State Board of Equalization
Notice to Creditors
Notice to Creditors/Liquor
Notice to Creditors/Assumption

Processing Documents

Amendment s
Seller Proc Letter
Seller Misc. Letter: Bulk

Buyer Proc Letter: Bulk

Buyer Misc. Letter: Bulk

New Lender Processing Letter
Mortgage Broker Process Letter
Private Lender Process Letter
Payoff Process Letter-Institution
Payoff Process Letter-Private
Existing Lender Process Letter
Other Disbursement Letter

Closing Documents

Seller Close Letter: Bulk
Buyer Close Letter: Bulk
New Lender Close Letter

Mortgage Broker Close Letter
Listing Broker Close Letter
Selling Broker Close Letter
Private Lender Close Letter
Payoff Close Letter-Institution
Payoff Close Letter-Private
Existing Lender Close Letter
Other Disbursement Letter

1031 Exchanges

Under section 1031 of the Internal Revenue Code, some or all of the profit or gain from the exchange of one property for another may not have to be immediately recognized for tax purposes.

A tax-free exchange is a legal method of deferring capital gains taxes by exchanging one qualified property for another qualified property. When real estate for investment or for production of income is exchanged for like-kind property, and follows strict Internal Revenue Service requirements, a tax-deferred exchange can take place.

In handling a transaction where the properties are involved in a tax deferred exchange, the escrow holder should be a specialist in exchanges. The law is very precise about whether an exchange qualifies as tax deferred, and the instruments used, the timing of recording and myriad other items must be confronted by the escrow holder in a completely accurate manner. A mistake as small as recording a document out of order could cause the exchange to be disqualified, all parties more than irritated and the escrow holder in great need of legal counsel.

Post Test

The following self test repeats the one you took at the beginning of this chapter. Now take the exam again--since you have read all the material-- and check your knowledge of escrow closing procedures.

True/False

1. Only sale escrows may be conducted by private escrow companies.

2. A loan escrow is used to transfer property which is being sold and funded by a subdivider.

3. A trust deed is sold whenever property transfers ownership.

4. An escrow can be required where fee title is not transferred.

5. Typical leasehold escrows will be a land lease or a space lease.

6. In commercial leasing, title insurance is never used.

7. The primary product in a mobilehome escrow is considered personal property.

8. A mobilehome never becomes real property.

9. Bulk transfer refers to the sale of a business.

10. Capital gains are deferred when a seller completes a 1031 tax free exchange.

chapter 15

ESCROW FOLDER

Focus

- **Introduction**
- **Procedure**
- **Computerized forms**

Pre-Test

The following is a self test to determine how much you know about conducting an escrow before reading this chapter. Take it without studying, then read the material presented in the text. At the end of the chapter you will find a repeat of this exam. Test your knowledge by answering the questions again, then check your improvement. (The answers are found at the end of the book.) Good luck.

True/False

1. The process of conducting an escrow involves two main steps.

2. There is only one kind of escrow.

3. In opening an escrow, the names of the parties, legal description and selling price, among other information, are collected by the escrow holder.

4. Escrow instructions are prepared to direct the escrow holder.

5. Escrow instructions need to be signed only by the seller to make an escrow valid.

6. The escrow holder never prepares a note and trust deed.

7. Closing costs are calculated before the escrow is opened.

8. The down payment is collected by the escrow holder.

9. The escrow holder coordinates with the lender.

10. Escrow instructions are commonly generated by computer.

Introduction

The process of conducting an escrow, while requiring the services of a highly skilled technician, is very simple. As we have seen, it involves three steps; opening the escrow, processing the escrow and finally closing the escrow.

The three basic requirements, however, involve a considerable amount of detail, knowledge, skill, and basic understanding of all the elements of each unique escrow. No two escrows are the same, and yet, every escrow can be linked to another by its similarities; opening, processing and closing.

Procedure

This chapter brings together everything you have learned about conducting an escrow. So far, you have seen forms, disclosures and other documents used by the escrow professional as you have studied each part of the escrow process separately. Here you have a summary of procedures as well as samples of documents you will need to conduct an escrow, from the first introductory document to the final closing documents.

Escrow Checklist

Prepare Escrow Instructions
According to region, bilateral or unilateral instructions, the initial phase of escrow begins with the purchase agreement and introductory documents to open escrow.

Gather Documentation
Grant deeds, trust deeds, quitclaim deeds, notes, bills of sale, security agreements, Uniform Commercial Code forms (financing statements, information requests, termination statements, assignments) must all be collected and prepared.

Order Title Report

The title report gives the escrow holder information about liens such as existing trust deeds, unpaid taxes, judgments or tax liens. Generally, the buyer has the right to approve or disapprove the preliminary title report as a contingency of the sale. The preliminary title report gives all the information included in the final title report which is usually insured in favor of the buyer, seller and/or lender.

Joint Escrow Instructions

Escrow instructions are for the purpose of communicating the intentions of the principals in a transaction to the escrow officer. The escrow officer has a stated time period to accomplish all the necessary tasks delegated by the instructions so the escrow will close in a timely manner according to the wishes of the parties. Commissions must be calculated if there is a broker involved, charges must be listed and made to the correct party and all contingencies must be completed.

SIGN Loan documents

In the presence of a notary public, the borrower agrees to all terms and signs the loan documents.

Prepare to Record

Upon completion of all terms of the agreement between the parties, the escrow officer will authorize the recording of documents necessary to the transfer. All documents, signed instructions and amendments have been deposited and are in the possession of the escrow holder. Good funds have been received and are in the possession of the escrow holder. All conditions of the contract have been satisfied.

Recordation

Upon recordation of grant deed, trust deed or other documents required for the transfer, the sale is complete. The seller gets the money, the broker gets the commission and the buyer gets the property, with the grant deed to follow as soon as it is mailed to him or her by the county recorder. Information about the transfer of ownership is forwarded to the fire insurance company and existing lenders or any other interested parties. A closing statement summarizing the disbursement of funds and costs of the escrow is prepared by the escrow officer and given to each of the parties.

References and Links

http://www.payoffassist.com/

Use this web site to streamline contacting Mortgage Lenders and Loan Servicers.

LANE GUIDE   (http://www.laneguide.com/)
Since 1957, the Lane Guide has been the leading creditors directory used by the industry to locate information concerning payoffs, ratings, verifications, bank/lender mergers, acquisition references and other types of financial information

The Lane Guide offers a complete reference on all banks, savings banks, finance companies, mortgage lenders, loan servicers, credit unions and other major creditors. With the Guide, you get instant access to loan service centers, main offices, loan departments, specialized departments and branch offices.

The Escrow Folder

The escrow folder is a legal file containing all the documents pertaining to the escrow. Checklists are printed directly on front, back and inside, to mark incoming and outgoing documents that need to signed, authorized, notarized, certified, and reviewed, and to account for all monies.

They function as general ledger for the critical transfer of money, and as a legal file for the contracts contained therein. Essentially, the escrow folder is where all the documents are collated, tacked down, and filed according to type and importance.

The front of the folder divides into two columns for buyer and seller, and then into subsets for lenders, lienholders, insurance agents, so that the escrow holder can look at what documents are outstanding at a glance.

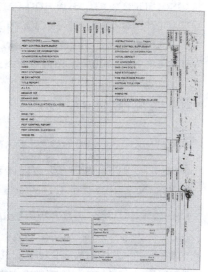

Inside the folder is the escrow status sheet which lists the numerous documents and requirements of the escrow and the date they are ordered, when they are delivered, and if they need signatures or further review. Like any legal file, they must be retained for a period of time, often up to seven years, and then warehoused for retrieval in the event of any legal action arising out of the sale of that property. Each office should develop a record retention policy to ensure that records are stored correctly, and readily available.

The Statute of Limitations for a claim for breach of contract is six years. Certain documents, such as corporate records, partnership agreements, audit reports, general ledgers, tax returns and deeds must be kept permanently.

Standard Documents

Jonathan J. Sellerman, Jr
Betty Jo Sellerman
8907 Elmhurst Avenue
Costa Mesa, CA 92626

Date: June 6, 1999
Escrow No: 1111-DEMO

Re: **8907 Elmhurst Avenue, Costa Mesa, CA 92626**

Dear Mr. & Mrs. Sellerman:

Thank you for selecting SMS to process your escrow. The enclosed items are required in your escrow, please review and comply as noted below and return to us as soon as possible.

SIGN AND RETURN the enclosed items, retain the copy for your records:
Escrow Instructions
Commission Instructions
Misc sign & return enclosure

COMPLETE IN FULL, SIGN AND RETURN the enclosed items:
CAL-FIRPTA 590 Form and/or Certificate
Statement of Information
Loan Information Sheet
IRS 1099 Reporting Form
Misc complete, sign & return enclosure

SIGN AND ACKNOWLEDGE BEFORE A NOTARY PUBLIC <u>EXACTLY</u> as your name(s)
appear on the enclosed items:
Grant Deed
Misc sign before a notary enclosure

Please Furnish the Following:
Misc furnish us with enclosure

All documents should be signed EXACTLY as your name(s) appear. Should your name(s) be misspelled, sign them correctly and advise us in writing when you return these papers.

We appreciate the opportunity to be of service to you in this transaction. Should you have any questions, please call us at the telephone number(s) referenced above.

SMS

Ella Escrowson
Escrow Officer

jjw

431

Escrow Officer: Debbie Weatherwax
Escrow No: 004860
Date: April 24, 1999

SALE ESCROW INSTRUCTIONS

INITIAL DEPOSIT	**5,000.00**
NEW FIRST TRUST DEED TO FILE	**180,000.00**
ADDIITIONAL CASH THROUGH ESCROW	**8,980.17**
TOTAL CONSIDERATION	**$193,980.17**

I/We will hand you the sum of **$8,980.17**, of which the sum of **$5,000.00** shall be handed escrow as the initial deposit upon opening of this escrow. I/We will further hand you any and all sufficient funds for closing costs, expenses and prorations between Buyer and Seller, prior to the close of this escrow.

I/We will deliver to you any executed instruments and or funds required to enable you to comply with these instructions, all of which you are authorized to use, provided that on or before **01/01/1999** you are in a position to order a standard policy of title insurance with the usual title company exceptions, provided that said policy has a liability of at least the amount of the above total consideration, covering the property described as follows:

All that tract and parcel of land located on the northwest corner of the subdivision more commonly known as Rainbow Ridge and being more fully described in Deed Book 123, page 891.

Commonly known as:

21128 Rose, Rancho Santa Margarita, CA 92691 (not verified by escrow holder)

Showing title vested in: **Robert Trabuco and Amelia Trabuco**

FREE FROM ENCUMBRANCES EXCEPT:
1. First installment(s) of the General and Special County, and City (if any) Taxes for the current fiscal year, not delinquent, and taxes for the ensuing year, if any, a lien not yet payable.
2. All taxes, bonds and assessments levied or assessed subsequent to the date of these instructions.
3. Covenants, conditions, restrictions, reservations, rights, rights of way, easements and the exception or reservation of water, oil, gas, minerals, carbons, hydrocarbons or kindred substances on or under said land, now of record, if any, or in the Deed to file.

SMS SETTLEMENT SERVICES IS LICENSED BY THE DEPARTMENT OF CORPORATIONS, STATE OF CALIFORNIA.

PRORATE OR ADJUST THE FOLLOWING ITEMS AS OF DATE OF CLOSE OF ESCROW:

Taxes (based on latest tax bill)   Homeowners Association Dues

Each party signing these instructions has read the additional escrow conditions, general provisions and instructions on the reverse side hereof and approves, accepts and agrees to be bound thereby as though the reverse side hereof appeared over their signatures.

SELLER: **BUYER:**

Jim Getz   Robert Trabuco

Mary Ann Getz   Amelia Trabuco

Escrow Officer: **Debbie Weatherwax**
Date: **April 24, 1999**

Escrow No: **004860**
Page 2

THE CLOSING OF THIS ESCROW IS CONTINGENT UPON:

A. Buyer and property qualifying for new loan set out above. Buyer's execution of loan documents shall constitute Buyer's approval of all terms and conditions contained therein and a satisfaction of this condition.

B. Buyer's approval of a preliminary title report covering the subject property together with any and all exceptions referred to therein, within 5 business days of Buyer's receipt of copies of same from Escrow does not deposit his written disapproval within time limit specified said preliminary title report shall be deemed approved.

INSTRUCTIONS:

1. A new hazard insurance policy to comply with lender's requirements will be delivered to escrow by buyer's agent. The buyer will deposit into his escrow sufficient funds to enable you to pay the premium at close of escrow.

AS A MEMORANDUM AGREEMENT ONLY WITH WHICH ESCROW HOLDER IS NOT TO BE CONCERNED AND/OR LIABLE.

2. All plumbing, electrical, heating and related systems and equipment are to be in working order at the close of escrow.

3. All carpets, drapes, window coverings, attached fixtures and appliances, except any which may be reserved herein, are to remain with subject property at the close of the escrow.

4. Seller herein agrees to maintain subject property in its present condition until possession of subject property is delivered to buyer.

5. Buyers to walk through subject property 7 days prior to close of escrow.

EACH PARTY SIGNING THESE INSTRUCTIONS HAS READ THE ADDITIONAL ESCROW CONDITIONS, GENERAL PROVISIONS AND INSTRUCTIONS ON THE REVERSE SIDE HEREOF AND APPROVES, ACCEPTS AND AGREES TO BE BOUND THEREBY AS THOUGH THE REVERSE SIDE HEREOF APPEARED OVER THEIR SIGNATURES.

SELLER: **BUYER:**

Jim Getz   **Robert Trabuco**

Mary Anne Getz   **Amelia Trabuco**

Escrow Officer: **Debbie Weatherwax**

Date: **April 24, 1999**

Escrow No: **004860**

page 3

BUYER:

SET OUT ON THE FINAL PAGE OF THESE INSTRUCTIONS ARE UNDERSTOOD AND APPROVED IN THEIR ENTIRETY BY EACH OF THE UNDERSIGNED. I AGREE TO PAY ON DEMAND BUYER'S CUSTOMARY COSTS AND CHARGES INCURRED HEREIN, INCLUDING BUT NOT LIMITED TO, RECORDING FEES, DOCUMENT PREPARATION FEES, ONE HALF OF YOUR ESCROW FEE, ANY COSTS INCURRED BY REASON OF ANY FINANCING OBTAINED OR ASSUMED BY ME, ONE-HALF OF ANY TRANSFER FEE CHARGED BY ANY ASSOCIATION COVERING THE SUBJECT PROPERTY, AND ANY OTHER CHARGE INCURRED FOR MY BENEFIT.

SELLER:

THE FOREGOING TERMS, CONDITIONS, PROVISIONS AND INSTRUCTIONS, TOGETHER WITH THE GENERAL PROVISIONS SET OUT ON THE FINAL PAGE OF THESE INSTRUCTIONS ARE UNDERSTOOD, APPROVED AND ACCEPTED IN THEIR

ENTIRETY BY EACH OF THE UNDERSIGNED. I WILL HAND YOU MY EXECUTED GRANT DEED AND/OR OTHER DOCUMENTS OR INSTRUMENTS REQUIRED FROM ME TO CAUSE TITLE TO BE AS SHOWN ABOVE, WHICH YOU ARE AUTHORIZED TO USE AND OR DELIVER WHEN YOU CAN COMPLY WITH THESE INSTRUCTIONS AND WHEN YOU CAN HOLD FOR MY ACCOUNT THE TOTAL CONSIDERATION AS SET FORTH ABOVE (LESS ANY AMOUNT TO BE DEBITED TO MY ACCOUNT SET FORTH BELOW), TOGETHER WITH ANY DOCUMENT(S) EXECUTED IN MY FAVOR.

FROM THE TOTAL CONSIDERATION DUE TO MY ACCOUNT AT THE CLOSE OF ESCROW, YOU ARE AUTHORIZED AND INSTRUCTED TO DEDUCT THE AMOUNT OF ANY REAL ESTATE BROKER'S COMMISSION TO BE PAID BY ME IN ACCORDANCE WITH SEPARATE INSTRUCTIONS, THE AMOUNT OF ANY FUNDS PAID TO ME OUTSIDE OF ESCROW, THE AMOUNT OWING UNDER ANY LIEN OR ENCUMBRANCE TO REMAIN OF RECORD AFTER CLOSE OF ESCROW, THE DEMAND OF ANY LIEN OR ENCUMBRANCE, REQUIRED TO BE PAID TO PLACE TITLE IN THE CONDITION AS CALLED FOR HEREIN, AND SELLER'S CUSTOMARY COSTS AND CHARGES INCURRED HEREIN, INCLUDING, BUT NOT LIMITED TO, THE PREMIUM FOR THE C.L.T.A. OWNER'S POLICY OF TITLE INSURANCE TO BE PROVIDED TO THE BUYER, THE AMOUNT OF ANY DOCUMENTARY TRANSFER TAX OWING ON THE DEED, ONE-HALF OF YOUR ESCROW FEE, RECORDING FEES FOR DOCUMENTS, INSTRUMENTS RECORDED FOR MY BENEFIT, ONE HALF OF ANY TRANSFER FEE CHARGED BY ANY ASSOCIATION COVERING THE SUBJECT PROPERTY, THE COST OF OBTAINING ANY STATEMENT(S) OR DEMAND CONCERNING ANY LIEN OR ENCUMBRANCE OF RECORD, AND ANY OTHER COST OR CHARGE INCURRED FOR MY BENEFIT.

EACH PARTY SIGNING THESE INSTRUCTIONS HAS READ THE ADDITIONAL ESCROW CONDITIONS, GENERAL PROVISIONS AND INSTRUCTIONS ON THE REVERSE SIDE HEREOF AND APPROVES, ACCEPTS AND AGREES TO BE BOUND THEREBY AS THOUGH THE REVERSE SIDE HEREOF APPEARED OVER THEIR SIGNATURES.

SELLER:	BUYER:
Jim Getz	**Robert Trabuco**
Mary Anne Getz	**Amelia Trabuco**

SMS

DocNet
Standard Documents

SALE ESCROW

OPENING DOCUMENTS:

Instruction: Sale
Instruction: Land contract
Instruction: AITD
CAR Deposit Receipt Phrases
Commission Instruction
Status Sheet: Broker/Lender
Status Sheet: Buyer
Status Sheet: Seller
Seller Open Letter

Buyer Open Letter
Loan Information Sheet
Statement of Information
Fire Insurance Info Form
Cal-FRPTA Notice/Disclosure
California 590-RE Form
PCOR

Vesting Worksheet:
Buyer/Borrower
Vesting Worksheet:
Trust/Corporation
1099 Tax Reporting Form

Listing/Selling Broker Open
Letter
New Lender Open Letter

Mortgage Broker Close Letter

Private Beneficiary Open Letter
Beneficiary Statement Request:
Private
Beneficiary Statement Request:
Institutional
Owner's Offset Statement
Rent Statement
Tenant Estoppel Certificate
Third Party Instruction
FRPTA: Notice to Buyer/Seller
FRPTA: Buyer's Exemption1445
FRPTA: Seller's Affidavit
Nonresident Withholding
Statement
Seller Tax Options
Request for Taxpayer ID Number

PROCESSING DOCUMENTS:

Title Open Transmittal
Preliminary title Report Approval
HOA Demand
Demand Request: Institutional
Demand Request: Private
FHA: 30 Day Notice
Instruction Reminder: Seller
Instruction Reminder: Buyer
Trust Certificate: Probate Section
18100.5
Trust Certification
Seller Amendment Letter
Buyer Amendment Letter
Broker Processing Letter
New Lender Processing Letter
Mortgage Broker Process Letter
Private Beneficiary Process Letter

Payoff Lender Process Letter
Fire Insurance Process Letter
Existing Lender Process Letter
Flood Insurance Process Letter
Earthquake Insurance Process
Letter
Pest Company Process Letter
Septic Company Process Letter
Irrevocable Demand: FROM
Escrow
Irrevocable Demand: TO
Escrow
Cancel Escrow Instructions

CLOSING DOCUMENTS

Request for Insurance
Title Docs Transmittal
Funding Letter: Mortgage
Funding Letter: New Lender
Wire Instructions
Buyer Close Letter
Buyer Title Policy Transmittal
Seller Close Letter
Broker Close Letter
New Lenders Close Letter
Mortgage Broker Close Letter
Private Beneficiary Close Letter
Payoff Lenders Close Letter
Existing Lender Close Letter
HOA Close Letter
Fire Insurance Close Letter
Earthquake Insurance Close
Letter
Pest Company Close Letter
Septic Company Close Letter
Nonresident Withholding
Statement
California 597-A Form
Closing Check List

SMS

AMENDMENT TO ESCROW INSTRUCTIONS

Date: **January 18, 1999**   Escrow No: **000020**

RE: **2165 Memory Lane, Santa Ana, CA 92705**

TO: Strategic Mortgage Services

My previous escrow instructions in the above numbered escrow are hereby amended and/or supplemented in the following particulars only:

Type Verbiage or Insert Amendment Clause Here

All other itmes and conditions shall remain the same.

EACH OF THE UNDERSIGNED STATES THAT EACH HAS READ THE FOREGOING INSTRUCTIONS, UNDERSTANDS THEM AND ACKNOWLEDGES RECEIPT OF A COPY OF THESE INSTRUCTIONS.

Michael M. Horton   Robert R. Mullins

Linda L. Horton   Margie M. Mullins

SMS

Escrow No. :1111-DEMO

Date: April 6, 1999

RE: 8907 Elmhurst Avenue, Costa Mesa, CA 92626

Escrow Officer: Ella Escrowson

INSTRUCTIONS TO PAY COMMISSION

Upon close of escrow, from funds received and/or held by you on my behalf you are instructed to pay;

Wimbush Realty
a licensed real estate broker, the sum of $5,300.00

Grubb & Ellis Company
a licensed real estate broker, the sum of $5,300.00

TO COMPLETE A TOTAL $10,600.00
COMMISSION IN THE SUM OF

The employment of said broker(s) to effect the transaction of the above described property described in said escrow is acknowledged by the undersigned, who has agreed to pay sum to said broker(s) as a commission for services rendered pursuant to said employment.

This is an IRREVOCABLE COMMISSION ORDER and cannot be amended or revoked, insofar as it relates to payment of commission, without the prior written consent of broker(s) named herein, who shall be deemed a party to the escrow for the sale and exclusive purpose of receiving said commission.

_____

Jonathan J. Sellerman,   Jr. Betty Jo Sellerman

Please mail payment(s) to address(s) below, unless payment is called for on the day this escrow is closed.

Frank Allen - Wimbush Realty

By:_____
License No. :11111111
Address :890 W. Baker Street, Costa Mesa, CA 92627

Mary Allen - Grubb & Ellis Company

By:_____
License No. :22222222
Address :4000 MacArthur Blvd., Newport Beach, CA 92660

SMS

Statement of Information

FILL OUT COMPLETELY AND RETURN TO STRATEGIC MORTGAGE SERVICES

ESCROW #00020-SMS   TRACT#   LOT#

Name_____ Social Security #_____ Driver's License#_____

Date of Birth_____ Place of Birth_____ Bus. Phone_____ Home Phone_____

Resided in USA since_____ Resided in California since_____

If you are married, please complete the following: Date Married_____at_____

Name of Spouse_____ Social Security #_____Driver's License #_____

Resided in USA since_____ Resided in California since_____

Previous Marriage or Marriages (if no previous marriage, write "None"):
Name of former spouse_____ Deceased___Divorced____Where____When____
Name of former spouse_____ Deceased___Divorced____Where____When____

Children by current or previous Marriages:
Name_____ Born_____ Name_____ Born_____
Name_____ Born_____ Name_____ Born_____

Information covering past 10 years:

Residence: _____
    Number/Street City   From   To

    _____
    Number/Street City   From   To

Employment _____
    Firm Name   Location

    _____
    Firm Name   Location

Spouse Employment: _____
    Firm Name   Location

    _____
    Firm Name   Location

Have you or your spouse owned or operated a business?
☐Yes   ☐No   If so please list names_____

I have never been adjudged, bankrupt, nor are there any unsatisfied judgments or other matters pending
against me which might affect my title to this property except as follow:

_____

The undersigned declare, under penalty of perjury, that the foregoing is true and correct.
Executed on_____ at_____
     date   city
            Signature

SMS SETTLEMENT SERVICES

RECEIPT FOR DEPOSIT

RECEIPT #002392

OFFICE: 999

DATE 02/27/1999   ESCROW NO.004861-DW

RECEIVED OF Bank of America

ESCROW NAME Getz/Trabuco

TYPE OF TRANSACTION Loan Proceeds

IN THE AMOUNT OF   IN THE FORM
$80,008.13   OF_____

BY_____

NOTICE OF RIGHT TO EARN INTEREST ON DEPOSITED FUNDS

Interest may be earned on all deposited funds by requesting the Escrow Officer who is handling your transaction to place the escrowed funds into an interest bearing account. The Escrow Officers Agent's charge to set up such an account is $50.00. Your funds will earn interest at the prevailing rate of interest paid by the federally insured financial institution where your funds would be deposited [for example, in a typical transaction, a $1,000.00 deposit for a thirty day (30) period with the prevailing interest rate of 6% per annum would earn $4.93].

(Accounting Copy)

SMS

REQUEST FOR DEMAND

December 29, 1999   Escrow No: **004860**

Attn: Payoff Department
All Lenders Mortgage
1212 N. Main Street
Santa Ana, CA 92705

RE: LOAN NUMBER: 1022290-09
    BORROWER: Jim Getz and Mary Anne Getz

An escrow has been opened with our company by the above reference borrowers and provides for the payment in full of the loan number referenced above. Your loan encumbers the real property described as:

See Exhibit A attached hereto and made a part hereof.

The property is commonly known as **21128 Rose, Rancho Santa Margarita, CA 92691**

We hereby request that you forward your **ORIGINAL DEMAND,** together with either (1) the original Note, Deed of Trust securing same and your executed Request for Full Reconveyance, or (2) your executed Full Reconveyance, to the following title company:

American Title Company
ATTN: Mary Ann Snow
10229 Main Street
Santa Ana, CA 92699
RE: TITLE ORDER No: 4860

Please fax a copy of your DEMAND to our office at (714) 549-0684 with an additional copy in the mail.

We wish to thank you for your cooperation and assistance. Please be sure to call our office if you have any questions concerning this matter.

Sincerely,

Debbie Weatherwax
Escrow Officer

RECORDING REQUESTED BY
SMS SETTLEMENT SERVICES
AND WHEN RECORDED MAIL TO:

| REC |
| RCF |
| MICRO |
| RTCF |
| LIEN |
| SMPF |
| PCOR |

Name: Robert Trabuco
Street Address: 21128 Rose
City, State: Mission Viejo, CA
Zip: 92691

Order No. 004860-DW

Space Above This Line for Recorder's Use

DEED OF TRUST WITH ASSIGNMENT OF RENTS

This DEED OF TRUST, made **January 1, 1999**, between **Robert Trabuco and Amelia Trabuco** herein called TRUSTOR,
whose address is **542 Paramount Drive, Chino Hills, CA**

SMS SETTLEMENT SERVICES, a California Corporation, herein called TRUSTEE and **Jim Getz, An Unmarried Man and Mary Anne Getz**, herein called BENEFICIARY, Trustor irrevocably grants, transfers and assigns to Trustee in Trust, with Power of Sale, that property in City of **Mission Viejo,** County of **Los Angeles**, California, described as:

All that tract and parcel of land located on the northwest corner of the subdivision more commonly known as Rainbow Ridge and being more fully described in Deed Book 123, page 891.

Together with the rents, issues and profits thereof, subject, however, to the right, power and authority hereinafter given to and conferred upon Beneficiary to collect and apply such rents, issues and profits. For the Purpose of Securing (1) payment of the sum of $180,000.00 with interest thereon according to the terms of a promissory note or notes of even date herewith made by Trustor, payable to order of Benficiary, and extensions or renewals thereof; (2) the performance of each agreement of Trustor incorporated by reference or contained herein or reciting it is so secured; (3) Payment of additional sums and interest thereon which may hereafter be loaned to Trustor, or his successors or assigns, when evidenced by a promissory note or notes reciting that they are secured by this Deed of Trust.

441

To protect the security of this Deed of Trust, and with respect to the property above described, Trustor expressly makes each and all of the agreements, and adopts and agrees to perform and be bound by each and all of the terms and provisions set forth in subdivision A of that certain Fictitious Deed of Trust reference herein, and it is mutually agreed that all of the provisions set forth in subdivision B of that certain Fictitious Deed of Trust recorded in the book and page of Official Records in the office of the county recorder of the county where said property is located, noted below opposite the name of such county:

Said agreements, terms and provisions contained in said Subdivision A and B, (identical in all counties are printed on the reverse side hereof) are by the within reference thereto, incorporated herein and made a part of this Deed of Trust for all purposes as fully as if set forth at length herein and Beneficiary may charge for a statement regarding the obligation secured hereby, provided the charge therefor does not exceed the maximum allowed by laws.

The foregoing assignment of rents is absolute unless initiated here, in which case, the assignment serves as additional security.

The undersigned Trustor, requests that a copy of any notice of default and any notice of sale hereunder be mailed to him at this address hereinbefore set forth.

Dated: __January 1, 1999__

STATE OF CALIFORNIA   **Robert Trabuco**
COUNTY OF_____   _____
                                            Amelia Trabuco
On_____before me.

a Notary Public in and for said County and State, personally appeared:

_____

_____

Personally known to me (or proved to me on the basis of satisfactory evidence whose name(s) is/are subscribed to the within instrument and acknowledged to me that he/she/they executed the same in his/her/their authorized capacity(ies) and that by his/her/their signature(s) on the instrument the person(s) or the entity upon behalf of which the person(s) acted, executed the instrument.

WITNESS my hand and official seal.

Signature_____   **(This area for official notorial seal)**

The following is a copy of Subdivision A and B of the fictitious Deed of Trust recorded in each county in California as stated in the foregoing Deed of Trust and incorporated by reference is said Deed of Trust as being a part thereof as if set forth at lenght therein.

A. To protect the security of this Deed of Trust, Trustor agrees:

(1) To keep said property in good condition and repair not to remove or demolish any building thereon; to complete or restore promptly and in good and workmanlike manner any building which may be constructed, damaged or destroyed thereon and to pay when due all claims for labor performed and materials furnished therefor; to comply with all laws affecting said property or requiring any alterations or improvements to be made thereon, not to commit or permit waste thereof; not to commit, suffer or permit any act upon said property in violation of law, to cultivate, irrigate, fertilize, fumigate, prune and do all other acts which from the character or use of said property may be reasonably necessary, the specific enumerations herein not excluding the general.

(2) To provide, maintain and deliver to Beneficiary fire insurance satisfactory to and with loss payable to Beneficiary. The amount collected under any fire or other insurance policy may be applied by Beneficiary upon any indebtedness secured hereby and in such order Beneficiary may determine, or at option of Beneficiary the entire amount so collected or any part thereof may be released to Trustor. Such application or release shall not cure or waive any default or notice of default hereunder or invalidate any act done pursuant to such notice.

(3) To appear in and defend any action or proceeding purporting to affect the security hereof or the rights or powers of Beneficiary or Trustee; and to pay all costs and expenses, including cost of evidence of title and attorney's fees in a reasonable sum, in any such action or proceeding in which Beneficiary or Trustee may appear, and in any suit brought by Beneficiary to foreclose this Deed.

(4) To pay: at least ten days before delinquency all taxes and assessments affecting said property, including assessments on appurtent water stock; when due, all incumbrances, charges and liens with interest, on said property or any part thereof, which appear to be prior or superior hereto; all costs, fees and expenses of this Trust.

Should Trustor fail to make any payment or to do any act as herein provided, then Beneficiary or Trustee, but without obligation so to do and without notice to or demand upon Trustor and without releasing Trustor from any obligation hereof, may: make or do the same in such manner and to such extent as either may deem necessary to protect the security hereof, Beneficiary or Trustee being authorized to enter upon said property for such purposes; appear in and defend any action or proceeding purporting to affect the security hereof or the rights or powers of Beneficiary or Trustee; pay, purchase, contest or compromise any incumbrance, charge or lien which in the judgment of either appears to be prior or superior hereto; and, in exercising any such powers, pay necessary expenses, employ counsel and pay his reasonable fees.

(5) To pay immediately and without demand all sums so expended by Beneficiary or Trustee, with interest from date of expenditure at the amount allowed by law in effect at the date hereof, and to pay for any statement provided for by law in effect at the date hereof regarding the obligation secured hereby any amount demanded by the Beneficiary not to exceed the maximum allowed by law at the time when said statement is demanded.

B. It is mutually agreed:

(1) That any award of damages in connection with any condemnation for public use of or injury to said property or any part therof is hereby assigned and shall be paid to Beneficiary who may apply or release such moneys received by him in the same manner and with he same effect as above provided for disposition of proceeds of fire or other insurance.

(2) That by accepting payment of any sum secured hereby after its due date, Beneficiary does not waive his right either to require prompt payment when due of all other sums so secured or to declare default for failure so to pay.

443

(3)   That at any time or from time to time, without liability therefor and without notice, upon written request of Beneficiary and presentation of this Deed and said note for endorsement, and without affecting the personal liability of any person for payment of the indebtedness secured hereby, Trustee may: reconvey any part of said property, consent to the making of any map or plate thereof; join in granting any easement thereon; or join in any extension agreement or any agreement subordinating the lien or charge hereof.

(4)   That upon written request of beneficiary stating stat all sums secured hereby have been paid, and upon said note to Trustee for cancellation and retention or other disposition as Trustee in its sole discretion may choose and upon payment of its fees; Trustee shall reconvey, without warranty, the property, then hereunder. The recitals in such reconveyance of any matter or facts shall be conclusive proof of the truthfulness thereof. The Grantee in such reconveyance may be described as "the person or persons legally entitled thereto."

(5)   That as additional security, Trustor hereby gives to and confers the right, power and authority, during the continuances of these Trusts, to collect the rents, issues and profits of said property, reserving unto Trustor the right, prior to any default by Trustor in payment of any indebtedness secured hereby or in performance of any agreement hereunder, to collect and retain such rents, issues and profits as they become due and payable. Upon any such default, Beneficiary may at any time without notice, either in person, by agent, or by a receiver to be appointed by a court, and without regard to the adequacy of any security for the indebtedness hereby secured, enter upon and take possession of said property or any part thereof, in his own name sue for or otherwise collect such rents, issues, and profits, including those past due and unpaid, and apply the same, less costs and expenses of operation and collection, including reasonable attorney's fees, upon any indebtedness secure hereby, and in such order as Beneficiary may determine. The entering upon and taking possession of said property, the collection of such rents, issues and profits and the application therof as aforesaid, shall not cure or waive any default hereunder or invalidate any act done pursuant to such notice.

(6)   That upon default by Trustor in payment of any indebtedness secured hereby or in performance of any agreement hereunder, Beneficiary may declare all sums secured hereby immediately due and payable by delivery to Trustee of written declaration of default and demand for sale and of written notice of default and of election to cause to be sold said property, which notice Trustee shall cause to be filed for record. Beneficiary also shall deposit with Trustee this Deed, said note and all documents evidencing expenditures secured hereby.

After the lapse of such time as may then be rquired by law following the recordation of said notice of default, and notice of sale having been given as then required by law, Trustee, without demand on Trustor, shall sell said property at the time and place fixed by it in said notice of sale, either as a whole or in separate parcels, and in such order as it may determine, at public auction to the highest bidder for cash in lawful money of the United States, payable at time of sale. Trustee may postpone sale of all or any portion of siad property by public announcement at such time and place of sale, and from time to time thereafter may postpone such sale by public announcment at the time fixed by the preceding postponement. Trustee shall deliver to such purchase its deed conveying the property so sold, but without any covenant or warranty, express or implied. The recitals in such deed of any matters or facts shall be conclusive proof of the truthfulness therof. Any person, including Trustor, Trustee, or Beneficiary as hereinafter defined, may purchase at such sale.

After deducting all costs, fees and expenses of Trustee and of this Trust, including cost of evidence of title in connection with sale, Trustee shall apply the proceeds of sale to payment of all sums expended under the terms hereof, not then repaid, with accrued interest at the amount allowed by law in effect at the date hereof; all other sums then secured hereby; and the remainder, if any, to the persons legally entitled thereto.

(7)   Beneficiary, or any successor in ownership of any indebtedness secured hereby, may from time to time, by instrument in writing, substitute a successor or succesors to any Trustee named herein or acting hereunder, which instrument, executed by the Beneficiary and duly acknowledged and recorded in the office of the recorder of the county or counties where said property is situated, shall be conclusive proof of proper substitution of such successor Trustee or Trustees, who shall, without

conveyance from the Trustee predecessor, succeed to all its title, estate, rights, powers and duties. Said instrument must contain the name of the original Trustor, Trustee and Beneficiary hereunder, the book and page where this Deed is recorded and the name and address of the new Trustee.

(8) That this Deed applies to, insures to the benefit of, and binds all parties hereto, their heirs, legatees, devisees, administrators, executors, successors and assigns. The term Beneficiary shall mean the owner and holder, including pledges, of the note secured hereby, whether or not named as Beneficiary herein. In this Deed, whenever the context so requires, the masculine gender includes the feminine and/or neuter, and the singular number includes the plural.

9) That Trustee accepts this Trust when this Deed, duly executed and acknowledged, is made a public record as provided by law. Trustee is not obligated to notify any party hereto of pending sale under any other Deed of Trust or of any action or proceeding in which Trustor, Beneficiary or Trustee shall be a party unless brought by Trustee.

DO NOT RECORD

TO SMS SETTLEMENT SERVICES COMPANY TRUSTEE   **REQUEST FOR FULL RECONVEYANCE**

The undersigned is the legal owner and holder of the note or notes, and of all other indebtedness secured by the foregoing Deed of Trust. Said note or notes, together with all other indebtedness secured by said Deed of Trust, have been fully paid and satisfied, and you are hereby requested and directed, on payment to you of any sums owing to you under the terms of said Deed of Trust, to cancel said note or notes above mentioned, and all other evidences of indebtedness secured by said Deed of Trust delivered to you herewith, together with the said Deed of Trust, and to reconvey, withour warranty, to the parties designated by the terms of said Deed of Trust, all the estate now held by you under the same.

Dated_____   _____

                                      _____

SIGNATURE MUST BE NOTARIZED

Please mail Deed of Trust,
Note and Reconveyance to_____

Do not lose or destroy this Deed of Trust OR THE NOTE which it secures. Both must be delivered to the Trustee for cancellation before reconveyance will be made.

South County Escrow Co.
8754 W. Camino Capistrano
San Juan Capistrano, CA 92624

1099 ESCROW REPORTING DOCUMENT   W-9

Escrow ID_____   Settlement Date:_____

Contract Sales Price:$_____

Property Address:_____

City_____   State_____   Zip_____

Buyer's Name:_____

Address:_____

City_____   State_____   Zip_____

CERTIFICATION - Under penalties of perjury, I certify that:
(1) The number shown on this form is my correct Taxpayer Identification Number
(2) I am not subject to backup withholding either because I have not been notified by the Internal Revenue Service (IRS) that I am subject to backup withholding as a result of a failure to report all interest or dividends or the IRS has notified me that I am no longer subject to backup withholding.
(3) The value of all cash, property and services I received is equal to my percent of ownership based on contract sales price.
Certification Instructions - You must cross out item (2) above if you have been notified by IRS that you are subject to backup withholding because of under reporting interest or dividends on your tax return. However, if after being notified by IRS that you were subject to backup withholding, you received another notification from IRS that you are no longer subject to backup withholding, do not cross out item (2).
Escrow officer is hereby authorized to forward this information to McGinnis & Zink.

Seller's name	Tax ID or Social Security No.	Percent of Ownership

Forwarding Address		Amount Withheld

City, State and Zip	Seller's Signature

Seller's name	Tax ID or Social Security No.	Percent of Ownership

Forwarding Address		Amount Withheld

City, State and Zip	Seller's Signature

PLEASE COMPLETE, SIGN AND RETURN
501 Parkcenter Drive, Santa Ana, CA 92705 (714) 550-1254
White: McGinnis & Zink Yellow: Branch

TITLE ORDER

December 29, 1999   ESCROW No.: 004860

ATTN; Mary Ann Snow
American Title Company
10229 Main Street
Santa Ana, CA 92699

RE: TITLE ORDER No.: 4860

PLEASE ACCEPT THIS AS OUR REQUEST FOR THE FOLLOWING POLICY(IES):
]CLTA $ 189,900.00   1.JOINT PROTECTION   ]ALTA $ 80,000.00

on property described as follows:

All that tract and parcel of land located on the northwest corner of the subdivision more commonly known as Rainbow Ridge and being more fully described in Deed Book 123, page 891.

Subject Property is commonly known as: 21128 Rose, Rancho Santa Margarita, CA 92691

Present Owner's Name: Jim Getz

WE ENCLOSE THE FOLLOWING:
1. Statements of information from Robert Trabuco Amelia Trabuco Jim Getz Mary Ann Getz
2. Grant Deed from Jim Getz, An Unmarried Man and Mary Ann Getz to Robert Trabuco and Amelia Trabuco
3. First Deed of Trust to record in favor of Bank of America, in the amount of $180,000.00
4. Note/Deed of Trust

UPON FURTHER AUTHORIZATION you are to record all instruments without collection when you can issue said form of Policy showing Title vesting in:

        Robert Trabuco and Amelia Trabuco

FREE FROM ENCUMBRANCES EXCEPT:
  1. ALL general and Special Taxes for the Fiscal Year 1999
  2. Covenants, Conditions, Restrictions, Easements and Rights of Way of record.
  3. Bonds and assessments not delinquent.
  4. Deeds of Trust now of record in the amount of $89,000.90
  5. New First Deed of Trust to record in favor of Bank of America

PLEASE ABSTRACT ALL DOCUMENTS AND ADVISE US IMMEDIATELY IF ANY CORRECTIONS ARE NEEDED

Please send the original policy(ies) and/or copies as appropriate to:

Bank of America   SMS SETTLEMENT SERVICES
27571 Trabuco Road   3160 Airway Avenue
Mission Viejo, CA 92674   Costa Mesa, CA 92621

If you have questions, please do not hesitate to contact our office.
Thank you.

Debbie Weatherwax
ESCROW OFFICER

January 17, 1999   Escrow No: 000020

Robert R. Mullins
306 Dublin Lane
Costa Mesa, CA 92626

RE: 2165 Memory Lane, Santa Ana, CA 92705

Dear Robert R. Mullins and Margie M. Mullins:

In connection with the above referenced escrow, we are enclosing the following items:

Please examine the following, and if they meet with your approval, sign and return. Copies are enclosed for your records.

> **Escrow Instructions**
> **Amendment(s)**
> **FHA/VA Supplemental Instructions**
> **Note**
> **Preliminary Title Report**

Please sign the following documents as indicated and return them to our office. Note that each signature on all documents **MUST BE ACKNOWLEDGED BY A NOTARY PUBLIC**. Please be sure to sign your name exactly as it is typed.

> **Grant Deed**
> **Quitclaim Deed**
> **Corporation Grant Deed**
> **Deed of Trust**

Please **complete**, sign and return the following:

> **Statement of Information**
> **Preliminary Change of Ownership**
> **Loan Information Sheet**

Your prompt attention to these items and their return to our office will assist us in the completion of your escrow. We are pleased to have been selected to service your escrow needs. If there is any way we may be of further assistance, please do no hesitate to contact our office.

Sincerely,

System A. User
Escrow Officer

December 29, 1999   Escrow NO. 004860

Robert Trabuco
21128 Rose
Rancho Santa Margarita, CA 92691

RE: **21128 Rose, Rancho Santa Margarita, CA 92691**

Dear Robert Trabuco and Amelia Trabuco:

The above referenced escrow closed on 01/01/1999. The following items enclosed for you and your records:

> **Check in the amount of $102.50**
> **Closing Statement**
> **HUD Settlement Statement**
> **Termite Report and Completion**

Please be advised that we will forward the Policy of Title Insurance to you upon our receipt of same. Any original documents recorded for your benefit will be forwarded to you directly from the County Recorder's office.

TAX INFORMATION

The next installment of property taxes must be paid by June 1, 2000 to avoid penalty. Tax bills are furnished to you as an accommodation of the Tax Assessor's Office, USUALLY by November 1st each year. In the event you do not receive a tax bill for this property at least a month prior to the delinquency date, contact the Tax Assessor's Office to request a duplicate billing. The payment of taxes is your responsibility; if they are not paid prior to the delinquency date, penalties will be assessed.

For any additional taxes which may be due by reason of the change in ownership. Supplemental Tax Bills will be sent to you from the Tax Collector separately from your regular tax bill. You normally must pay these taxes by a delinquency date which is separate from the regualr tax billing. Please read these supplemental tax bills for the particulars concerning same and contact the Tax Assessor's Office with any questions you may have.

It has been a pleasure handling this transaction for you. Please do not hesitate to contact our office if you have any questions regarding this matter.

Sincerely,

Debbie Weatherwax
Escrow Officer

LOAN INFORMATION SHEET

January 18, 1995   Escrow No: 000020

RE: 2165 Memory Lane, Santa Ana, CA 92705

In order to proceed with the above referenced escrow, we need the following information about your property. **PLEASE COMPLETE.** **SIGN, AND RETURN** this form to our office as soon as possible.

FIRST   Name of Lender _____
LOAN: Address _____
                 Loan Number _____ Approximate unpaid balance _____

SECOND   Name of Lender _____
LOAN: Address _____
                 Loan Number _____ Approximate unpaid balance _____

ADDITIONAL ENCUMBRANCE

Third Trust Deed ☐   Pool Loan ☐   Home Improvement Loan ☐   Lien ☐

Lienholder Name _____
Address _____
Account No_____ Approximate unpaid balance _____

If your property is affected by a Community Association please complete the following:

Name of Association _____
Name of Management Company_____
Address _____
Account No_____

If you have shares of Water Stock please complete the following:

Name of Water Company _____
Address: _____

FORWARDING ADDRESS AFTER CLOSE OF ESCROW:

_____
_____

INSURANCE INFORMATION

Name of Insurance Company_____

Agent's name _____ Phone No. _____
Address _____
Policy Number _____ Expiration Date_____

We, the undersigned, certify that the above information is true and correct to the best of our knowledge.

_____   _____
Michael M. Horton   Linda L. Horton

3160 Airway Ave. Costa Mesa, CA 92626 (714) 549-5700 (714) 549-0684

YEAR

CALIFORNIA FORM

Withholding Exemption Certificate

1995   (For use by Individuals, corporations, partnerships and estates)

590

File this form with your withholding agent.

Name
Michael M. Horton and Linda L. Horton

Address (number and street)
2165 Memory Lane

Telephone number

City
Santa Ana, CA 92705

State

ZIP code

Complete the appropriate line: Individuals - Social security no. **545-33-5345** ☑ Married ☐ Single

Corporations - California corporation no. _____ (Issued by Secretary of State)

Partnerships and - F.E.I.N. _____

To **Strategic Mortgage Services** _____
      (Withholding Agent or Payer)

Individuals:

Certificate of Residency

I hereby declare under penalty perjury that I am a resident of California and that I reside at the address shown above.

Signature _____ Date _____

Certificate of Residency of Deceased Person

I hereby certify under penalty of perjury, as executor of the above named person's estate that decedent was a California resident at the time of death.

Name of Executor (type or print)_____ Date _____

Signature _____

Certificate of Principal Residence (Real estate sales only)

I hereby certify under penalty of perjury that the California real property located at **2165 Memory Lane** _____
Santa Ana, CA 92705 was my principal residence within the meaning of IRC Section 1034.

Signature _____ Date _____

Corporations:

I hereby certify the above-named corporation has a permanent place of business in California at the address shown above or is qualified to do business in California.

Signature _____ Date _____

Title of corporate officer_____

Tax Exempt Entities and Non Profit Organizations:

I hereby certify, under penalty of perjury, that the above-named entity is exempt from tax under California or Federal law.

Name and Title _____

Signature _____ Date _____

Trusts:

I hereby certify, under penalty of perjury, that at least one trustee of the above-named trust is a California resident.

Name and Title _____

Signature _____ Date _____

PRELIMINARY CHANGE OF OWNERSHIP REPORT

To be completed by transferee (buyer) prior to transfer of subject property in accordance with Section 480.03 of the Revenue and Taxation Code. A Preliminary Change of Ownership Report must be filed with each conveyance in the County Recorder's office for the county where the property is located; this particular form may be used in all 58 counties of California.

THIS REPORT IS NOT A PUBLIC DOCUMENT

FOR RECORDER'S USE ONLY

SELLER/TRANSFEROR: Michael M. Horton and Linda L. Horton
BUYER/TRANSFEREE: Robert R. Mullins and Margie M. Mullins
ASSESSOR'S PARCEL NUMBER(S) 123-45-6789
PROPERTY ADDRESS OR LOCATION:

2165 Memory Lane
Santa Ana, CA 92705

MAIL TAX INFORMATION TO:

Name   Robert R. Mullins
Address 2165 Memory Lane

Costa Mesa, CA 92626

NOTICE: A lien for property taxes applies to your property on March 1 of each year for the taxes owing in the following fiscal year, July 1 through June 30. One-half of these taxes is due November 1, and one-half is due February 1. The first installment becomes delinquent on December 10, and the second installment becomes delinquent on April 10. One tax bill is mailed before November 1 to the owner of record. **IF THIS TRANSFER OCCURS AFTER MARCH 1 AND ON OR BEFORE DECEMBER 31, YOU MAY BE RESPONSIBLE FOR THE SECOND INSTALLMENT OF TAXES DUE FEBRUARY 1.**

The property which you acquired may be subject to a supplemental assessment in an amount to be determined by the Orange County Assessor. For further information on your supplemental roll obligation, please call the Orange County Assessor at 714-834-2727.

PART I: TRANSFER INFORMATION   Please answer all questions.

YES	NO		
☐	☑	A.	Is this transfer solely between husband and wife (Addition of a spouse, death of a spouse, divorce settlement, etc.)?
☐	☑	B.	Is this transaction only a correction of the name(s) of the person(s) holding title to the property (For example, a name change upon marriage)?
☐	☑	C.	Is this document recorded to create, terminate, or reconvey a lender's interest in the property?
☐	☑	D.	Is this transaction recorded only to create, terminate, or reconvey a security interest (e.g. cosigner)?
☐	☑	E.	Is this document recorded to substitute a trustee under a deed of trust, mortgage, or other similar document?
☐	☑	F.	Did this transfer result in the creation of a joint tenancy in which the seller (transferor) remains as one of the joint tenants?
☐	☑	G.	Does this transfer return property to the person who created the joint tenancy (original transferor)?
		H.	Is this transfer of property:
☐	☑		1. to a trust for the benefit of the grantor, or grantor's spouse?
☐	☑		2. to a trust revocable by the transferor?
☐	☑		3. to a trust from which the property reverts to the grantor within 12 years?
☐	☑	I.	If this property is subject to a lease, is the remaining lease term 35 years or more including written options?
☐	☑	J.	Is this a transfer from parents to children or from children to parents?
☐	☑	K.	Is this transaction to replace a principal residence by a person 55 years of age or older?
☐	☑	L.	Is this transaction to replace a principal residence by a person who is severely disabled as defined by Revenue and Code Section 69.5?

If you checked yes to J, K, or L, an applicable claim form must be filed with the County Assessor.
Please provide any other information that would help the Assessors to understand the nature of the transfer.

IF YOU HAVE ANSWERED "YES" TO ANY OF THE ABOVE QUESTIONS EXCEPT J, K, OR L, PLEASE SIGN AND DATE, OTHERWISE COMPLETE BALANCE OF THE FORM.

PART II: OTHER TRANSFER INFORMATION

A. Date of transfer if other than recording date _____.
B. Type of transfer. Please check appropriate box.
   ☑ Purchase   ☐ Foreclosure   ☐ Gift   ☐ Trade or Exchange   ☐ Merger, Stock, or Partnership Acquisition
   ☐ Contract of Sale - Date of Contract _____
   ☐ Inheritance - Date of Death _____   ☐ Other: Please explain: _____
   ☐ Creation of Lease   ☐ Assignment of a Lease   ☐ Termination of a Lease
   Date lease began _____
   Original term in years (including written options) _____
   Remaining term in years (including written options) _____
C. Was only a partial interest in the property transferred? ☐ Yes   ☑ No   If yes, indicate the percentage transferred _____%

PRELIMINARY CHANGE OF OWNERSHIP REPORT

Please answer, to the best of your knowledge, all applicable questions, sign and date. If a question does not apply, indicate with "N/A."

PART III: PURCHASE PRICE AND TERMS OF SALE

A. CASH DOWN PAYMENT OR Value of Trade or Exchange (excluding closing costs) — Amount $5,000.00

B. FIRST DEED OF TRUST @ 7.57% interest for 30 years. Pymts./Mo.=$857.00 (Prin. & Int. only) — Amount $80,000.00

☐ FHA	☑ Fixed Rate	☑ New Loan
☑ Conventional	☐ Variable Rate	☐ Assumed Existing Loan Balance
☐ VA	☐ All inclusive D.T. ($ _____ Wrapped)	☑ Bank or Savings & Loan
☐ Cal-Vet	☐ Loan Carried by Seller	☐ Finance Company

Balloon Payment ☐ Yes ☑ No   Due Date _____ Amount $_____

C. SECOND DEED OF TRUST @ _____% interest for _____years. Pymts/Mo.=$_____(Prin. & Int. only)   Amount $_____

☐ Bank or Savings & Loan	☐ Fixed Rate	☐ New Loan
☐ Loan Carried by Seller	☐ Variable Rate	☐ Assumed Existing Loan Balance

Balloon Payment ☐ Yes ☐ No   Due Date _____ Amount $_____

D. OTHER FINANCING: Is other financing involved not covered in (b) or (c) above? ☐ Yes ☑ No   Amount $_____
Type_____ @ _____% interest for _____years. Pymts./Mo.=$_____(Prin. & Int. only)

☐ Bank or Savings & Loan	☐ Fixed Rate	☐ New Loan
☐ Loan Carried by Seller	☐ Variable Rate	☐ Assumed Existing Loan Balance

Balloon Payment ☐ Yes ☑ No   Due Date _____ Amount $_____

E. IMPROVEMENT BOND ☐ Yes ☑ No   Outstanding Balance: Amount $_____

F. TOTAL PURCHASE PRICE (or acquisition price, if traded or exchanged, include real estate commission if paid.)

Total Items A through E $ 100,000.00

G. PROPERTY PURCHASED ☑ Through a broker ☐ Direct from seller ☐ Other (explain)_____

If purchased through a broker, provide broker's name and phone number: Century One Real Estate (714) 555-7676
_____

Please explain any special terms or financing and any other information that would help the Assessor understand the purchase price and terms of sale.
_____
_____
_____

PART IV: PROPERTY INFORMATION

A. IS PERSONAL PROPERTY INCLUDED IN PURCHASE PRICE
(other than a mobilehome subject to local property tax)? ☐ Yes ☑ No
If yes, enter the value of the personal property included in the purchase price $_____ (Attach itemized list of personal property).

B. IS THIS PROPERTY INTENDED AS YOUR PRINCIPAL RESIDENCE? ☑ Yes ☐ No
If yes, enter date of occupancy _____/_____/_____ or intended occupancy 02/01/1995
Month Day Year   Month Day Year

C. TYPE OF PROPERTY TRANSFERRED:

☑ Single-family residence	☐ Agricultural	☐ Timeshare
☐ Multiple-family residence (no. of units: _____)	☐ Co-op/Own-your-own	☐ Mobilehome
☐ Commercial/Industrial	☐ Condominium	☐ Unimproved lot
☐ Other (Description: _____)		

D. DOES THE PROPERTY PRODUCE INCOME? ☐ Yes ☑ No

E. IF THE ANSWER TO QUESTION D IS YES, IS THE INCOME FROM:
☐ Lease/Rent ☐ Contract ☐ Mineral Rights ☐ Other - Explain: _____

F. WHAT WAS THE CONDITION OF PROPERTY AT THE TIME OF SALE?
☑ Good ☐ Average ☐ Fair ☐ Poor

Enter here, or on an attached sheet, any other information that would assist the Assessor in determining the value of the property such as the physical condition of the property, restrictions, etc.
_____
_____
_____

I certify that the foregoing is true, correct and complete to the best of my knowledge and belief.

Signed_____   Dated_____
NEW OWNER/CORPORATE OFFICER

Please Print Name of New Owner/Corporate Officer Robert R. Mullins and Margie M. Mullins

Phone Number where you are available from 8:00 a.m. - 5:00 p.m. (714) 555-2323
(NOTE: The Assessor may contact you for further information)

If a document evidencing a change of ownership is presented to the recorder for recordation without the concurrent filing of a preliminary change of ownership report, the recorder may charge an additional recording fee of twenty dollars ($20).

1099-S INPUT

IMPORTANT

All areas and data fields
with numbers must be completed
before submissions to SMS.

COMPANY NUMBER	OFFICE NUMBER	TYPE	ORDER/ESCROW FILE NO.	ACTUAL CLOSING DATE
(1)Co#244	(2)Off#1	(3)	(4)5072-J	(5)

SUBJECT PROPERTY INFORMATION

Street Address or Brief Form of Legal Description (for vacant land, use APN, county, state

City	State	Zip Code

TRANSACTION DATA

CONTRACT SALES PRICE (line 401 HUD-1 form If this is an exchange, provide total dollar value of cash, notes and debt relief received by exchangeer.	NO. OF 1099-S forms required for the sale of this property.	2 OR MORE 1099-S FORMS If 2 or more 1099-S forms are required, record the dollar amount for this seller based on the seller's declaration.	BUYERS PART OF REAL ESTATE TAX Show any real estate tax, on a residence, charged to the buyer at settlement.	CONTINGENT TRANSACTION Is this a contingent transaction wherein gross proceeds cannot be determined with certainty at time of closing?	EXCHANGE Was (or will there be) other property or services received?
$321,000.00				yes	yes

SELLER INFORMATION-PLEASE PRINT CLEARLY

Seller's Last Name	Seller's First Name	M.I.
Seller's Forwarding Street Address		
City	State	Zip Code (or country if not USA)
Seller's Social Security Number	or	Seller's Tax Identification Number

You are required by law to provide your closing agent with your correct Taxpayer Identification Number. If you do not' provide your correct Taxpayer Identification Number, you may be subject to civil or criminal penalties imposed by law .

Under penalties of perjury, I certify that the number shown above is my correct Taxpayer Identification Number.

Seller's Signature

REQUEST FOR DEMAND

January 18, 1995   Escrow No: 000020

Attn: **Payoff Department**
Bank of the West
6729 Bristol St.
Costa Mesa, CA 92626

RE: LOAN NUMBER: 789123
     BORROWER: Michael M. Horton and Linda L. Horton

An escrow has been opened with our company by the above referenced borrowers and provides for the payment in full of the loan number referenced above. Your loan encumbers the real property described as:

     See Exhibit A attached hereto and made a part hereof.

This property is commonly known as: **2165 Memory Lane, Santa Ana, CA 92705**

We hereby request that you forward your **ORIGINAL DEMAND**, together with either (1) the original Note, Deed of Trust securing same and your executed Request for Full Reconveyance, or (2) your executed Full Reconveyance, to the following title company:

     New Land Title
     ATTN: Timothy West
     114 5th Street
     Santa Ana, CA 92705
     RE: TITLE ORDER No: 94-8976

Please fax a copy of your DEMAND to our office at (714) 549-0684 with an additional copy in the mail.

We wish to thank you for your cooperation and assistance. Please be sure to call our office if you have any questions concerning this matter.

Sincerely,

System A. User
Escrow Officer

3160 Airway Ave. Costa Mesa, CA 92626 (714) 549-5700 (714) 549-0684

AMORTIZATION SCHEDULE
Robert and Amelia Trabuco

Principal Amount:	$180,000.00	Term (Months):	120			
Interest Rate:	8.25	Payment Frequency:	Monthly		Start Date:	03/01/1995
Payment Amount:	$2,207.75	Loan Start Date:	02/27/1995		End Date:	01/01/2005

Pmt No.	Due Date	Payment Amount	Interest Paid	Principal Paid	Principal Balance	Unpaid Interest	Balance Due	Modification
1	03/01/95	$2,207.75	$82.50	$2,125.25	$177,874.75		$177,874.75	
2	04/01/95	2,207.75	1,222.89	984.86	176,889.89		176,889.89	
3	05/01/95	2,207.75	1,216.12	991.63	175,898.26		175,898.26	
4	06/01/95	2,207.75	1,209.30	998.45	174,899.81		174,899.81	
5	07/01/95	2,207.75	1,202.44	1,005.31	173,894.50		173,894.50	
6	08/01/95	2,207.75	1,195.52	1,012.23	172,882.27		172,882.27	
7	09/01/95	2,207.75	1,188.57	1,019.18	171,863.09		171,863.09	
8	10/01/95	2,207.75	1,181.56	1,026.19	170,836.90		170,836.90	
9	11/01/95	2,207.75	1,174.50	1,033.25	169,803.65		169,803.65	
10	12/01/95	2,207.75	1,167.40	1,040.35	168,763.30		168,763.30	
	Total Paid For Year		$10,840.80	$11,236.70				
11	01/01/96	2,207.75	1,160.25	1,047.50	167,715.80		167,715.80	
12	02/01/96	2,207.75	1,153.05	1,054.70	166,661.10		166,661.10	
13	03/01/96	2,207.75	1,145.80	1,061.95	165,599.15		165,599.15	
14	04/01/96	2,207.75	1,138.49	1,069.26	164,529.89		164,529.89	
15	05/01/96	2,207.75	1,131.14	1,076.61	163,453.28		163,453.28	
16	06/01/96	2,207.75	1,123.74	1,084.01	162,369.27		162,369.27	
17	07/01/96	2,207.75	1,116.29	1,091.46	161,277.81		161,277.81	
18	08/01/96	2,207.75	1,108.78	1,098.97	160,178.84		160,178.84	
19	09/01/96	2,207.75	1,101.23	1,106.52	159,072.32		159,072.32	
20	10/01/96	2,207.75	1,093.62	1,114.13	157,958.19		157,958.19	
21	11/01/96	2,207.75	1,085.96	1,121.79	156,836.40		156,836.40	
22	12/01/96	2,207.75	1,078.25	1,129.50	155,706.90		155,706.90	
	Total Paid For Year		$13,436.60	$13,056.40				
23	01/01/97	2,207.75	1,070.49	1,137.26	154,569.64		154,569.64	
24	02/01/97	2,207.75	1,062.67	1,145.08	153,424.56		153,424.56	
25	03/01/97	2,207.75	1,054.79	1,152.96	152,271.60		152,271.60	
26	04/01/97	2,207.75	1,046.87	1,160.88	151,110.72		151,110.72	
27	05/01/97	2,207.75	1,038.89	1,168.86	149,941.86		149,941.86	
28	06/01/97	2,207.75	1,030.85	1,176.90	148,764.96		148,764.96	
29	07/01/97	2,207.75	1,022.76	1,184.99	147,579.97		147,579.97	
30	08/01/97	2,207.75	1,014.61	1,193.14	146,386.83		146,386.83	
31	09/01/97	2,207.75	1,006.41	1,201.34	145,185.49		145,185.49	
32	10/01/97	2,207.75	998.15	1,209.60	143,975.89		143,975.89	
33	11/01/97	2,207.75	989.83	1,217.92	142,757.97		142,757.97	
34	12/01/97	2,207.75	981.46	1,226.29	141,531.68		141,531.68	
	Total Paid For Year		$12,317.78	$14,175.22				
35	01/01/98	2,207.75	973.03	1,234.72	140,296.96		140,296.96	
36	02/01/98	2,207.75	964.54	1,243.21	139,053.75		139,053.75	
37	03/01/98	2,207.75	955.99	1,251.76	137,801.99		137,801.99	
38	04/01/98	2,207.75	947.39	1,260.36	136,541.63		136,541.63	
39	05/01/98	2,207.75	938.72	1,269.03	135,272.60		135,272.60	
40	06/01/98	2,207.75	930.00	1,277.75	133,994.85		133,994.85	
41	07/01/98	2,207.75	921.21	1,286.54	132,708.31		132,708.31	
42	08/01/98	2,207.75	912.37	1,295.38	131,412.93		131,412.93	
43	09/01/98	2,207.75	903.46	1,304.29	130,108.64		130,108.64	
44	10/01/98	2,207.75	894.50	1,313.25	128,795.39		128,795.39	
45	11/01/98	2,207.75	885.47	1,322.28	127,473.11		127,473.11	
46	12/01/98	2,207.75	876.38	1,331.37	126,141.74		126,141.74	
	Total Paid For Year		$11,103.06	$15,389.94				
47	01/01/99	2,207.75	867.22	1,340.53	124,801.21		124,801.21	
48	02/01/99	2,207.75	858.01	1,349.74	123,451.47		123,451.47	
49	03/01/99	2,207.75	848.73	1,359.02	122,092.45		122,092.45	
50	04/01/99	2,207.75	839.39	1,368.36	120,724.09		120,724.09	
51	05/01/99	2,207.75	829.98	1,377.77	119,346.32		119,346.32	
52	06/01/99	2,207.75	820.51	1,387.24	117,959.08		117,959.08	
53	07/01/99	2,207.75	810.97	1,396.78	116,562.30		116,562.30	

AMORTIZATION SCHEDULE
Robert and Amelia Trabuco

Principal Amount:	$180,000.00	Term (Months):	120				
Interest Rate:	8.25	Payment Frequency:	Monthly		Start Date:	03/01/1995	
Payment Amount:	$2,207.75	Loan Start Date:	02/27/1995		End Date:	01/01/2005	

Pmt No.	Due Date	Payment Amount	Interest Paid	Principal Paid	Principal Balance	Unpaid Interest	Balance Due	Modification
54	08/01/99	$2,207.75	$801.37	$1,406.38	$115,155.92		$115,155.92	
55	09/01/99	2,207.75	791.70	1,416.05	113,739.87		113,739.87	
56	10/01/99	2,207.75	781.96	1,425.79	112,314.08		112,314.08	
57	11/01/99	2,207.75	772.16	1,435.59	110,878.49		110,878.49	
58	12/01/99	2,207.75	762.29	1,445.46	109,433.03		109,433.03	
	Total Paid For Year		$9,784.29	$16,708.71				
59	01/01/00	2,207.75	752.35	1,455.40	107,977.63		107,977.63	
60	02/01/00	2,207.75	742.35	1,465.40	106,512.23		106,512.23	
61	03/01/00	2,207.75	732.27	1,475.48	105,036.75		105,036.75	
62	04/01/00	2,207.75	722.13	1,485.62	103,551.13		103,551.13	
63	05/01/00	2,207.75	711.91	1,495.84	102,055.29		102,055.29	
64	06/01/00	2,207.75	701.63	1,506.12	100,549.17		100,549.17	
65	07/01/00	2,207.75	691.28	1,516.47	99,032.70		99,032.70	
66	08/01/00	2,207.75	680.85	1,526.90	97,505.80		97,505.80	
67	09/01/00	2,207.75	670.35	1,537.40	95,968.40		95,968.40	
68	10/01/00	2,207.75	659.78	1,547.97	94,420.43		94,420.43	
69	11/01/00	2,207.75	649.14	1,558.61	92,861.82		92,861.82	
70	12/01/00	2,207.75	638.43	1,569.32	91,292.50		91,292.50	
	Total Paid For Year		$8,352.47	$18,140.53				
71	01/01/01	2,207.75	627.64	1,580.11	89,712.39		89,712.39	
72	02/01/01	2,207.75	616.77	1,590.98	88,121.41		88,121.41	
73	03/01/01	2,207.75	605.83	1,601.92	86,519.49		86,519.49	
74	04/01/01	2,207.75	594.82	1,612.93	84,906.56		84,906.56	
75	05/01/01	2,207.75	583.73	1,624.02	83,282.54		83,282.54	
76	06/01/01	2,207.75	572.57	1,635.18	81,647.36		81,647.36	
77	07/01/01	2,207.75	561.33	1,646.42	80,000.94		80,000.94	
78	08/01/01	2,207.75	550.01	1,657.74	78,343.20		78,343.20	
79	09/01/01	2,207.75	538.61	1,669.14	76,674.06		76,674.06	
80	10/01/01	2,207.75	527.13	1,680.62	74,993.44		74,993.44	
81	11/01/01	2,207.75	515.58	1,692.17	73,301.27		73,301.27	
82	12/01/01	2,207.75	503.95	1,703.80	71,597.47		71,597.47	
	Total Paid For Year		$6,797.97	$19,695.03				
83	01/01/02	2,207.75	492.23	1,715.52	69,881.95		69,881.95	
84	02/01/02	2,207.75	480.44	1,727.31	68,154.64		68,154.64	
85	03/01/02	2,207.75	468.56	1,739.19	66,415.45		66,415.45	
86	04/01/02	2,207.75	456.61	1,751.14	64,664.31		64,664.31	
87	05/01/02	2,207.75	444.57	1,763.18	62,901.13		62,901.13	
88	06/01/02	2,207.75	432.45	1,775.30	61,125.83		61,125.83	
89	07/01/02	2,207.75	420.24	1,787.51	59,338.32		59,338.32	
90	08/01/02	2,207.75	407.95	1,799.80	57,538.52		57,538.52	
91	09/01/02	2,207.75	395.58	1,812.17	55,726.35		55,726.35	
92	10/01/02	2,207.75	383.12	1,824.63	53,901.72		53,901.72	
93	11/01/02	2,207.75	370.57	1,837.18	52,064.54		52,064.54	
94	12/01/02	2,207.75	357.94	1,849.81	50,214.73		50,214.73	
	Total Paid For Year		$5,110.26	$21,382.74				
95	01/01/03	2,207.75	345.23	1,862.52	48,352.21		48,352.21	
96	02/01/03	2,207.75	332.42	1,875.33	46,476.88		46,476.88	
97	03/01/03	2,207.75	319.53	1,888.22	44,588.66		44,588.66	
98	04/01/03	2,207.75	306.55	1,901.20	42,687.46		42,687.46	
99	05/01/03	2,207.75	293.48	1,914.27	40,773.19		40,773.19	
100	06/01/03	2,207.75	280.32	1,927.43	38,845.76		38,845.76	
101	07/01/03	2,207.75	267.06	1,940.69	36,905.07		36,905.07	
102	08/01/03	2,207.75	253.72	1,954.03	34,951.04		34,951.04	
103	09/01/03	2,207.75	240.29	1,967.46	32,983.58		32,983.58	
104	10/01/03	2,207.75	226.76	1,980.99	31,002.59		31,002.59	
105	11/01/03	2,207.75	213.14	1,994.61	29,007.98		29,007.98	
106	12/01/03	2,207.75	199.43	2,008.32	26,999.66		26,999.66	

AMORTIZATION SCHEDULE
Robert and Amelia Trabuco

Principal Amount:	$180,000.00	Term (Months):	120			Start Date:	03/01/1995
Interest Rate:	8.25	Payment Frequency:	Monthly				
Payment Amount:	$2,207.75	Loan Start Date:	02/27/1995			End Date:	01/01/2005

Pmt No.	Due Date	Payment Amount	Interest Paid	Principal Paid	Principal Balance	Unpaid Interest	Balance Due	Modification
	Total Paid For Year		$3,277.93	$23,215.07				
107	01/01/04	$2,207.75	$185.62	$2,022.13	$24,977.53		$24,977.53	
108	02/01/04	2,207.75	171.72	2,036.03	22,941.50		22,941.50	
109	03/01/04	2,207.75	157.72	2,050.03	20,891.47		20,891.47	
110	04/01/04	2,207.75	143.63	2,064.12	18,827.35		18,827.35	
111	05/01/04	2,207.75	129.44	2,078.31	16,749.04		16,749.04	
112	06/01/04	2,207.75	115.15	2,092.60	14,656.44		14,656.44	
113	07/01/04	2,207.75	100.76	2,106.99	12,549.45		12,549.45	
114	08/01/04	2,207.75	86.28	2,121.47	10,427.98		10,427.98	
115	09/01/04	2,207.75	71.69	2,136.06	8,291.92		8,291.92	
116	10/01/04	2,207.75	57.01	2,150.74	6,141.18		6,141.18	
117	11/01/04	2,207.75	42.22	2,165.53	3,975.65		3,975.65	
118	12/01/04	2,207.75	27.33	2,180.42	1,795.23		1,795.23	
	Total Paid For Year		$1,288.57	$25,204.43				
119	01/01/05	1,807.57	12.34	1,795.23				
	Total Paid For Year		$12.34	$1,795.23				
	Total Paid for Loan		$82,322.07	$180,000.00				

458

1004 E. Taft Avenue
Orange, CA 92865
(800) 767-7832

Escrow No.   CRISTY2
Reference: 2566 Broadway
              Laguna Beach, CA 91002

Closing Date: October 3, 2000
              Page 1

CLOSING STATEMENT

Steve Silvers
Susan Sanders
257 Ocean Blvd.
Corona Del Mar, CA 92665

Brandon Bowers
Brenda Bowers
2566 Broadway
Laguna Beach, CA 91002

SELLER:			BUYER:	
- - DEBITS - -	- - CREDITS - -		- - DEBITS - -	- - CREDITS - -
		Consideration:		
	150,000.00	Total Consideration		150,000.00
		Deposits:		
		Deposit		
		By: Brandon Bowers		2,500.00
		Deposit		
		By: Brandon Bowers		27,000.00
		Existing & New Encumbrances:		
		New Encumbrance		95,000.00
		Golden Coin Bank		
30,000.00		New Encumbrance		30,000.00
		Steve Silvers		
		Adjustments:		
	200.00	Credit for Ceiling Fan	200.00	
		Credit from Selling Broker		2,000.00
		Prorations:		
	84.00	Beach Front Homeowners	84.00	
		at $ 90.00 per month		
		From 10/03/00 to 11/01/00		
867.87		County Taxes		867.87
		at $ 1698.00 per 6 months		
		From 07/01/00 to 10/03/00		
		Payoff(s):		
95,742.10		Loan Payoff		
		Re: Lucky Lender		
1,170.55		Interest @ 12.75%		
		From 09/01/00 to 10/06/00		
100.00		Reconveyance Fee		
100.00		Statement / Forwarding Fee		
		New Loan Charges:		
		Re: Golden Coin Bank		
		Interest @ 8.5%	663.70	
		From 10/02/00 to 11/01/00		
		Discount Points	950.00	
1,100.00		**Origination fee**		
		Document Preparation	500.00	
		Lender's Inspection Fee	100.00	
		Impounds: Taxes	937.50	
		6 months @ $156.25 per month		
		Impounds: Fire Insurance	91.66	
		2 months @ $45.83 per month		
		Aggregate Account Adjustment	-325.00	
		Re: Steve Silvers		
	238.36	Interest @ 10%	238.36	
		From 10/03/00 To 11/01/00		
		Re: Fat Jack Lender		
		*Yield Spread POC $ 1,200.00		
		Disbursements Paid:		
		Fire Insurance	550.00	
		pd to: Red Hot Fire Insurance		
65.00		Pest Inspection		
		pd to: Bug B Gone		
90.00		Dues paid by Seller October		
		pd to: Beach Front Homeowners		
		Transfer Fee	50.00	
		pd to: Coast Villas Management		
		Dues paid by Buyer November	90.00	
		pd to: Beach Front Homeowners		
9,000.00		Commission		
		Commission of $ 4,500.00		
		pd to: Century 21 Surf and Sand		
		Commission of $ 4,500.00		
		pd to: Star Agency		
325.00		Home Warranty Plan		
		pd to: We Fix it Warranty		
		Ref: 369852		
800.00		Credit card payment		
		pd to: Bankroll Visa		
1,200.00		Credit card payment		
		pd to: Paymore Payment Center		
		Title Charges:		
800.00		Owner's Title Policy		
		Lender's Title Policy	500.00	
		Taxes: Paid by Title Company	1,698.00	
50.00		Sub-title Fee	50.00	
165.00		County Document Transfer Tax		
		Record Grant Deed	25.00	
		Record Trust Deed	75.00	
25.00		Record Release/Reconveyance		
		Escrow Fees:		
500.00		Seller's Portion of Escrow Fee	500.00	
25.00		Order Demand Statement		
25.00		Prepare Grant Deed	25.00	
		Loan Tie-In Fee	100.00	
		Federal Express/Messenger Fees	35.00	
		Funds Held:		
350.00		Roof Repair Completion		
		Check Herewith	$ 229.65	
		Check Herewith		
$ 8,021.84				
$ 150,522.36	$ 150,522.36	Total	$ 157,367.87	$ 157,367.87

SAVE FOR INCOME TAX PURPOSES

1004 E. Taft Avenue
Orange, CA 92865
(800) 767-7832

Escrow No. CRISTY1
Reference: 2165 Memory Lane
            Santa Ana, CA 92705

Estimated Close Date: September 13, 2000
Report Print Date: July 14, 2000

Seller
ESTIMATED CLOSING STATEMENT

SELLER:
Michael Horton
Linda Horton

	- - DEBITS - -	- - CREDITS - -
Consideration:		
Total Consideration		100,000.00
Adjustments:		
Seller credit for Furniture		1,000.00
Prorations:		
Beach Front Homeowners		51.00
at $ 85.00 per month		
From 09/13/00 to 10/01/00		
County Taxes	287.28	
at $ 718.20 per 6 months		
From 07/01/00 to 09/13/00		
Payoff(s):		
Loan Payoff	42,721.11	
Re: Lucky Lender		
Interest @ 12.75%	223.85	
From 09/01/00 to 09/16/00		
Reconveyance Fee	75.00	
Statement / Forwarding Fee	50.00	
New Loan Charges:		
Origination fee	950.00	
Disbursements Paid:		
Pest Inspection	65.00	
pd to: Bug B Gone		
Dues for Oct. from Seller	85.00	
pd to: Beach Front Homeowners		
Commission	6,000.00	
Commission of $ 3,000.00		
pd to: Century 21 Surf and Sand		
Commission of $ 3,000.00		
pd to: Sure Lock Homes		
Home Warranty Plan	325.00	
pd to: We Fix It Warranty		
Ref: 8632152		
Upgrades	2,500.00	
pd to: Stewart Design House		
Title Charges:		
Owner's Title Policy	525.00	
Sub-Title Fee	75.00	
County Document Transfer Tax	110.00	
Record Release/Reconveyance	20.00	
Title-Wire/Mess Fees	25.00	
Lender's Endorsement(s)	125.00	
Escrow Fees:		
Seller's Portion of Escrow Fee	500.00	
Order Demand Statement	20.00	
Prepare Grant Deed	25.00	
Notary Fee**	25.00	
Check Herewith	$ 46,318.76	
Totals	$ 101,051.00	$ 101,051.00

NOTICE: This estimated closing statement is subject to changes, corrections or
        additions at the time of final computation of closing escrow statement.

_____   _____
Michael Horton   Linda Horton

1004 E. Taft Avenue
Orange, CA 92865
(800) 767-7832

Escrow No.   CRISTY1
Reference: 2165 Memory Lane
             Santa Ana, CA 92705

Estimated Close Date: September 13, 2000
Report Print Date: July 14, 2000

Buyer
ESTIMATED CLOSING STATEMENT

BUYER:
Robert Mullins and Margie Mullins as trustees
Anybody Cruz

	- - DEBITS - -	- - CREDITS - -
Consideration:		
Total Consideration	100,000.00	
Deposits:		
Deposit		
By: Robert Mullins and Margie Mull		5,000.00
Deposit		
By: Robert Mullins and Margie Mull		20,500.00
Existing & New Encumbrances:		
New Encumbrance		80,000.00
The Money Store		
Adjustments:		
Seller credit for Furniture	1,000.00	
Credit from Listing Broker		300.00
Prorations:		
Beach Front Homeowners	51.00	
at $ 85.00 per month		
From 09/13/00 to 10/01/00		
County Taxes		287.28
at $ 718.20 per 6 months		
From 07/01/00 to 09/13/00		
New Loan Charges:		
Re: The Money Store		
Interest @ 9%	374.79	
From 09/12/00 To 10/01/00		
Discount Points	800.00	
*Appraisal Fee POC $ 50.00		
Document Preparation	300.00	
Processing Fee	100.00	
Impounds: Taxes	240.00	
6 months @ $40 per month		
Impounds: Fire Insurance	45.00	
2 months @ $22.5 per month		
Aggregate Account Adjustment	-325.00	
Re: Fat Jack Lender		
Appraisal Fee	125.00	
Credit Report	50.00	
*Yield Spread POC $ 1,200.00		
Disbursements Paid:		
Fire Insurance	300.00	
pd to: Red Hot Fire Insurance		
Transfer Fee	50.00	
pd to: Coast Villas Management		
Dues for Nov. from Buyer	85.00	
pd to: Beach Front Homeowners		
Title Charges:		
Lender's Title Policy	375.00	
Taxes: Paid by Title Company	718.20	
Sub-Title Fee	75.00	
Record Grant Deed	20.00	
Record Trust Deed	75.00	
Escrow Fees:		
Seller's Portion of Escrow Fee	500.00	
Loan Tie-In Fee	100.00	
Check Herewith	$ 1,028.29	
Totals	$ 106,087.28	$ 106,087.28

NOTICE: This estimated closing statement is subject to changes, corrections or
        Additions at the time of final computation of closing escrow statement.

_____   _____
Robert Mullins and Margie Mullins as trustees   Anybody Cruz

461

1004 E. Taft Avenue
Orange, CA 92865
(800) 767-7832

Escrow No. CRISTY3
Reference: 2165 Memory Lane
            Mission Viejo, CA 92705

Closing Date: October 10, 2000

Borrower
CLOSING STATEMENT

BORROWER:
Michael Horton
Linda Horton
Robert Mullins and Margie Mullins Trustee
2165 Memory Lane
Mission Viejo, CA 92705

	- - DEBITS - -	- - CREDITS - -
New Loan:		
New Encumbrance		150,000.00
The Money Store		
Payoff(s):		
Loan to be Paid Off	124,321.50	
Re: Lucky Lender		
Interest @ 12.75%	173.71	
From 10/01/00 To 10/05/00		
Reconveyance Fee	75.00	
Statement / Forwarding Fee	50.00	
New Loan Charges:		
Re: The Money Store		
Interest @ 8%	953.42	
From 10/03/00 To 11/01/00		
Discounts Points	2,250.00	
Origination Fee	3,000.00	
Document Preparation	150.00	
Tax Service	75.00	
Photo Inspection Fee	100.00	
PROCESSING FEE	200.00	
Impounds for Taxes	90.00	
2 months @ $45 per month		
Impounds for Fire Insurance	45.00	
2 months @ $22.5 per month		
Aggregate Account Adjustment	-325.00	
Re: Fat Jack Lender		
*Appraisal Fee POC $ 125.00		
*Credit Report POC $ 75.00		
*Yield Spread POC $ 1,020.00		
Disbursements Paid:		
Fire Insurance	500.00	
pd to: Red Hot Fire Insurance		
Dues paid by Borrower Aug/Sept	180.00	
pd to: Beach Front Homeowners		
Demand Fee	50.00	
pd to: Coast Villas Management		
credit card payment	800.00	
pd to: Bankroll Visa		
credit card payment	1,200.00	
pd to: Paymore Payment Center		
Title Charges:		
Lenders Title Policy	385.00	
Sub-Title Fee	100.00	
Record Trust Deed	75.00	
Record Conveyance	25.00	
Title Wire Fee	20.00	
Lender's Endorsements	125.00	
Title Messenger Fees	45.00	
Escrow Fees:		
Escrow Fees	350.00	
Order Demand Statement	25.00	
Notary Fee*	20.00	
Messenger Fee	45.00	
Check Herewith	$ 14,896.37	
Totals	$ 150,000.00	$ 150,000.00

SAVE FOR INCOME TAX PURPOSES

GOOD FAITH ESTIMATE OF SETTLEMENT CHARGES

Borrower:

Creditor:
Westmark Mortgage Corp.
535 Anton boulevard, Suite 500
Costa Mesa, CA 92626

Loan Number:

Date:

The information provided below reflects estimates of the charges which you are likely to incur at the settlement of your loan. The fees listed are estimates--the actual charges may be more or less. Your transaction may not involve a fee for every item listed.

The numbers listed beside the estimates generally correspond to the numbered lines contained in the HUD-1 settlement statement which you will be receiving at settlement. The HUD-1 settlement statement will show you the actual cost for items paid at settlement.

LOAN AMOUNT: $ 118,750.00

ITEMIZATION OF PREPAID FINANCE CHARGES:
801	Loan Origination Fee 1.25%(Lender)	$ 1,484.38
810	Tax Servisce	75.00
811	Processing Fee	200.00
813	UNDERWRITING	375.00
814	TAX SERVICE	75.00
901	Prepaid Interest (5/14/99-6/01/99)	489.78
1002	Mortgage Insurance Reserves	

TOTAL PREPAID FINANCE CHARGE $ 2,901.03
AMOUNT FINANCED   115,848.97

OTHER SETTLEMENT CHARGES:

AMOUNTS PAID TO OTHERS ON YOUR BEHALF BY CREDITOR
803	Appraisal Fee to Truman Bailey	295.00
804	Credit Report Fee	55.00
903	Property Insurance to Insurance Co.	400.00
1001	Property Insurance Reserves (2 mo.)	66.68
1004	County Tax Reserves (4 mo.)	520.00
1101	Settlement or Closing Fee	400.00
1106	Notary Fees to ESCROW COMPANY	10.00
1108	Title Insurance to TITLE COMPANY	300.00
1201	Recording Fees	50.00

TOTAL OTHER SETTLEMENT CHARGES   2,097.52
LOAN PROCEEDS $ 113,751.45

These estimates are provided pursuant to the Real Estate Settlement Procedures Act of 1974 (RESPA). Additional information can be found in the HUD Special Information booklet, chich is to be provided to you by your mortgage broker or lender.

I (WE) HEREBY ACKNOWLEDGE RECEIVING AND READING A COMPLETEDS COPY OF THIS DISCLOSURE.

Date   Date

463

Federal Truth-In-Lending Disclosure Statement

Borrower:

Creditor:
WESTMARK MORTGAGE CORP.
535 ANTON BOULEVARD, SUITE 500
COSTA MESA, CA 92626

Loan Number: 2-0111-2457

4/19/99

ANNUAL PERCENTAGE RATE	FINANCE CHARGE	AMOUNT FINANCED	TOTAL OF PAYMENTS
The cost of your credit as a yearly rate.	The dollar amount the credit will cost you.	The amount of credit provided to you or on your behalf.	The amount you will have paid after you have made all payments as scheduled
9.2730%	$229,540.84	$115,848.97	$345,389.81

Your payment schedule will be:

No. of Pmts.	Amt.of Pmts.	Monthly Pmts Begin	No. of Pmts.	Amt. of Pmts.	Monthly Pmts. Begin	No. of Pmts.	Amt. of Pmts.	Monthly Pmts. Begin
359	959.42	7/01/99						
1	958.03	6/01/2029						

INSURANCE: The following insurance is required to obtain credit: *Property
You may obtain the insurance from anyone that is acceptable to creditor.

SECURITY: You are giving a security interest in the real property being purchased.
Property Address: 3210 Juniper Court, Hanford, CA 93230

FILING FEES: $50.00

LATE CHARGE: If a payment is more than 15 days late, you will be charged 5% of the payment.

PREPAYMENT: If you pay off your loan early, you will not have to pay a penalty. You will not be entitled to a refund of part of the finance charge.

ASSUMPTION: Someone buying your property cannot assume the remainder of your loan on the original terms.

All dates and numerical disclosures except the late payment disclosures are estimates.

See your contract documents for any additional information about nonpayment, default, any required repayment in full before the scheduled ate, and prepayment refunds and penalties.

Name	Date	Name	Date

INSTALLMENT NOTE
(INTEREST INCLUDED)
(THIS NOTE CONTAINS AN ACCELERATION CLAUSE)

$189,000   Mission Viejo   ,California, 1/1/99

In installments and at the times hereinafter stated, for value received, Robert Trabuco and Amelia Trabuco

promise to pay to Jim Getz and Mary Anne Getz

, or order

at 21128 Rose, Rancho Santa Margarita, CA 92626

the principal sum of One Hundred Eighty Thousand   dollars

with interest from January 1, 1999   on the amounts of

principal remaining from time to time unpaid, until said principal sum is paid, at the rate of 8.9   percent

per annum. Principal and interest due in monthly installments of One Thousand Five Hundred Dollars, $1,500, or more on the 15th day of each and every month, beginning on the 15th day of February, 1999.

and continuing until said principal sum has been fully paid. AT ANY TIME, THE PRIVILEGE IS RESERVED TO PAY MORE THAN THE SUM DUE. Should the interest not be so paid, it shall be added to the principal and thereafter bear like interest as the principal, but such unpaid interest so compounded shall not exceed an amount equal to simple interest on the unpaid principal at the maximum rate permitted by law. Should default be made in the payment of any of said installments when due, then the whole sum of principal and interest shall become immediately due and payable at the option of the holder of this note.

If the trustor shall sell, convey, or alienate said property, or any part thereof, or any interest therein, or shall be divested of his title or any interest therein in may manner or way, whether voluntarily or involuntarily, without the written consent of the beneficiary being first had and obtained, beneficiary shall have the right, at its option, to declare any indebtedness or obligations secured hereby, irrespective of the maturity date specified in any note evidencing the same, immediately due and payable.

Should suit be commenced to collect this note or any portion thereof, such sum as the Court may deem reasonable shall be added hereto as attorney's fees. Principal and interest payable for lawful money of the United States of America. This note is secured by a certain DEED OF TRUST to the SMS SETTLEMENT SERVICES, a California corporation, as TRUSTEE.

_____   _____
Robert Trabuco   Amelia Trabuco

RECORDING REQUESTED BY
New Land Title Company
AND WHEN RECORDED MAIL TO:

Name: Robert R. Mullins
Street Address: 2185 Memory Lane
City, State: Costa Mesa, CA 92626
Zip

REC
RCF
MICRO
RTCF
LIEN
SMPF
PCOR

Order No. 56748932-SMS

Space Above This Line for Recorder's Use

QUITCLAIM DEED

THE UNDERSIGNED GRANTOR(S) DECLARE(S)
City of : <u>Costa Mesa</u>

Conveyance tax is $_____
Parcel No. 123-45-6789

DOCUMENTARY TRANSFER TAX $_____
☐Computed on full value of interest of property conveyed
☐Full value less value of liens or encumbrances remaining at the time of sale

FOR A VALUABLE CONSIDERATION, receipt of which is hereby acknowledged, Michael L. Horton and Lisa M. Horton, Husband and Wife as Joint Tenants do (does) hereby REMISE, RELEASE AND FOREVER QUITCLAIM to Robert R. Mullins and Margie M. Mullins, Husband and Wife as Joint Tenants

the following real property in the city of
Costa Mesa, county of Orange, state of California

Lot 12 in Tract 2316 as recorded in Book 42 pages 5-10 inclusive of Miscellaneous Maps in t he office of the County Recorder of the County of Orange State of California and described as follows: commencing at a point on the Southerly line thereof 450.8 feet West of the Southeast corner thereof, thence North 68 degrees 58 minutes West 100 fee, the nce North 23 degrees 02 minutes East 60 feet, thence South 66 degrees 58 minutes East one hundred feet, thence South 23 degrees 02 minutes West 60 feet to the point of beginning.

Dated:_____

STATE OF CALIFORNIA
COUNTY OF_____

On_____ before me.

a Notary Public in and for said County and State, personally appeared:

_____

_____   _____

Personally known to me (or provided to me on the basis of satisfactory evidence whose name(s) is/are subscribed to the within instrument and acknowledged to me that he/she/they executed the same in his/her/their authorized capacity(ies) and that by his/her/their signature(s) on the instrument the person(s) or the entity upon behalf of which the person(s) acted, executed the instrument.

WITNESS my hand and official seal.

Signature _____

_____
Michael M. Horton

_____
Linda L. Horton

(This area for official notorial seal)

RECORDING REQUESTED BY
New Land Title Company
AND WHEN RECORDED MAIL TO:

Name: Robert R. Mullins
Street Address: 2185 Memory Lane
City, State: Costa Mesa, CA 92626
Zip

| REC |
| RCF |
| MICRO |
| RTCF |
| LIEN |
| SMPF |
| PCOR |

Order No. 56748932-SMS

Space Above This Line for Recorder's Use

GRANT DEED

THE UNDERSIGNED GRANTOR(S) DECLARE(S)
City of : <u>Costa Mesa</u>

Conveyance tax is $_____
Parcel No. 123-45-6789

DOCUMENTARY TRANSFER TAX $_____
☐Computed on full value of interest of property
conveyed
☐Full value less value of liens or encumbrances
remaining at the time of sale

FOR A VALUABLE CONSIDERATION, receipt
of which is hereby acknowledged, Michael L.
Horton and Lisa M. Horton, Husband and Wife as
Joint Tenants do (does) hereby GRANTS to
Robert R. Mullins and Margie M. Mullins, Husband
and Wife as Joint Tenants

the following real property in the city of Costa
Mesa, county of Orange, state of California

Lot 12 in Tract 2316 as recorded in Book 42 pages 5-10 inclusive of Miscellaneous Maps in the office of
the County Recorder of the County of Orange State of California and described as follows: commencing at
a point on the Southerly line thereof 450.8 feet West of the Southeast corner thereof, thence North 68
degrees 58 minutes West 100 fee, thence North 23 degrees 02 minutes East 60 feet, thence South 66
degrees 58 minutes East one hundred feet, thence South 23 degrees 02 minutes West 60 feet to the point of
beginning.

Dated:_____

STATE OF CALIFORNIA
COUNTY OF_____ –

On_____before me.

a Notary Public in and for said County and State, personally appeared:

_____

_____

Personally known to me (or providedto me on the basis of satisfactory evidence
whose name(s) is/are subscribed to the within instrument and acknowledged to
me that he/she/they executed the same in his/her/their authorized capacity(ies)
and that by his/her/their signature(s) on the instrument the person(s) or the entity
upon behalf of which the person(s) acted, executed the instrument.

WITNESS my hand and official seal.

Signature_____

Michael M. Horton
_____

Linda L. Horton
_____

(This area for official notorial seal)

Post Test

The following self test repeats the one you took at the beginning of this chapter. Now take the exam again--since you have read all the material-- and check your knowledge of conducting an escrow.

True/False

1. The process of conducting an escrow involves two main steps.

2. There is only one kind of escrow.

3. In opening an escrow, the names of the parties, legal description, and selling price, among other information, are collected by the escrow holder.

4. Escrow instructions are prepared to direct the escrow holder.

5. Escrow instructions need to be signed only by the seller to make an escrow valid.

6. The escrow holder never prepares a note and trust deed.

7. Closing costs are calculated before the escrow is opened.

8. The down payment is collected by the escrow holder.

9. The escrow holder coordinates with the lender.

10. Escrow instructions are commonly generated by computer.

A

A.L.T.A. owner's policy
An owner's extended title insurance policy.

A.L.T.A. title policy
A type of title insurance policy issued by title insurance companies that expands the risks normally insured against under the standard type policy to include unrecorded mechanic's liens; unrecorded physical easements; facts a physical survey would not show; water and mineral rights; and rights of parties in possession, such as tenants and buyers under unrecorded instruments.

abstract of judgment
A summary of a court decision.

abstract of title
Written summary of all useful documents discovered in a title search.

acceleration clause
Clause in a loan document describing events causing entire loan to come due.

acceptance
An unqualified agreement to the terms of an offer.

Acknowledgment
(1) A signed statement, made before a notary public, by a named person confirming the signature on a document and that it was made of free will.

actual notice
A fact, such as seeing the grand deed or knowing a person inherited a property by will.

adjustable rate mortgage
A note whose interest rate is tied to a movable economic index.

administrator
A person appointed by the probate court to administer the estate of a deceased person. His or her duties include making an inventory of the assets, managing the property, paying the debts and expenses, filing necessary reports and tax returns, and distributing the assets as ordered by the probate court.

affidavit
A statement or declaration reduced to writing sworn to or affirmed before some officer who has authority to administer an oath or affirmation.

affidavit of title/ownership
A statement, in writing, made under oath by seller or grantor, acknowledged before a Notary Public in which the seller/affiant identifies themselves and indicates marital status; certifies by examination of title on contract, there are no judgments, bankruptcies, or divorces, no unrecorded deeds, contracts, unpaid repair, or improvements, or defects of title known to seller; and seller possesses property.

after-acquired title
Any benefits that come to a property after a sale must follow the sale and accrue to the new owner.

agency
A legal relationship in which a principal authorizes an agent to act as the principal's representative when dealing with third parties.

agency relationship
A special relationship of trust by which one person (agent) is authorized to conduct business, sign papers, or otherwise act on behalf of another person (principal).

agreement
A mutual exchange of promises (either written or oral). Although often used as synonymous with contract, technically it denotes mutual promises that fail as a contract for lack of consideration.

agreement of sale
(1) A contract for the sale of real property where the seller gives up possession, but retains the title until the purchase price is paid in full. (2) Also called contract for sale or land contract.

agricultural property
Property zoned for use in farming, including the raising of crops and livestock.

air rights
Rights in real property to the reasonable use of the air space above the land surface.

airspace
The interior area which an apartment, office or condominium occupies. Airspace is considered real property to a reasonable height. For example, an owner or developer of condominiums may sell the airspace as real property.

alienate
(1) To transfer, convey, or sell property to another. (2) The act of transferring ownership, title, or interest.

alienation clause
(1) A clause in a loan document allowing lender to call the balance of the loan due upon the sale of the property. (2) Also called the **due-on-sale** clause.

all-inclusive trust deed
A purchase money deed of trust subordinate to—but still including—the original loan.

amendment
Change to escrow instructions. Any changes must be made by mutual agreement between buyer and seller. The escrow agent does not have the authority to make changes in the contract upon the direction of either the buyer or seller, unless both agree to the change, in the form of an amendment. A change to an existing contract by mutual agreement of the parties.

amortization
The liquidation of a financial obligation on an installment basis.

amortized loan
(1) A loan to be repaid, interest and principal, by a series of regular payments that are equal or nearly equal, without any special balloon payment prior to maturity. (2) Also called a Level Payments Loan.

annual percentage rate
The relationship of the total finance charge to the total amount to be financed as required under the Truth-in-Lending Act.

appraisal
An unbiased estimate or opinion of the property value on a given date.

appraisal report
A written statement where an appraiser gives his or her opinion of value.

arm's length transaction
A transaction, such as a sale of property, in which all parties involved are acting in their own self-interest and are under no undue influence or pressure from other parties.

assessed value
Value placed on property by a public tax assessor as a basis for taxation.

assessor's parcel number (APN)
The official identification number for a specific property. The assessor, who has the responsibility of determining assessed values, to determine property tax. Also referred to as account, folio or UPC number, and appears in legal property descriptions.

assignment
The transfer of entire leasehold estate to a new person.

assignment of rents
An agreement between property owner and holder of a trust deed or mortgage by which holder receives, as security, the right to collect rents from tenants of property in event of default by borrower.

assignment of rents clause
A clause in a deed of trust or mortgage, providing that in the event of default, all rents and income from the secured property will be paid to the lender to help reduce the outstanding loan balance.

assumption clause
A clause in a document that allows a buyer to take over existing loan and agree to be liable for the repayment of the loan.

attachment
The process by which the court holds the property of a defendant pending outcome of a lawsuit.

attachment lien
(1) When the court holds the real or personal property of a defendant as security for a judgment pending the outcome of a lawsuit. (2) Aka as a writ of attachment.

attorney-in-fact
(1) The person holding the power of attorney. (2) A competent and disinterested person who is authorized by another person to act in his or her place in legal matters.

B

balloon mortgage
(ginniemae.gov) Mortgage with final lump sum payment that is greater than preceding payments and pays the loan in full.

balloon payment
Under an installment loan, a final payment that is substantially larger than any other payment and repays the debt in full.

bare legal title
The title to real property passes to a third party called a trustee who holds the 'bare legal title,' and forecloses in event of default. Also called naked legal title. The trustee has bare title and the owner has equitable ownership or possession.

bargain and sale deed
Any deed that recites a consideration and purports to convey the real estate; a bargain and sale deed with a covenant against the grantor's act is one in which the grantor warrants that grantor has done nothing to harm or cloud the title.

beneficiary
The lender under a deed of trust.

beneficiary statement
A statement of the unpaid balance of a loan and describes the condition of the debt.

bequest
A gift of personal property by will.

bilateral contract
An agreement in which each person promises to perform an act in exchange for another person's promise to perform.

bill of sale
A written agreement used to transfer ownership in personal property.

blanket loan
A loan secured by several properties. The security instrument used can be a blanket deed of trust or a blanket mortgage.

Boot
Extra cash or non like-kind property put into an exchange.

breach of contract
A failure to perform on part or all of the terms and conditions of a contract.

bridge loan
(1) A loan to "bridge" the gap between the termination of one mortgage and the beginning of another, such as when a borrower purchases a new home before receiving cash proceeds from the sale of a prior home, aka 'swing loan.'

broker agreement
A contract between a borrower and a mortgage broker. It describes what the broker will do for the borrower, and the terms of the agreement, including compensation.

bulk transfer law
The law concerning any transfer in bulk (not a sale in the ordinary course of the seller's business).

bundle of rights
An ownership concept describing all the legal rights that attach to the ownership of real property.

business opportunity
Any type of business that is for lease or sale.

buydown
A cash payment, usually measured in points, to a lender in order to reduce the interest rate a borrower must pay. The seller may increase the sales price to cover the cost of the buydown.

C

CC&Rs (See *covenants, conditions and restrictions*)

C.L.T.A. standard policy A
policy of title insurance covering only matters of record.

California Land Title Association
A trade organization of the state's title companies.

CAL-VET Program
A program administered by the State Department of Veterans Affairs for the direct financing of farm and home purchases by eligible California veterans of the armed forces.

capital assets
Assets of a permanent nature used in the production of an income, such as land, buildings, machinery and equipment, etc. Under income tax law, it is usually distinguishable from "inventory" which comprises assets held for sale to customers in ordinary course of the taxpayer's trade or business.

capital gain
At resale of a capital item, the amount by which the net sale proceeds exceed the adjusted cost basis (book value). Used for income tax computations. Gains are called short or long term based upon length of holding period after acquisition. Usually taxed at lower rates than ordinary income.

carryback financing
Financing by a seller who takes back a note for part of the purchase price.

cashout refinancing loan
A loan that refinances a prior mortgage and that provides additional cash to the borrower. Funds, usually to pay off debts, or renovate.

certificate of eligibility
Issued by Department of Veterans Affairs – evidence of individual's eligibility to obtain VA loan.

certificate of reasonable value
The Federal VA appraisal commitment of property value.

certificate of taxes due
A written statement or guaranty of the condition of the taxes on a certain property made by the County Treasurer of the county wherein the property is located. Any loss resulting to any person from an error in a tax certificate shall be paid by the county which such treasurer represents.

certificate of title
A written opinion by an attorney that ownership of the particular parcel of land is as stated in the certificate.

certificate of occupancy
A certificate issued by local building authorities that indicates new construction is in compliance with codes and may be occupied.

chain of title
A chronological history of property's ownership. Also, sequential record of changes in ownership showing the connection from one owner to the next. A complete chain of title is desirable whenever property is transferred and required by title insurance companies if they are writing a policy on a property.

chattel
Personal property.

chattel mortgage
A claim on personal property (instead of real property) used to secure or guarantee a promissory note. (See definition of *Security Agreement and Security Interest.*)

chattel real
An item of personal property connected to real estate; for example, a lease.

clause
A distinct section of a writing; *specifically* : a distinct article, stipulation, or proviso in a formal document e.g. a clause in a deed of trust or mortgage, providing that in the event of default, all rents and income from the secured property will be paid to the lender to help reduce the outstanding loan balance.

closing
(1) Process by which all the parties to a real estate transaction conclude the details of a sale or mortgage. The process includes the signing and transfer of documents and distribution of funds.

closing costs
The miscellaneous expenses buyers and sellers normally incur in the transfer of ownership of real property over and above the cost of the property. A general term to describe the fees that a borrower will pay at closing. Sometimes called "settlement fees."

closing statement
An accounting of funds made to the buyer and seller separately. Required by law to be made at the completion of every real estate transaction.

cloud on title
Any condition that affects the clear title of real property or minor defect in the chain of title which needs to be removed.

Code of Civil Procedure
One of the 25 California codes that contain the statutes passed by the state legislature. It contains most of the procedural requirements for enforcing rights granted by other codes, including the procedures for evictions, foreclosures, and lawsuits.

Code of Ethics
A set of rules and principles expressing a standard of accepted conduct for a professional group and governing the relationship of members to each other and to the organization.

codicil
A change in a will before the maker's death.

collateral
Something of value given as security for a debt.

commission
A fee for services rendered usually based on a certain percentage of the sales price of a property.

commission split
The previously agreed upon division of money between a broker and sales-associate when the brokerage has been paid a commission from a sale made by the associate.

commitment
A pledge or a promise or firm agreement to do something in the future, such as a loan company giving a written commitment with specific terms of mortgage loan it will make.

common area
An entire common interest subdivision except the separate interests therein.

common interest subdivision
Individuals owning a separate lot or unit, with an interest in the common areas of the entire project. The common areas are usually governed by a homeowners association.

community property
All property acquired by a husband and wife during a valid marriage (excluding certain separate property).

community property with right of survivorship
A law allowed a husband and wife to hold title to their property.

co-mortgagor (ginnemae.gov)
One who is individually and jointly obligated to repay a mortgage loan and shares ownership of the property with one or more borrowers. (See *co-signer*)

complete escrow
All terms of the escrow instructions have been met.

compound interest
Interest paid on original principal and also on the accrued and unpaid interest which has accumulated as the debt matures.

concurrent ownership
(1) When property is owned by two or more persons or entities at the same time. (2) Also known as co-ownership.

condition
Similar to a covenant, a promise to do or not to do something. The penalty for breaking a condition is return of the property to the grantor Also, Conditions, Covenants and Restrictions-CC&Rs found in Homeowners Associations master deed.

condition precedent
A condition which requires something to occur before a transaction becomes absolute and enforceable; for example, a sale that is contingent on the buyer obtaining financing.

condition subsequent
A condition which, if it occurs at some point in the future, can cause a property to revert to the grantor; for example, a requirement in a grant deed that a buyer must never use the property for anything other than a private residence.

conditional sale contract
A contract for the sale of property stating that delivery is to be made to the buyer, title to remain vested in the seller until the conditions of the contract have been fulfilled.

conditional use permit
Allows a land use that may be incompatible with other uses existing in the zone.

condominium
A housing unit consisting of a separate fee interest in a particular specific space, plus an undivided interest in all common or public areas of the development. Each unit owner has a deed, separate financing and pays the property taxes for their unit.

condominium declaration
The document which establishes a condominium and describes the property rights of the unit owners.

conforming loans
Loans which conform to Fannie Mae guidelines, which sets loan limits to a certain amount.

consideration
Something of value—such as money, a promise, property or personal services.

construction loan
A loan made to finance actual construction or improvement on land. Funds are usually disbursed in increments as the construction progresses.

constructive eviction
Conduct by a landlord that impairs tenant's possession of the premises making occupancy hazardous.

constructive notice
Notice given by recording a document or taking physical possession of the property.

Consumer Credit Protection Act
A federal law that includes the Truth-in-Lending Law.

contiguous
In close proximity; connected.

contingent
Conditional, uncertain, conditioned upon the occurrence or nonoccurrence of some uncertain future event.

contract
A legally enforceable agreement made by competent parties, to perform or not perform a certain act.

contract date

The date the contract is created. The contract is created when the final acceptance was communicated back to the offeror.

contract of sale

(1) A contract for the sale of real property where the seller gives up possession but retains title until the total of the purchase price is paid off. (2) Also called installment sales contract, a contract of sale, an agreement of sale, a conditional sales contract, or a land sales contract.

contractual intent

An intention to be bound by an agreement; thereby, thus preventing jokes and jests from becoming valid contracts.

covenant

A promise to do or not do certain things.

conventional loan

Any loan made by lenders without any governmental guarantees.

convey

To transfer ownership or title.

conveyance

The transfer of title to land by use of a written instrument.

cooperative

Ownership of an apartment unit in which the owner has purchased shares in the corporation that holds title to the entire building. A residential multifamily building.

co-signer

A second party who signs a promissory note together with the primary borrower.

cotenancy

Ownership of an interest in a particular parcel of land by more than one person; e.g., tenancy in common, joint tenancy.

covenants, conditions and restrictions (CC&Rs)

Restrictions are placed on certain types of real property and limit the activities of owners. Covenants and conditions are promises to do or not to do certain things. Consequence for breaking those promises may either be money damages in the case of covenants, or the return of the property to the grantor, in the case of conditions.

credit report

Report generated by a credit reporting agency (such as Trans Union, Experion or Equifax). Shows history of on-time and late payments on mortgages, credit cards, rent, utilities, and other debts. Credit reports are used with other information to generate a credit score to reflect credit risk.

credit score

Number showing the lender how likely a person will repay a loan--whether they are a good or poor credit risk. This score can be a very big factor in determining whether a person gets a loan, from whom, and what interest rate and fees they will be charged for the loan. The score is generated by a mathematical formula that considers the credit reports and other factors. It may also be referred to as **FICO** score (**Fair Isaac Company- see myfico.com**) or Beacon score or some other name-these are companies that create credit scores.

D

damages

The indemnity recoverable by a person who has sustained an injury, either in his or her person, property, or relative rights, through the act or default of another. Loss sustained or harm done to a person or property.

Declaration of Homestead

The recorded document that protects a homeowner from foreclosure by certain judgment creditors.

Declaration of Restrictions

A written legal document which lists covenants, conditions and restrictions (CC&Rs). This document gives each owner the right to enforce the CC&Rs.

deed

A formal transfer by a party.

deed in lieu of foreclosure

A deed to real property accepted by a lender from a defaulting borrower to avoid the necessity of foreclosure proceedings by the lender.

deed of trust

In some states loans are secured by means of a document called a deed of trust, instead of a mortgage document. (See *Trust Deed*)

document preparation fee
An amount of money charged for the preparation of mortgage loan documents. This charge will be shown on the HUD-1 Settlement Statement and is part of "closing costs."

deed restrictions
Limitations in the deed to a property that dictate certain uses that may or may not be made of the property.

default
Failure to pay a debt or on a contract.

default judgment
A judgment entered in favor of the plaintiff when the defendant fails to appear in court.

defeasance clause
The clause in a mortgage that gives the mortgagor the right to redeem mortgagor's property upon the payment of mortgagor's obligations to the mortgagee.

deficiency judgment
A judgment against a borrower for the balance of a debt owed when the security or the loan is not sufficient enough to pay the debt.

delivery (of a deed)
The unconditional, irrevocable intent of a grantor immediately to divest (give up) an interest in real estate by a deed or other instrument.

deposit receipt
Contract that acts as the receipt for earnest money given by the buyer to secure an offer, as well as being the basic agreement, between the buyer and seller.

devise
A gift of real property by will.

disclosure statement
The statement required by the Truth-in-Lending Law whereby a creditor must give a debtor a statement showing the finance charge, annual percentage rate, and other required information.

discount points
The amount of money the borrower or seller must pay the lender to get a mortgage at a stated interest rate, the amount is equal to the difference between the principal balance on the note and the lesser amount which a purchaser of the note would pay the original lender for it under market conditions. A point equals one percent of the loan.

discount rate
The interest rate that is charged by the Federal Reserve Bank to its member banks for loans.

discounting a note
Selling a note for less than the face amount or the current balance.

documentary transfer tax
A state enabling act allowing a county to adopt a documentary transfer tax to apply on all transfers of real property located in the county. Notice of payment is entered on face of the deed or on a separate paper filed with the deed.

due-on-sale clause
An acceleration clause granting the lender the right to demand full payment of the mortgage upon a sale of the property.

E

earthquake insurance
Covers a building and its contents, but includes a large percentage deductible on each. A special policy or endorsement exists because earthquakes are not covered by standard homeowners or most business policies.

earnest money
Down payment made by a purchaser of real estate as evidence of good faith. A deposit or partial payment.

easement
(1) The right to use another's land for a specified purpose, sometimes known as a right-of-way. (2) The right to enter or use someone else's land for a specified purpose.

EFT
Electronic Funds Transfer, also known as a wire transfer. Banks routinely wire monies from account to account via EFT so as to avoid any accrual of interest.

electronic signature
Signatures via fax or email or websites are considered valid for many documents except those requiring recording, . Allows for certain transactions to be confirmed electronically, however, for purposes of real estate, escrow, and banking, electronic signatures are not allowed for signature required under the Uniform Commercial Code.

emancipated minor
Someone who is legally set free from parental control/ supervision.

Encroachment

The unauthorized placement of permanent improvements that intrude on adjacent property owned by another.

encumbrance

An interest in real property that is held by someone who is not the owner.

Environmental Impact Report

(1) A study of how a development will affect the ecology of its surroundings. (2) Also known as EIR.

Equal Credit Opportunity Act

Federal act to ensure that all consumers are given an equal chance to obtain credit.

equitable title

(1) The interest held by the trustor under a trust deed. (2) Selling a note for less than the face amount or the current balance.

equity

The difference between the appraised value and the loan. Also, dollar amount of a home that is paid for. Calculate equity by taking the market value of the home and subtracting debt. Ex.: A house worth $150,000 with $65,000 owed on a first mortgage and $15,000 owed on a home equity line of credit. Take $150,000 - $80,000 (65,000 + 15,000) to arrive at $90,000 or the equity of the home.

escalation

The right reserved by the lender to increase the amount of the payments/or interest upon the happening of a certain event.

escalator clause

A clause in a contract providing for the upward or downward adjustment of certain items to cover specified contingencies, usually tied to some index or event. Often used in long term leases to provide for rent adjustments, to cover tax and

maintenance increases.

escrow

A small and short-lived trust arrangement. Escrow Money, property, a deed, or a bond put into the custody of a third party for delivery to a grantee only after the fulfillment of the conditions specified.

escrow agent

The neutral third party holding funds or something of value in trust for another.

escrow holder

Acts as a neutral agent of both buyer and seller. An independent third party legally bound to carry out the written provisions of an escrow agreement; a neutral, bonded third party who is a dual agent for the principals; sometimes called an escrow agent.

escrow instructions

Written directions, signed by a buyer and seller, detailing the procedures necessary to close a transaction and directing the escrow agent how to proceed.

estate

The ownership interest or claim a person has in real property. A legal interest in land; defines the nature, degree, extent and duration of a person's ownership in land.

estate for life

A possessory, freehold estate in land held by a person only for the duration of his or her life or the life or lives of another.

evidence of title

Proof of property ownership.

exchange

A means of trading equities in two or more properties, treated as a single transaction through a single escrow.

execute/ executed contract

To perform or complete; to sign.

All parties have performed completely.

executor/executrix

A person named in a will to handle affairs of the deceased.

executory contract

A contract in which obligation to perform exists on one or both sides.

express contract Parties declare the terms and put their intentions in words, either oral or written.

extended policy An extended title insurance policy.

F

Federal Housing Administration (FHA)

A federal government agency that insures private mortgage loans for financing of homes and home repairs.

Federal National Mortgage Association
"Fannie Mae" a quasi-public agency converted into a private corporation whose primary function is to buy and sell FHA and VA mortgages in the secondary market.

fees
Money paid or is charged up front to get a mortgage loan. fees are paid in cash or financed as part of the loan. If financed, loan balance increases equity is reduced. The fees appear on the Good Faith Estimate and HUD-1 Settlement Statement. Many of these fees are negotiated. (See Up Front Fees, finance charge, underwriting, warehousing fees)

fee simple
The greatest possible interest a person can have in real estate.

fee simple absolute
(1)The largest, most complete ownership recognized by law. (2)An estate in fee with no restrictions on its use. (3)Property transferred or sold with no conditions or limitations on its use.

fee simple estate
The most complete form of ownership.

fee simple qualified/defeasible
(1) An estate in which the holder has a fee simple title, subject to return to the grantor if a specified condition occurs. (2) Also known as fee simple defeasible.

FICO
Credit scores calculated by Fair Isaac Company are often referred to as FICO. Normally an average of credit scores taken by 3 national credit bureaus. (See Credit Score)

fictitious business name
(1) A business name other than the name of the person who has registered the business. (2) Also known as assumed name. (3) A name that does not include the last name of the owner in the name of the business, and known as DBA or "doing business as."

Fiduciary
A relationship that implies a position of trust or confidence.

fiduciary duty
That duty owned by an agent to act in the highest good faith toward the principal and not to obtain any advantage over the latter by the slightest misrepresentation, concealment, duress of pressure

fiduciary relationship
A relationship that implies a position of trust or confidence.

finance charge
The dollar amount the credit will cost and is composed of any direct or indirect charge as a condition of obtaining credit. Also, disclosure that appears on the Truth-in-Lending Act Disclosure Statement, intended to show cost of loan as a dollar amount. Includes (1) interest that will be charged over the life of the loan and (2) some upfront fees (prepaid finance charges).

financing statement
(1) A written notice filed with the county recorder by a creditor who has extended credit for the purchase of personal property; establishes the creditor's interests in the personal property which is security for the debt. (2) A document used to record debt.

fire insurance
Coverage protecting property against losses caused by a fire or lightning that is usually included in homeowners or commercial multiple peril policies.

first mortgage
A mortgage superior to any other mortgages.

first trust deed
A legal document pledging collateral for a loan (See "trust deed") that has first priority over all other claims against the property except taxes and bonded indebtedness. That trust deed is superior to any other.

fiscal year
Starts on July 1 and runs through June 30 of the following year; used for real property tax purposes.

fixed rate full amortized loan
A loan with two distinct features. First, the interest rate remains fixed for the life of the loan. Second, the payments remain level for the life of the loan and are structured to repay the loan at the end of the loan term.

fixed rate loan
The most common type of loan. The principal and interest are calculated for the term of the loan. Payments are determined by dividing the total by the number of payments in the term of the loan. Regular payments of fixed amounts, to include both interest and principal are made. This payment pays off the debt completely by the end of the term.

fixture
(1) Personal property that has become affixed to real estate.

flood certification fee
Fee charged to determine if the property lies in a flood zone and whether flood insurance is required.

forbearance
Forgiving a debt or obligation.

foreclosure
A legal procedure by which mortgaged property in which there has been default on the part of the borrower is sold to satisfy the debt.

fraud
An act meant to deceive in order to get someone to part with something of value.

freehold estate
An estate in real property which continues for an indefinite period of time.

foreclosure
A legal procedure by which mortgaged property in which there has been default on the part of the borrower is sold to satisfy the debt.

fully amortized note
A note that is fully repaid at maturity by periodic reduction of the principal.

G

general lien
A lien on all the property of a debtor.

gift deed
Used to make a gift of property to a grantee, usually a close friend or relative.

gift tax
Tax that can be due when you give property or other assets to someone.

goodwill
An intangible, salable asset arising from the reputation of a business; the expectation of continued public patronage.

Good Faith Estimate
Lenders are required to give borrowers with a "good faith estimate" of all fees due at closing within three days of applying for a loan. These fees, also called settlement costs, cover expenses associated with home loans: inspections, title insurance, taxes and other charges. Costs average between 3 and 5 percent of the sale price.

Government National Mortgage Association
(1) An agency of HUD, which functions in the secondary mortgage market, primarily in social housing programs. (2) Also known as Ginnie Mae.

government recording fees and taxes
Fees and taxes required to be paid to the local government where your mortgage documents are filed.

government survey
A method of specifying the location of parcel of land using prime meridians, base lines, standard parallels, guide meridians, townships and sections.

graduated payment adjustable mortgage
A loan in which the monthly payment graduates by a certain percentage each year for a specific number of years, then levels off for the remaining term of the loan.

grant
A technical legal term in a deed of conveyance bestowing an interest in real property on another. The words "convey" and "transfer" have the same effect.

grant deed
A type of deed in which the grantor warrants that he or she has not previously conveyed the property being granted, has not encumbered the property except as disclosed, and will convey to the grantee any title to the property acquired later.

grantee
The person receiving the property, or the one to whom it is being conveyed.

grantor
The person conveying, or transferring, the property.

granting clause
The clause in a deed or mortgage that conveys the property and usually states "To grant and release" from grantor to grantee.

gross income
Total income from property before any expenses are deducted.

ground lease
A lease for only the land.

guarantee of title
An assurance of clear title.

H

habendum clause
The "to have and to hold" clause which may be found in a deed.

hard money loan
Any loan made on real property in exchange for cash.

hazard insurance
A property insurance policy that protects the owner and lender against physical

hazards to property such as fire and windstorm damage.

"hold harmless" clause
Protects the broker from incorrect information.

holder
The party to whom a promissory

note is made payable.

holder in due course
A person who has obtained a negotiable instrument (promissory note, check) in the ordinary course of business before it is due, in good faith and for value, without knowledge that it has been previously dishonored.

home equity loan
A cash loan made against the equity in the borrower's home.

homeowners' association
A group of property owners in a condominium or other subdivision neighborhood, who manage common areas, collect dues, and establish property standards.

homeowners' exemption
A $7,000 tax exemption available to all owner-occupied dwellings.

homeowners' insurance
Policy covering house, garage and other structures on the property, as well as personal possessions inside the house such as furniture, appliances and clothing, against threats from wind, storms, fire, and theft, and additional living expenses, known as Loss of Use, in the event of a disaster. Accidental injuries caused to third parties and/or their property (such as a guest slipping and falling down improperly maintained stairs) is covered under liability. Coverage for flood and earthquake damage is excluded and must be purchased separately.

homestead
A piece of land that is owned and occupied as a family home.

HUD/Hud 1
US Department of Housing Urban Development/Settlement statement of all costs and fees in closing escrow.

Hypothecation
A process which allows a borrower to remain in possession of the property while using it to secure a loan.

I

intestate
Dying without leaving a will.

implied contract
An agreement shown by acts and conduct rather than written words.

impound account
A trust account set up for funds set aside for future costs relating to a property.

improvements
Valuable additions made to property to enhance value or extend useful remaining life.

injunction
A court order forcing a person to do or not do an act.

installment note
A note which provides for a series of periodic payments of principal and interest, until amount borrowed is paid in full. This periodic reduction of principal amortizes the loan.

instrument
A formal legal document such as a contract, deed or will.

interest
The charge for the use of money.

interest rate
The percentage charged for the use of money.

interpleader action
A court proceeding initiated by the stakeholder of property who claims no proprietary interest in it for the purpose of deciding who among claimants is legally entitled to the property.

involuntary lien
When the owner does not pay taxes or the debt owed, a lien may be placed against his or her property without permission.

J

joint tenancy
When two or more parties own real property as co-owners, with the right of survivorship.

judgment
The final legal decision of a judge in a court of law regarding the legal rights of

parties to disputes.

judgment lien
The final determination of the rights of parties in a lawsuit by the court.

judicial foreclosure
Foreclosure by court action.

jumbo loans
Loans which exceed the Fannie Mae guidelines for loan size and amount. Jumbo loans may have different guidelines from a "conforming" loan.

junior mortgage
A second mortgage; one that is subordinate or has an inferior priority to the

first mortgage.

junior trust deed
Any trust deed that is recorded after a first trust deed, whose priority is less than that first trust deed.

L

land contract
A contract for the sale of real property where the seller gives up possession, but retains the title until the purchase price is paid in full; also known as a contract of sale or agreement of sale.

leasehold
(1) An agreement, written or unwritten, transferring the right to exclusive possession and use of real estate for a definite period of time. (2)Also known as a rental agreement or lease.

leasehold estate
A tenant's right to occupy real estate during the term of the lease. This is personal property interest.

legacy
A gift of personal property by will.

legal description
A land description recognized by law; a description by which property can be definitely located by reference to government surveys or approved recorded maps.

legal title
Title that is complete and perfect regarding right of ownership.

lender
A company or person that makes mortgage loans, such as a mortgage banker, credit union, bank, or savings and loan. Lender's name will appear on the promissory note.

lessee
(1) Tenant. (2) Renter.

lessor
(1) Landlord (2) property owner (3) The person who owns the property and signs the lease to give possession and use to the tenant.

less-than-freehold estate
(1)The lessee's interest. (2)An estate owned by a tenant who rents real property.

lien
(1) A claim on the property of another for the payment of a debt. (2) A legal obligation to pay.

life estate
An estate that is limited in duration to the life of its owner or the life of another designed person.

limited partnership
A partnership of at least one general partner and one limited partner.

liquidated damages clause
Clause in a contract that allows parties to the contract to decide in advance the amount of damages to be paid, should either party breach the contract.

listing agreement
A written contract by which a principal, or seller, employs a broker to sell real estate.

loan application
The loan application is a source of information on which the lender bases a decision to make the loan; defines the terms of the loan contract, gives the name of the borrower, place of employment, salary, bank accounts, and credit references, and describes the real estate that is to be mortgaged. It states the amount of loan being applied for and repayment terms. (Also known as a "1003")

loan assumption
A buyer assumes the exiting loan when a property is sold. The buyer takes over primary liability for the loan, with the original borrower secondarily liable if there is a default.

loan closing
When all conditions have been met, the loan officer authorizes the recording of the trust deed or mortgage. The disbursal procedure of funds is similar to the closing of a real estate sales escrow. The borrower can expect to receive less than the amount of the loan, as title, recording, service, and other fees may be withheld, or can expect to deposit the cost of these items into the loan escrow. This process is sometimes called "funding" the loan.

loan commitment
Lender's contractual commitment to make a loan based on the appraisal and underwriting.

loan term
Length of time until loan is due and payable

loan-to-value ratio
The percentage of appraised value to the loan. (Also known as LTV)

lot, block and tract system
(1) A process where developers divide parcels of land into lots. Each lot in a subdivision is identified by number, as is the block in which it is located; each lot and block is in a referenced tract. This process is required by the California Subdivision Map Act.

M

maker
The borrower who executes a promissory note and becomes primarily liable for payment to the lender.

manufactured home
A home built in a factory after June 15, 1976 and must conform to the U.S. government's Manufactured Home Construction and safety Standards.

marketable title
Good or clear saleable title reasonably free from risk of litigation over possible defects.

material fact
Any fact that would seem likely to affect the judgment of the principal in giving consent to the agent to enter into the particular transaction on the specified terms.

mechanic's lien
A lien placed against a property by anyone who supplies labor, services, or materials used for improvements on real property and

did not receive payment for the improvements.

Mello-Roos Act
Allows developers to make improvements (roads, parks, schools, fire stations) while making each homeowner pay for the improvements. These improvements are listed in the property taxes.

meridian
A survey line running north and south, used as a reference when mapping land.

metes and bounds
Land description that delineates boundaries and measures distances between landmarks to identify property.

mineral rights
The legal interest in the valuable items found below the surface of a property (i.e., gold and coal).

minor
A person under 18 years of age.

misrepresentation
(1) Making a false statement or concealing a material fact. (2) A false statement of fact.

mobile home
A factory-built home manufactured prior to June 15, 1976, constructed on a chassis and wheels, and designed for permanent or semi-attachment to land.

money encumbrance
An encumbrance that affects the title.

monument
A fixed landmark used in a metes and bounds land description.

mortgage
A legal document used as security for a debt. Also, mortgage or Trust Deed (TD). A mortgage is a promise in which principal agrees to put up their home as security for a loan. The mortgage is the instrument which secures the Promissory Note, in which buyer or borrower promises to repay the loan at a certain date. This document allows the lender to force a sale of their home (foreclosure), if, for example, they fail to make payments, to pay property taxes or insurance, or keep other promises. In some states the mortgage document is called a *"Deed of Trust."*

481

mortgage banker
A person whose principal business is the originating, financing, closing, selling, and servicing of loans secured by real property for institutional lenders on a contractual basis.

mortgage broker
A person or company that obtains a mortgage loan for the borrower from another lender. A mortgage broker will not always be representing the borrower and will not necessarily be looking after the borrower's best interests.

mortgage insurance
Also called PMI or MI. Insurance that may be required when a loan is greater than 80% of the value of the home. This insurance protects the lender in the event a borrower fails to make his or her loan payments. The borrower ordinarily pays the cost of MI or PMI, in the form of monthly premiums added to the mortgage payments.

mortgage yield
The amount received or returned from an investment expressed as a percentage.

mortgagee
The lender under a mortgage.

mortgagor
The interest rate stated in the note.

mutual assent
(1) An agreement between the parties in a contract. (2) The offer and acceptance of a contract.

mutual consent
(1) The offer by one party and acceptance by another party. (2) Also known as mutual assent or "meeting of the minds".

mutual mortgage insurance (MMI)
A fee for an insurance policy charged the borrower to protect lender under an FHA loan, in the event of foreclosure on the property.

naked legal title
Title lacking the rights and privileges commonly associated with ownership may be held by trustee under a trust deed.

negative amortization
Occurs when monthly installment payments are insufficient to pay the interest, so any unpaid interest is added to the principal due.

negligence
The failure to act as a reasonable person. The performance of an act that would not be done by a reasonable person.

negotiable instrument
Any written instrument that may be transferred by endorsement or delivery.

net lease
The tenant pays an agreed-upon sum as rent, plus certain agreed-upon expenses per month (i.e., taxes, insurance and repairs).

neutral depository
An escrow business conducted by someone who is a licensed escrow holder.

nominal interest rates
The interest rate that is named or stated in loan documents.

notary public
A licensed public officer who takes or witnesses the acknowledgement.

note
An evidence of a debt.

notice of completion
A notice filed by the owner or general contractor after completion of work on improvements, limiting the time in which mechanic's liens can be filed against the property.

notice of default
A notice to a defaulting party that there has been a nonpayment of a debt.

notice of non-responsibility
When an owner discovers unauthorized work on the property, he or she must file a notice. This is a notice that must be recorded and posted on the property to be valid, stating the owner is not responsible for work being done. This notice releases the owner from the liability for work done without permission.

notice of right to cancel
Under federal law, borrower or buyer may be permitted to cancel or "rescind" a mortgage loan within a specified time, generally three days, after you have signed loan documents in a refinance, second mortgage or other mortgage loans which do not involve the purchase of a home. The lender is required to give the borrower notice in writing of this right to cancel or rescind and the deadline to cancel. (See Right of Rescission)

O

1 month/1 year
For escrow purposes, 30 days=1 month/ for escrow and proration purposes 1 year = 12 months, 52 weeks.

1031 exchange
(1) A method of deferring tax liability. (2) Also known as a "tax-free" exchange.

obligor
(1)One who is bound by a legal obligation. (2) A person, delinquent in paying child support, whose name is listed by the Child Support Services.

offer
A presentation or proposal for acceptance to form a contract.

option
A contract to keep open, for a set period of time, an offer to purchase or lease property.

"or more" clause
A clause in a mortgage or trust deed that allows a borrower to pay it off early with no penalty.

ownership
The right of one or more persons to possess and use property to the exclusion of all others. A collection of rights to the use and enjoyment of property.

ownership in severalty
Property owned by one person or entity.

P

paramount title
Title which is superior or foremost to all others.

parcel map
Map showing a parcel of land that will be subdivided into less than five parcels or units, and shows land boundaries, streets, and parcel numbers.

partial reconveyance
A clause in a trust deed or mortgage permitting the release of a parcel or part of a parcel from the lien of that security instrument. The release usually occurs upon the payment of a specified sum of money.

partially amortized note
A promissory note with a repayment schedule that is not sufficient to amortize the loan over its term.

partition action
A court action to divide a property held by co-owners.

partnership
A form of business in which two or more persons join their money and skills in conducting the business.

personal property
Anything movable that is not real property.

plaintiff
In a court action, the one who sues; the complainant.

planned development
A planning and zoning term describing land not subject to conventional zoning to permit clustering of residences or other characteristics of the project which differ from normal zoning. Sometimes called a planned unit development (PUD).

points
Charges levied by the lender based on the loan amount. Each point equals one percent of the loan amount; for example, two points on a $100,000 mortgage is $2,000. Discount points are used to buy down the interest rate. Points can also include a loan origination fee, which is usually one point. See *Discount Points*.

power of attorney
A legal document that gives another person the legal authority to act on his or her behalf.

power of sale
A clause in a trust deed or mortgage that gives the holder the right to sell the property in the event of default by the borrower.

preliminary title report
An offer to issue a policy of title insurance in the future for a specific fee.

prepaid items of expense
Prorations of prepaid items of expense which are credited to the seller in the closing escrow statement.

prepayment clause
A clause in a trust deed that allows a lender to collect a certain percentage of a loan as a penalty for an early payoff.

prepayment penalty
Penalty for the payment of a note before it actually becomes due. A fee or charge imposed upon a debtor who desires to pay off their loan before its maturity.

presumption
An assumption of fact that the law requires to be made from another fact or group of facts found or otherwise established
in the section.

principal
(1) In a real estate transaction, the one (seller) who hires the broker to represent him or her in the sale of the property. (2) The amount of money borrowed.

principal note
The promissory note which is secured by the mortgage or trust deed.

priority
The order in which deeds are recorded.

private grant
The granting of private property to other private persons.

private mortgage insurance
Mortgage guarantee insurance available to conventional lenders on the first part of a high risk loan.

private restrictions
Created at the time of sale or in the general plan of a subdivision.

pro rata
In proportion; according to a certain percentage or proportion of a whole.

probate
The legal process to prove a will is valid.

probate sale
A court-approved sale of the property of a deceased person.

procuring cause
A broker who produces a buyer "ready, willing and able" to purchase the property for the price and on the terms specified by the seller, regardless of whether the sale is completed.

promissory note
The evidence of the debt.

property taxes
Taxes used to operate the government in general.

prorate
(1) The division and distribution of expenses and/or income between the buyer and seller of property as of the date of closing or settlement. (2) The process of making a fair distribution of expenses, through escrow, at the close of the sale.

purchase money mortgage or trust deed
A trust deed or mortgage given as part or all of the purchase consideration for real property. In some states the purchase money mortgage or trust deed loan can be made by a seller who extends credit to the buyer of property or by a third party lender (typically a financial institution) that makes a loan to the buyer of real property for a portion of the purchase price to be paid for the property. In many states there are legal limitations upon mortgages and trust deed beneficiaries collecting deficiency judgments against the purchase money borrower after the collateral hypothecated under such security instruments has been sold through the foreclosure process.

Q

quiet title action
(1) A court proceeding to clear a cloud on the title of real property. (2) Also known as action to quiet title.

quitclaim deed
Transfers any interest the grantor may have at the time the deed is signed with no warranties of clear title.

R

radon
Colorless, odorless, gas that is a carcinogen detected by a spectrometer.

range lines
Government survey imaginary vertical lines six miles east and west of the meridian to form columns.

rate
The percentage of interest charged on the principal.

rate & term
The note rate (percentage) and the period of time during which loan payments are made must be specified on the promissory note to be binding.

rate lock
Locks in the interest rate. Refers to the agreement between the borrower and the lender or broker that as long as the loan is closed within a certain period of time (for example, 30 or 60 days), the interest rate on the loan will be set (locked) at an agreed-upon rate.

ratification
The approval of a previously authorized act, performed on behalf of a person, which makes the act valid and legally binding.

Real Estate Settlement Procedures ACT (RESPA)
A federal law requiring disclosure to borrowers of settlement (closing) procedures and costs by means of a pamphlet and forms prescribed by the United States Department of Housing and Urban Development.

Real Estate Transfer Disclosure Statement
A document that the seller must provide to any buyer of residential property (one-to-four units).

real property
Land (air, surface, mineral, water rights), appurtenances and anything attached, and

immovable by law. Also included in real property are the interests, benefits and rights inherent in owning real estate, i.e., the "bundle of rights." Current usage makes the term real property synonymous with real estate.

reconveyance deed
Conveys title to property from a trustee back to the borrower (trustor) upon payment in full of the debt secured by the trust deed.

recording
The process of placing a document on file with a designated public official for public notice. This public official is usually a county officer known as the County Recorder who designates the fact that a document has been presented for recording by placing a recording stamp upon it indicating the time of day and the date when it was officially placed on file.

recording fees
Fees charged by the local government to record loan documents (for example, the mortgage). These fees will be charged to the borrower and shown on the Settlement Statement (HUD-1).

red flag
Something that alerts a reasonably observant person of a potential problem.

redemption period
A period of time established by state law during which a property owner has the right to recover real estate after a foreclosure or tax sale by paying the sales price plus interest and costs.

refinancing
The payoff of an existing obligation and assuming a new obligation in its place. To finance anew, or extend or renew existing financing.

release clause
A provision found in many blanket mortgage or trust deeds enabling the borrower to obtain partial release from the loan of specific parcels.

request for notice
A notice that is sent, upon request, to any parties interested in a trust deed, informing them of a default.

rescission
Legal action taken to repeal a contract either by mutual consent of the parties or by one

party when the other party has breached a contract.

Right of Rescission
The right of a consumer to nullify a contract within three business days of signing it without paying a penalty or down payment. Federal law allows for cooling-off period when obtaining a home equity loan or line of credit, or refinance with another lender. Allows borrower to rescind, or cancel some types of home loans and walk away without losing money. The right of rescission provides a three-day period when borrower can back out of the loan before getting the borrowed money, no questions asked. Within 20 days, the lender must give up its claim to the property as collateral and must refund any fees paid. This provision is included in the Truth-in-Lending Act (TILA).

restriction
A limitation placed on the use of property and may be placed by a private owner, a developer or the government. It is usually placed on property to assure that land use is consistent and uniform within a certain area.

revocation
The canceling of an offer to contract by the person making the original offer.

right of survivorship
The right of a surviving tenant or tenants succeeds to the entire interest of the deceased tenant; the distinguishing feature of a joint tenancy.

risk analysis
A study made, usually by a lender, of the various factors that might affect the repayment of a loan.

485

risk rating
A process used by a lender to decide on the soundness of making a loan and to reduce all the factors affecting the repayment of the loan to a qualified rating of some kind.

rollover mortgage
A loan that allows the rewriting of a new loan at the termination of a prior loan.

S

S corporation
A corporation that operates like a

corporation but is treated like a partnership for tax purposes.

sales contract
A contract by which buyer and seller agree to terms of a sale.

sales tax
Collected as a percentage of the retailing sales of a product, by a retailer, and forwarded to the State Board of Equalization.

satisfaction
Discharge of a mortgage or trust deed from the records upon payment of the debt.

section
An area of land, one square mile, or 640 acres; 1/36 of a township.

security
Evidence of obligations to pay money.

security agreement
A document commonly used to secure a loan on personal property.

security deposit
Money given to a landlord to prepay for any damage other than just normal wear and tear.

security interest
The interest of a creditor (lender) in the property of a debtor (borrower).

Settlement Statement
A mortgage loan closing form required by HUD that is often called a HUD-1. It provides details of all charges and payments made in connection with your loan, and shows to whom they are distributed.

severalty
Ownership of real property by one person or entity.

shared appreciation mortgage (SAM)
Lender and borrower agree to share a certain percentage of the appreciation in market value of the property.

sheriff's deed
A deed given to a buyer when property is sold through court action in order to satisfy a judgment for money or foreclosure of a mortgage.

simple interest
Interest computed on the principal amount of a loan only as distinguished from compound interest.

sole proprietorship
A business owned and operated by one person.

special assessments
Taxes used for specific local purposes.

special warranty deed
A deed in which the grantor warrants or guarantees the title only against defects arising during grantor's ownership of the property and not against defects existing before the time of grantor's ownership.

specific lien
A lien placed against a certain property, such as a mechanic's lien, trust deed, attachment, property tax lien or lis pendens.

specific performance
An action brought in a court to compel a party to carry out the terms of a contract.

standard policy
A policy of title insurance covering only matters of record.

Statute of Frauds
A state law which requires that certain contracts must be in writing to prevent fraud in the sale of land or an interest in land.

Statute of Limitations
The period of time limited by statute within which certain court actions may be brought by one party against another.

straight note
A promissory note in which payments of interest only are made periodically during the term of the note, with the principal payment due in one lump sum upon maturity; may also be a note with no payments on either principal or interest until the entire sum is due.

"subject to" clause
A buyer takes over the existing loan payments, without notifying the lender. The buyer assumes no personal liability for the loan.

subordination clause
A clause in which the holder of a trust deed permits a subsequent loan to take priority.

subrogation
Replacing one person with another in regard to a legal right or obligation. The substitution of another person in place of the creditor, to whose rights he or she succeeds in relation to the debt. The doctrine is used very often where one person agrees to stand surety for the performance of a contract by another person.

succession
The legal transfer of a person's interest in real and personal property under the laws of descent.

T

tax deed
A deed given to a successful bidder at a tax auction.

tax delinquent property
Property that has unpaid taxes.

tax lien
When income or property taxes are not paid.

tax sale
Sale of property after a period of non-payment of taxes.

tax-deferred exchange
The trade or exchange of one real property for another without the need to pay income taxes on the gain at the time of trade. Also call a tax-free exchange.

tenancy
(1)The interest of a person holding property by any right or title. (2)A mode or method of ownership or holding title to property.

tenancy in common
When two or more persons, whose interests are not necessarily equal, are owners of undivided interests in a single estate.

tenancy in partnership
Ownership by two or more persons who form a partnership for business purposes.

tenant
A renter.

tenants by the entireties
Under certain state laws, ownership of property acquired by a husband and wife during marriage, which property is jointly and equally owned. Upon death of one spouse it becomes the property of the survivor.

term
The period of time during which loan payments are made. At the end of the loan

term, the loan must be paid in full. (See Rate & Term)

testate
A person who dies leaving a valid will.

testator / testatrix
A person who has made a will.

third party
A person who may be affected by the terms of an agreement but who is not a party to the agreement.

timely manner
An act must be performed within certain time limits described in a contract.

time is of the essence clause
A clause in a contract that emphasizes punctual performance as an essential requirement of the contract.

title
Evidence that the owner of land is in lawful possession.

title companies
Companies who perform a title search on the property and issue a title policy for the lender and the purchaser to ensure that there is a valid mortgage lien against the property and title is clear.

title insurance
An insurance policy that protects the named insured against loss or damage due to defect in the property's title.

title plant
The storage facility of a title company in which it has accumulated complete title records of properties in its area.

title report
A report which discloses condition of the title, made by a title company preliminary to issuance of title insurance policy.

title theory
Mortgage arrangement whereby title to mortgaged real property vests in the lender.

Some states give greater protection to mortgage lenders and assume lenders have title interest. Distinguished from Lien Theory States.

"to let", "to demise"
These phrases mean the same as "to rent."

trade fixture
An item of personal property, such as a shelf, cash register, room partition or wall mirror, used to conduct a business.

transfer fee
A charge made by a lending institution holding or collecting on a real estate mortgage to change its records to reflect a different ownership. Also called Transfer Tax or Charge, a government tax or charge usually based on a percentage of the property value or loan amount and imposed by state or local law.

transferability
The title must be marketable with an unclouded title.

trust account
An account separate and apart and physically segregated from broker's own funds, in which broker is required by law to deposit all funds collected for clients.

trust deed
A security instrument that conveys naked legal title of real property.

trust funds
Money or other things of value received from people by a broker to be used in real estate transactions.

trustee
Holds naked legal title to property as a neutral third party where there is a deed of trust.

trustee's deed
A deed given to a buyer of real property at a trustee's sale.

trustee's sale
The forced sale of real property, by a lender, to satisfy a debt.

trustor
The borrower under a deed of trust.

Truth in Lending Act (TILA)
1) A federal law that requires borrowers to be informed about the cost of borrowing money. (2)Also known as Regulation Z. (See Right of Rescission)

Truth-in-Lending Disclosure Statement
Federal law requires for this document for all consumer loans. It provides key information to enable borrowers to shop around and compare loan terms from various lenders.

U

underwriting
The process of evaluating a borrower's risk factors before the lender will make a loan.

underwriting fee
A fee charged by lender to evaluate whether the borrower charged to the borrower and shown on the Settlement Statement (HUD-1) qualifies for a mortgage loan.

undivided interest
The buyer receives an undivided interest in a parcel of land as a tenant in common with all the other owners.

undue influence
Using unfair advantage to get agreement in accepting a contract.

unearned increment
An increase in value to real estate that comes about from forces outside the control of the owners, such as a favorable shift in population.

unenforceable contract
A contract that was valid when made but either cannot be proved or will not be enforced by a court.

Uniform Commercial Code
A code that establishes a unified and comprehensive method for regulation of security transactions in personal property.

unilateral contract
A contract where a party promises to perform without expectation of performance by the other party.

unilateral rescission
Legal action taken to repeal a contract by one party when the other party has breached a contract.

unity

Equal right of possession or undivided interest. For example, each tenant has the right to use the whole property. None of the owners may exclude any co-owner from the property, nor claim any portion of the property for exclusive use.

Up Front Costs

Costs or fees charged to the borrower at or before closing a loan, such as application fees, appraisal fees, points, broker fees, credit report fees, real estate taxes, etc. They can be paid in several ways: (1) they can be paid by the borrower in cash; or (2) they can be added to the loan amount and financed over the life of the loan.

usury

The act of charging a rate of interest in excess of that permitted by law.

V

VA loan

A loan made to qualified veterans for the purchase of real property wherein the Department of Veteran's Affairs guarantees the lender payment of the mortgage.

valid

Legally binding.

valid contract

A binding and enforceable contract; a document that has all the basic elements required by law.

valuable consideration

Each party to a contract must give up something to make the agreement binding.

valuation

The process of estimating market value.

value

(1) The present and future anticipated enjoyment or profit from the ownership of property. (2)Also known as worth.

variable-rate mortgage (VRM)

A mortgage where the interest rate varies according to an agreed-upon index, thus resulting in a change in the borrower's monthly payments. Mortgages used prior to 1982 replaced by ARMs.

variance

An exception granted to existing zoning regulations for special reasons.

vendee

The buyer under a contract of sale (land contract).

vendor

The seller under a contract of sale (land contract).

veneer

Thin sheets of wood.

verification

Sworn statement before a duly qualified officer to correctness of contents of an instrument.

vested/ vesting

Owned by. The way title will be taken.

Veteran's Exemption

Entitles a resident of California who has been in the military during wartime to take a $4,000 real estate tax emption.

void / void contract

An agreement which is totally absent of legal effect. Contract that has no legal effect due to incapacity or illegal subject matter.

voidable

An agreement which is valid and enforceable on its face, but may be rejected by one or more of the parties.

voluntary lien

When an owner chooses to borrow money, using the property as security for the loan.

W

waiver

The relinquishment or refusal to accept a right.

warehousing

The process of assembling into one package a number of mortgage loans, prior to selling them to an investor.

warehousing fees

Charges included in home loans on the settlement statement or closing costs.

warranty deed

No longer used in California; a deed used to transfer title to property, guaranteeing that the title is clear and the grantor has the right to transfer it.

will
A written instrument whereby a person makes a disposition of his or her property to take effect after their death.

writ of execution
A legal document issued by a court forcing the sale of a property to satisfy a judgment.

writ of possession
A legal action granted by the court to the landlord if the tenant does not move out or answer a lawsuit.

yield
The interest earned by an investor on an investment (or by a bank on the money it has loaned). Also, called return.

yield rate
The yield expressed as a percentage of the total investment. Also, called rate of return.

Z

zone
Area set off by authorities for specific use; subject to certain restrictions or restraints.

zoning
The regulation of structures and uses of property within selected districts.

zoning ordinance
Regulates land use for individual projects.

INDEX

ANSWERS TO PRETESTS AND POST TESTS

Chapter 1	Chapter 2	Chapter 3	Chapter 4
1. T	1. T	1. T	1. F
2. F	2. T	2. T	2. T
3. T	3. T	3. F	3. T
4. F	4. F	4. F	4. T
5. F	5. F	5. T	5. F
6. T	6. T	6. T	6. T
7. T	7. F	7. T	7. T
8. F	8. F	8. F	8. T
9. T	9. T	9. T	9. F
10. F	10. T	10. T	10. F

Chapter 5	Chapter 6	Chapter 7	Chapter 8
1. T	1. F	1. T	1. T
2. F	2. T	2. T	2. T
3. T	3. T	3. F	3. F
4. F	4. F	4. F	4. T
5. F	5. F	5. T	5. T
6. F	6. T	6. F	6. F
7. F	7. T	7. T	7. F
8. T	8. F	8. F	8. T
9. F	9. F	9. F	9. F
10. T	10. F	10. T	10. T

Chapter 9	Chapter 10	Chapter 11	Chapter 12
1. F	1. F	1. T	1. T
2. T	2. T	2. T	2. F
3. T	3. T	3. F	3. F
4. T	4. F	4. F	4. T
5. T	5. F	5. F	5. T
6. T	6. T	6. F	6. T
7. T	7. F	7. T	7. F
8. F	8. F	8. F	8. T
9. F	9. T	9. T	9. T
10. F	10. T	10. T	10. T

Chapter 13	Chapter 14	Chapter 15
1. F	1. F	1. F
2. F	2. F	2. F
3. T	3. F	3. T
4. T	4. T	4. T
5. F	5. T	5. F
6. T	6. F	6. F
7. T	7. F	7. F
8. F	8. F	8. T
9. T	9. T	9. T
10. T	10. T	10. T